Students Taking Charge in Grades 6-12

Discover how to design innovative learning environments that increase student ownership so they can achieve at high levels and meet rigorous standards. *Students Taking Charge* shows you how to create student-centered classrooms that empower learners through problem-based learning and differentiation, where students pose questions and actively seek answers. Technology is then used seamlessly throughout the day for information, communication, collaboration, and product generation.

You'll find out how to:

♦ Design an *Authentic Learning Unit*, which is at the core of the *Learner-Active, Technology-Infused Classroom*, aimed at engaging students;

♦ Understand the structures needed to support its implementation and empower students;

♦ Build the facilitation strategies that will move students from engagement to empowerment to efficacy.

This new 6–12 edition offers a more detailed look into secondary school implementation. With the book's practical examples and step-by-step guidelines, you'll be able to start designing your innovative classroom immediately!

Nancy Sulla is an author, national speaker, and thought leader in transforming learning environments to build student engagement, empowerment, and efficacy. As the creator of the *Learner-Active, Technology-Infused Classroom*™ and founder of IDE Corp. (Innovative Designs for Education), Dr. Sulla leads her educational consulting firm in the pursuit of equity-focused instructional design, positioning students to change the world. Learn more at nancysulla.com.

Students Taking Charge in Grades 6–12

Inside the Learner-Active, Technology-Infused Classroom

Nancy Sulla

Routledge
Taylor & Francis Group

NEW YORK AND LONDON

First published 2019
by Routledge
711 Third Avenue, New York, NY 10017

and by Routledge
2 Park Square, Milton Park, Abingdon, Oxon, OX14 4RN

Routledge is an imprint of the Taylor & Francis Group, an informa business

Library of Congress Cataloging-in-Publication Data
A catalog record has been requested for this book

ISBN: 978-0-415-34920-8 (hbk)
ISBN: 978-0-415-34919-2 (pbk)
ISBN: 978-1-315-22922-5 (ebk)

Typeset in Palatino
by Apex CoVantage, LLC

Portions of this book were previously published as *Students Taking Charge: Inside the Learner Active, Technology-Infused Classroom,* © 2011.

Visit the eResources: www.routledge.com/9780415349192

Dedication

To the three pillars in my work: God, who always has a great plan for
my days; *Team IDE*—a dedicated group of people who push my
thinking and innovate better than any team I know; and the amazing
educators who take the words on these pages and put them into action
in schools, giving me inspiration and fueling my continued work.

Contents

Meet the Author

Nancy Sulla is an author, national speaker, and thought leader in transforming learning environments to build student engagement, empowerment, and efficacy. As the creator of the *Learner-Active, Technology-Infused Classroom*™ and founder of IDE Corp. (Innovative Designs for Education), Dr. Sulla leads her educational consulting firm in the pursuit of equity-focused instructional design, positioning students to change the world. She holds a B.A. in Education from Fairleigh Dickinson University, an M.A. in computer science from Montclair State University, and an Ed.D. in Educational Administration from Fordham University. Her diverse background includes teaching at the elementary, middle school, high school, and college levels; working as a computer programmer and systems analyst; and leading teachers as a district administrator prior to launching IDE Corp. Learn more at nancysulla.com.

eResources

Keep an eye out for the eResources icon 🔖 throughout this book, which indicates a resource is available online. Resources mentioned in this book can be downloaded, printed, used to copy/paste text, and/or manipulated to suit your individualized use. You can access these downloads by visiting the book product page on our website: www.routledge.com/products/9780415349192. Then click on the tab that reads "eResources" and select the file(s) you need. The file(s) will download directly to your computer.

Introduction

I am pleased to offer this new edition of *Students Taking Charge*, focusing on 6–12 classrooms, thus allowing me to provide you with even more examples and strategies. As always, my thinking continues to evolve, so this edition offers new insights into designing student-driven classrooms, building student engagement, empowerment, and efficacy. I am indebted to the many teachers who run *Learner-Active, Technology-Infused Classrooms*, tweet about them, and share their stories with me. Their experiences help educators collectively take school to the next level.

Passion lies at the intersection of a dream and success. Those who are passionate about their craft typically have a dream of what can be, and have had glimpses of that dream in small pockets of success along the way. That combination fuels a desire to keep moving forward, regardless of personal sacrifice, fully believing that this is the road on which they are meant to travel.

The field of education is graced with many passionate teachers—those who believe that all students can learn and are fueled by those moments when students perform beyond their expectations. The Greek philosopher Heraclitus said that you can never step in the same river twice, because the river is constantly changing. So it is with the classroom. Each day brings newness: students are constantly changing, growing, and learning; passionate teachers are continually honing their craft; society possesses a momentum that repeatedly presents new challenges for schools.

Passionate teachers see beyond the barriers; they know there is a better way to prepare young people for their future and to unleash in them all the potential they possess. They explore new ways of approaching teaching and learning, and, fueled by isolated and sometimes small encounters with success, they forge ahead. I have no doubt that the relentless pursuit of instructional innovation by the passionate few will overcome the barriers of resistance and create innovative, adaptive learning environments that will both serve and form society in ways beyond our current imagination.

My own passion for changing the world through education is fueled by the *Learner-Active, Technology-Infused Classroom* students who thank me and share their stories; their dedicated teachers who challenge themselves daily and work tirelessly to make their students' educational experiences more productive and meaningful; and their school and district leaders who courageously find ways to make it happen, battle the status quo, and take the risk to forge a new and innovative path for school. I am blessed to be joined by the amazing group of educators at IDE Corp. Their passion and dedication to the educators and students we serve is inspiring; they challenge my thinking and enhance the collective work we do.

My Journey

My vision for the *Learner-Active, Technology-Infused Classroom* was inspired by many moments throughout my life. When I was ten, I began running a summer school program for the neighborhood children; by the time I was twelve, I was charging fees and holding graduation ceremonies for parents. In some ways, it was a one-room schoolhouse; I had neighborhood children of all ages anxious to come to my school for the three days a week it was open, including those who were gifted, those with learning difficulties, and a teenager with cerebral palsy. To meet their needs, I assigned varying work and spent a lot of my time working in small groups and with individual students. I still look back in amazement that the neighborhood kids hated to miss a day of summer school, given that we truly worked the entire time! One bright and talented young man had been attending my school since age three. When his mom had her first parent–teacher conference, his teacher pointed out how far ahead he was from his peers, no doubt because of the private school he was attending. Today, the young man is a judge, and I like to think his early experiences in "school" helped to fuel his own passion for his craft.

An early experience in my teaching career inspired me to solidify my vision and articulate it so that others could join my quest for the ultimate learning environment. It was the late 1970s, my second year in teaching and first year teaching middle school. I was assigned the lower-level math students who had repeatedly failed the state tests. I remember starting class asking my eighth graders to take out their books, only to find that few had brought them. Paper? Pencil? My efforts to recreate the traditions experienced in my own schooling seemed futile. One day, I asked my students to simply show up for class the next day—no books, no paper, no pencils. They all complied. I had pushed back the desks and arranged the chairs in a circle. I explained that I wanted to keep my job and they needed to learn math, and I asked them for the solution to my dilemma. My students pointed out that math instruction was boring and they didn't see the point.

I suggested that perhaps I could design projects that would make the learning more meaningful; they agreed to give it a try.

I don't remember the first project I designed, nor the entire complement, but I do recall a few. We created scale drawings of birdhouses to build; we used paper plates to create polyhedral disco balls (it was, after all, the 1970s, and John Travolta's nephews were in my classes). In those days, teachers could take their students out to play kickball on a nice day. My students would head out with clipboards to track the progress of the game; once inside, they would run the statistics on the game and analyze it in light of previous games. When the state tests arrived, my students did quite well, with almost all of them passing. I remember my principal asking me what I did; I didn't know. He persisted and pointed out that my students performed particularly well on percentages, but I simply shrugged my shoulders and admitted I hadn't gotten to that chapter yet.

Years later, I realized what had happened. I had designed higher-order problems for my students to solve, and then provided them with the resources and support they needed to learn. I realized, too, that the problems did not encompass only the skills in a single chapter of the textbook; they spanned many chapters. I would venture to say we worked with percentages, for example, in most of the problems. I saw the power of students learning from a *felt need* in an authentic context, and that year and the successes my teaching style yielded never left me. The personal computer had not even been invented yet.

It was the invention of the desktop computer and its arrival in schools that further fueled my vision for the classroom. Teachers are faced with a classroom of students with varying needs and interests; computers provide them with a wealth of opportunities to help students learn. In the early 1980s, I was a district-level administrator, when I decided to make "an offer to innovate" to a couple of teachers. Alysse Daches and Cyndie Bach taught fourth and fifth grade, respectively. They were both among the daring few who purchased desktop computers for their homes. I asked how they would like to have five desktop computers for their classrooms, and they jumped at the chance. Over the course of the next few months, I saw a new vision for the classroom spring to life. On one visit they told me they felt guilty that the computers sat vacant while they were teaching lessons; I suggested that perhaps they could reduce the number of whole-class lessons in favor of other means of providing instruction. On another visit they told me how challenging it was for the children to push together desks of all different sizes and attempt to work collaboratively. I replaced the desks with forty-two-inch round tables. Structure by structure, strategy by strategy, my vision for instruction took shape. More than twenty years later, with myriad classroom teachers implementing the *Learner-Active, Technology-Infused Classroom* across the grade levels, I wrote the first edition of this book to capture the essence of this instructional framework to share with passionate teachers everywhere. This second edition is split into two books to offer a more detailed look into 6–12 implementation and K-5 implementation, allowing me to provide even more detail and examples for you to understand the framework and implementation strategies.

Your Journey

This book is intended to be a three-fold guide to:

♦ Designing an *Authentic Learning Unit*, which is the foundation of the *Learner-Active, Technology-Infused Classroom*, aimed at engaging students;

♦ Understanding the structures needed to support its implementation and empower students;

♦ Building the facilitation strategies that will move students from engagement to empowerment to efficacy.

Therefore, it's best if you pause after each chapter and spend some time designing the various components of the unit. Every six months, reread the book and you'll learn even more! The early chapters delve into designing an appropriate core problem for students to solve and the analytic rubric to provide them with clearly articulated expectations. Chapter 4 addresses differentiation techniques to further engage students in grappling with content. Chapter 5 focuses on the many structures of the *Learner-Active, Technology-Infused Classroom* that empower students to take charge of their own learning. Chapter 6 drives home the importance of teacher facilitation— a new role for teachers—in this environment. Chapter 7 addresses physical classroom design, which will prove to be more useful for those who have more control over their physical classroom space than for those who do not. The ten principles of the *Learner-Active, Technology-Infused Classroom* are woven throughout and then addressed more fully in Chapter 8. Chapter 9 closes the book with special considerations, such as a priming plan and designing a *Learner-Active, Technology-Infused School*; it also offers thoughts on how the *Learner-Active, Technology-Infused Classroom* addresses many of the instructional needs and programs present in schools today.

I hope this book helps to fuel your passion and provide you with many ideas for innovatively designing your classroom.

1

The Why for Your Instructional Design Journey

Change the World!

"Design Your Own Destiny." Those are the words that greet middle school students in one of our *Learner-Active, Technology-Infused Schools* as they enter each day. Those words resonate with the "why?" of the *Learner-Active, Technology-Infused Classroom*: positioning students to change the world. Students deserve an education that positions them to tackle any challenge, pursue any goal, and be outfitted with the skills to meet with success. Before schools can consider what that should look like, they need to identify the why, their purpose. Why should we put all this energy, thought, money, and time into teaching children? My answer to that question is: efficacy!

Efficacious people can identify a goal, build a plan, and put it in motion; and if they don't achieve that goal they can reflect on why and make adjustments for the next attempt. Efficacious people are driven by their passion to make a difference in their own lives and the lives of others; they make life happen, rather than letting life just happen to them. Efficacious people can take steps to lead a happy life, be a productive citizen, and, moving beyond themselves, change the world! What would it take to create classrooms and schools that produce efficacious human beings and world citizens?

Imagine a learning environment in which students pose questions and actively seek answers, pursuing solutions to problems they want to solve. They decide how they will use their time, take charge of setting and achieving goals, and work individually to build skills and collaboratively develop solutions to real-world problems. Technology is used throughout the day, seamlessly, as students and teachers need it—from handheld devices to tablets to laptops to virtual reality headsets. Students walk to a flat-screen monitor on the wall and talk to students in another part of the world. Teachers move around the room, sitting with students who share their accomplishments, asking probing questions and gathering assessment data that will shape tomorrow's instructional plans. You hear students talking about content; their vocabulary is sophisticated; their thinking processes are evident through their discussions and reflections. They are intent on the task at hand, yet not everyone is working on the same thing at the same time. No one is off task. Every now and then you hear a cheer or a student exclaim "I got it!" as they dive into the next phase of a project. Students shift from current activities to others without the prompting of the teacher. No one watches the clock; no one wants to leave. This is a snapshot of the *Learner-Active, Technology-Infused Classroom*. Students in this classroom take learning seriously and pursue it vigorously. Teachers in this classroom masterfully craft and co-create learning experiences with their students that emanate from real-world situations; they facilitate learning, ensuring that each student achieves at the highest level. Parents are partners in the learning process, often via the Internet, working with teachers and students as one cohesive unit to ensure that the students are given the best foundation possible for the rest of their lives.

You may recognize aspects of your own classroom or those of your colleagues. Pockets of innovation exist in schools; it's time to stop celebrating pockets of change, incremental improvements, and isolated innovative teachers. It's time to take bold steps to secure the future of our students and the world.

School and Society

Schools both serve and form society. They serve society by building in their students the skills, concepts, and information needed to thrive in today's world. When the sundial gave way to the analog clock, people needed new skills. When the slide rule gave way to the calculator, school curriculum changed. The school community must continually consider changes in society, particularly technological changes, scientific breakthroughs, and historical events, and ensure that the curriculum is designed to shape successful world citizens.

In addition to critical subject-area content mastery, students need to build skills in creativity, innovation, critical thinking, problem solving, communication, collaboration, information literacy, technological literacy, initiative, self-direction, socializing, cross-cultural engagement, productivity, leadership, flexibility, adaptability, accountability, and responsibility. How do you build "ility"? Most of these skills cannot be approached as a subject. A student cannot take a class in flexibility and adaptability. These skills that fall outside of subject-area content are acquired based on *how* teachers teach more than *what* they teach.

"**If schools serve society by *what* they teach, then they form society by *how* they teach.**"

If schools serve society by *what* they teach, then they form society by *how* they teach. Schools that place a great emphasis on individual competition develop citizens who are well-suited for that, but may not be as able or willing to work collaboratively. Schools that place a great emphasis on project management, time management, and resourcefulness develop citizens who are better prepared to lead self-reliant, productive lives. This is a connection that schools often fail to realize, and it is why teachers and administrators must very carefully develop an ongoing, purposeful, instructional design plan that not only considers the written curriculum—the what—but also shapes the teaching and learning process in the classroom—the how. Both should connect to a powerful purpose, in the case of this book, positioning students to change the world.

In today's society, an event in one part of the world affects others around the world. Countries around the world comprise a global, interdependent system. Our economies, commerce, health, environment, and more are interconnected, which presents both opportunities and challenges. Beyond the realm of Earth, countries are engaged in a new space race to colonize Mars.

> In order for schools to meet the needs of a global society, they must prepare students to be problem-finders, innovators, and entrepreneurs. . . . Today's students are ready to make the leap from passive recipients of information to active participants in a classroom that will prepare them for their future.
>
> (Sulla, 2015, p. 5)

Moving Beyond "It's Always Been That Way"

Consider this anecdote I once heard. A mother is cooking a ham dinner. She cuts off the end of the ham, places the larger piece in the pan, and begins to roast it. Her young daughter says, "Mommy, why do you cut off the end of the ham?" Mom responds, "You know, I'm not sure but my mother always did that. Go ask Grandma." The young girl goes into the living room and asks her grandmother the same question. The response is, "I don't know; my mom did that so I did too," and the girl turned to her great-grandmother and asked why. The elderly woman responded, "Well, otherwise it wouldn't fit in my roasting pan!"

What a wonderful anecdote for the ills of perpetuating the dominant paradigm of schooling. Teachers always stood in the front of the room when I was in school, so that must be where you stand. We always had textbooks,

[handwritten note: There are ills of perpetuating the dominant paradigm of schooling]

so they must be a necessary part of school. We've always had students write and solve problems on the board, so that must be a necessary component of mathematics instruction. It's time to think through what schooling looks like and make some significant adjustments to past practices. That's not to say you discard everything you currently do. Rather, you keep what works and make some adjustments. The important thing is to keep your mind continually open to change and be willing to shift some of your beliefs as to what the teaching and learning process could look like.

Shifting your belief system is not an easy process; it requires unlearning some of what you've learned in the past. Authors Ron Heifetz and Marty Linksy (2002) distinguished between technical and adaptive change. Technical change focuses on implementing known solutions to problems. For example, if students are not performing up to your desired level, use a rubric to offer them clearly articulated expectations. You learn how to use a rubric, implement its use, and teach others. That's technical change, and it is the focus of most professional development and college courses today in the field of education. It is a transaction of knowledge. Adaptive change, on the other hand, focuses on developing solutions to problems for which none yet exists. It represents an underlying transformation of thought and action. Designing classrooms to meet a new, emerging generation of learners is a problem for which there can be no available solution, given that students and society are continually changing. Adaptive change requires a change in one's belief system.

From a Compliance Model to an Efficacy Model

When you walk into a *Learner-Active, Technology-Infused Classroom*, you immediately notice how engaged students are. You look around the room and note that all students are on task and look very focused on whatever they are doing. Conventional classrooms are based on a compliance model of education: the teacher has rules, goals, and assignments, and wants students to comply with those. The understanding is that through compliance, by following the teacher's lead, students will learn; and, while that approach might produce temporary test score results, it will, in and of itself, fall short of producing long-term retention of learning and will do little to produce efficacious learners. Thus, a different model of education is needed to produce efficacious citizens who can change the world.

The first step toward an efficacy model is positioning students to engage with content at deep levels. This is one of the key goals for instructional design, as you'll read about in the next section. As students build the ability to engage in activities and with content, they will be better positioned to be empowered to take charge of their own learning. In the *Learner-Active, Technology-Infused Classroom*, many structures and strategies are put in place to empower students. With engagement and empowerment as the foundation, shifting focus from being empowered by others to empowering yourself leads to efficacy. The *Learner-Active, Technology-Infused Classroom* is an efficacy model of education.

Achieving Instructional Equity *Equity vs. Equality*

A wonderfully diverse world means diverse learners with diverse needs. The equity discussion has schools challenged to provide not an equal but an equitable education for all by giving each student what he or she needs to succeed. At the core of equity is opportunity and access. Imagine classrooms in which students have myriad opportunities to thrive academically, and access to the instructional approach they need and desire.

In his book *For White Folks Who Teach in the Hood . . . And the Rest of Y'All Too*, Christopher Emdin (2016) defines reality pedagogy as:

> An approach to teaching and learning that has a primary goal of meeting each student on his or her own cultural and emotional turf. It focuses on making the local experiences of the student visible and creating contexts where there is a role reversal of sorts that positions the student as the expert in his or her own teaching and learning, and the teacher as the learner. It posits that while the teacher is the person charged with delivering the content, the student is the person who shapes how best to teach that content. Together, the teacher and students co-construct the classroom space.
>
> (p. 27)

In the *Learner-Active, Technology-Infused Classroom*, student voice and choice are at the forefront. Students work with teachers to identify problems they wish to solve and ways in which to learn what they need to achieve their goals. Teachers facilitate through small-group and one-on-one conversations with students to gain a better understanding of students' abilities, successes, challenges, and needs so they can be a powerful resource in their students' learning journey. It is a classroom where all students thrive. The *Learner-Active, Technology-Infused Classroom* is an instructional equity model for education.

Three Critical Goals for Instructional Design

At the core of the *Learner-Active Technology-Infused Classroom* lie three critical goals for instructional design: engage students in learning, build greater responsibility for student learning, and ensure academic rigor.

Engaged Learners

Busy students are not necessarily engaged students, nor are seemingly happy students who are working in groups. Although "hands-on" activities are wonderful, what you truly want are "minds-on" activities. If you assume students are engaged in learning, take a closer look to see if what they are doing is directly related to academically rigorous content and if they are understanding and thinking deeply about that content. Suppose middle school students are learning about the impact of invasive species on the carrying capacities of species in an ecosystem. Consider the following scenarios as we peek into three classrooms:

♦ Students are locating information in books and from the Internet to construct a food web and energy pyramid for an ecosystem being overrun by a non-native species.

♦ Students are designing a hyperlinked computer presentation on a food web and energy pyramid for an ecosystem being overrun by a non-native species, incorporating animation and sound, developing hyperlinks to provide further information on various species.

♦ A group of students is developing a presentation on the future of the Great Lakes if the growth of the Asian carp population goes unchecked, along with suggestions for how to slow the population growth.

Although all three scenarios cover the content of food webs and energy pyramids, it is important to consider how students spend the bulk of their time. In the first scenario, students are most likely engaged in finding and reporting information. Doing so will lead them to some level of knowledge of the science topics, but the work is primarily "regurgitation" of content: copying and pasting; taking data in one form and presenting it in another. This is a prevalent activity in the compliance model of education. The second scenario assumes students have already found their information and are reporting it using a digital presentation, sharing "known" information with others. Their engagement, however, is now in the digital presentation software. Again, although the students are focusing on important skills, as the teacher, you must consider what content is the *goal* of instruction. In this case, students are engaged in the use of software, not understanding the food chain. The third scenario has students "grappling" (Sulla, 2015) with the content itself—understanding the cause-and-effect relationships that exist and using higher-order thinking to consider future situations; they are identifying problems and posing solutions for them based on personal interest and curiosity. All three of these scenarios might occur when learning about

Regurgitation → Known → Grappling

ecosystem interdependencies and the cycles of matter and energy transfer in an ecosystem; the key is the *amount* of time allocated to each and which is the end goal. In the case of the third scenario, students will absolutely have to search for "known" information, and they will have to develop a mode of presentation. That presentation, however, will focus on convincing others of the merit of their solution to the problem, the "unknown" that students have created as the goal of the unit of study.

Current standards demand a higher level of understanding and application of content than ever before.

> The word "understand" means to know how something works and to grasp the meaning of it. The definition intimates personal, often long-term, experience with the subject. . . . Achieving understanding involves deconstructing information, making connections to existing knowledge, making and testing predictions, and constructing new meaning—in short, grappling.
>
> (Sulla, 2015, p. 30)

The bulk of students' time should be spent on grappling with "known" content to provide an "unknown" solution to a problem. Engaged learners need to be grappling with curricular content in significant ways much of the time, no matter what their ages.

Student Responsibility for Learning

Student responsibility for learning is a concept that most educators embrace but few foster. Teachers are often frustrated that students don't come to class prepared, haven't done their homework, and so forth. If you take a closer look at most classrooms, students enter the room and wait for the teacher to tell them what to do; or they follow a "do now" written on the board, that the teacher created. You'll hear teachers saying phrases like "clear your desks," "take out your notebook and a pen," "put your homework out on your desk," "quiet down," "speak up," and more. Teachers will call on students to speak; distribute materials; give, collect, grade, and return assignments; and tell students what their grades are. In this type of environment, students are asked to follow along compliantly; the teacher decides what, when, and how students are learning. This model typically does not actually produce learning; it might produce a short-term bump in test scores relying on short-term memory, but the goal of schooling must be long-term retention of learning. Many of us who succeeded in spite of the compliance model of education had other things going for us: parents who served as models and mentors, a national respect for education as the way out of poverty post-World War II, the ability to construct meaning from information, and so forth.

Imagine a classroom in which seventh-grade students walk through the door; retrieve their folders, or log onto a website that includes their current work and a schedule that they developed the prior day; read through comments from the teacher; and start working on activities they decided upon. Students determine what resources they'll need to accomplish their tasks, and they sign up for them, including *small-group mini-lessons* offered by the teacher. They use *analytic rubrics* to guide their work and assess their own progress; they share with the teacher how they're progressing and what they need to be more successful. The teacher facilitates learning through a carefully structured environment that allows students to take responsibility for the classroom. Student responsibility for learning requires clearly articulated expectations and consequences, structures that students use to meet with success, and guidance and feedback from the teacher.

Imagine a classroom in which eleventh-grade students are working in pairs with counterparts in another part of the world, collaborating to address the global food shortage. Some students are independently conducting research; others are videoconferencing with their partners to share information and ideas. A student who is having difficulty interpreting a graph and has been unable to obtain help from his team accesses a digital *help board* and enters his name and help topic. Soon, the teacher joins him to analyze the graph. About twenty minutes into the class period on this particular day, the students transition from what they are doing to attend to a brief lecture by the teacher on the topic of precision agriculture.

Academic Rigor

If students are engaged in learning and taking greater responsibility for their own learning, then ensuring academic rigor is easy. The battle cry of most schools is to increase test scores, even if scores are already relatively high; but you can't force students to learn. In 1998, William Glasser determined that students choose to learn based on a sense of belonging, freedom, power, and fun. Sousa (2017) found that for information to move into long-term memory, it must have sense and meaning. Presenting content followed by practice, absent of these conditions, will not necessarily increase understanding and will, most likely, not lead to long-term retention. It may bring about a small, temporary bump in test scores, but weeks later the students will have little to show for their work, and little foundation to build upon the following year, which leaves the next year's teacher reteaching that which was forgotten.

I met with a group of teachers representing second grade through twelfth grade to discuss rethinking instruction. During the discussion, an eleventh-grade teacher commented, "Well not only do I have to concentrate on history, but I have to teach them how to write. I don't know what your curriculum is in middle school, but many of my eleventh graders can't write in paragraphs!" A middle school language arts teacher quickly defended her curriculum with, "I spend a lot of time on paragraph construction because they come to me with no knowledge; but they leave my classroom with strong writing skills. Our district needs to teach paragraph writing in the elementary grades." A second-grade teacher who happened to have a stack of student stories with her pulled them out and said, "I don't know what you're talking about. My second graders write great paragraphs." We passed around the student writing samples and the upper-grade teachers were incredulous. The first teacher to speak exclaimed, "If they write this well in second grade, what happens to them between then and high school?!"

Many students can memorize content for the moment; if you engage students' minds in grappling with content through meaningful, authentic problems, they will build knowledge and understanding for the long term. If you increase students' responsibility for learning, offering them freedom and power, they will be able to accomplish more, not remaining dependent on others to continue moving forward; they will strengthen their executive function skills to enable them to take increasingly greater responsibility for their learning. You can then increase academic rigor through well-crafted assignments, questions, differentiation, collaboration, and more.

> "if you engage students' minds in grappling with content through meaningful, authentic problems, they will build knowledge and understanding for the long term."

A Synergy

When the goals of engagement with content, responsibility for learning, and academic rigor are working in concert, the outcome is powerful and lasting learning (see Figure 1.1). This synergy is critical to the success of the *Learner-Active, Technology-Infused Classroom.*

Figure 1.1. Three Critical Goals

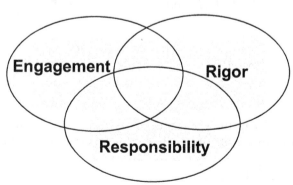

The Students We Teach

The Internet has significantly changed how people communicate, work, collaborate, engage in commerce, and think. Educators need to understand how our technologically advanced world has affected today's students and design classrooms that better suit their learning modalities.

As early as 1998, Don Tapscott described the ten themes of the then-emerging digital (or net) generation. They possess a *strong independence and autonomy*, considering they can easily access and challenge information. They reveal an *emotional and intellectual openness*, based on their willingness to post their thoughts and opinions on websites. They are *inclusive*, using technology as a means through which to develop a community of diverse individuals with whom they interact. They believe in *free expression and strong views*, having unparalleled access to information and forums. They are *innovative*, continually looking for ways to improve the world around them. They are *preoccupied with maturity*, seeking to meld into groups of people who are older than they. They engage in *investigations*, willing to surf the Internet in search of the answers they seek. They thrive on *immediacy*, spurred on by the instantaneous connection offered by modern cellular phones and the Internet. They are *sensitive to corporate interest*, skeptical that media messages are designed to serve corporate needs. They are mindful of *authentication and trust*, given that, with the open architecture of the Internet, they must continually question what they see and hear. Tapscott (2009) later reinforced this, pointing out how these characteristics have been solidified in these students' adult lives. These adults are now parents of children in school, and yet their digital experiences were nowhere near as sophisticated as those of their children. This and future generations of students deserve formal learning environments that honor their unique characteristics.

Consider a few effects of technology on the digital generation. In a technologically advanced world, you:

◆ Can post opinions through blogs, share videos, upload podcasts, create personal social networking pages, and more. The result is that your students *thrive on expressing themselves in a variety of ways*.

◆ Go to websites and they welcome you, know what you're interested in, and refer to you by name. You create digital avatars that represent you online. The result is that your students *expect personalization*.

◆ Send instant digital messages to whom you want, engage in online environments with whom you want, control your tablet's screen layout, customize your cell phone, and wear technology on your wrist. The result is that your students *demand freedom*.

- Engage in online, interactive environments with others around the world, socializing, creating, and gaming. The result is that your students *thrive on social interaction*.

- "Google" people, use the Internet to learn to pronounce a word, watch a YouTube video to learn a skill, go to the UN website to learn about world hunger, check the weather, and get the news. The result is that your students *demand immediate information—* what they want, when they want it.

- Digitally message several people while searching the Web, engaging in an online discussion, streaming a television program, and posting to social media. The result is that your students *want to be everywhere at once*.

- Grieve the loss of others through social networking pages, raise money for starving people in third-world countries, raise money to support taking a stand against genocide in other parts of the world, and organize political events. The result is that your students are *socially aware and active*.

In our students' lives, the digital world is ever present and melded with the real world. "Very few adults have had any real long-term exposure to the digitally infused life experiences of the students who populate our schools" (Jukes, Schaaf, & Mohan , 2017, p. 31). The digital nature of our students speak to the need to design classrooms that are engaging, authentic, differentiated, resource-rich, collaborative, and that foster greater student responsibility for learning. In short, these are classrooms that support efficacy.

Stories From the Field

A seventh-grade science teacher has been working on making his contact with students more meaningful and focused on grappling with content. On Friday, he had planned to take the students outside with paper airplanes to conduct some physics experiments around flight. In the past, he would stand in the front of the room giving the entire class directions on folding a paper airplane, as all of the students followed along. Realizing this is a lower-order activity, he instead videotaped his hands making the airplane as he offered verbal directions. He set up a video station and instructed students to sign up in groups of three throughout the week to assemble their airplanes. Students reported enjoying this approach. One noted, "You know, sometimes when a teacher is talking you kinda zone out. And you can't rewind them. Now we can!" Students worked on this independently while the teacher joined other students to discuss the results of their current experiments. Two pairs of students were conducting an experiment on molecular movement that generates heat. They each set up three beakers of water: one cold, one room temperature, and one hot. They then introduced a drop of food coloring in each beaker and watched to see how quickly the water throughout the entire beaker changed color, if at all. The teacher listened to one pair's description and then mused, "I wonder what would happen if you used yellow food coloring instead of blue." The students were eager to set up a second experiment and try it. He listened to the other pair's similar description and then offered, "I wonder what would happen if you used mineral oil instead of water." Again, students jumped at the opportunity to see what would happen. Imagine a classroom in which students are engaged in grappling with content, fueled by the teacher asking probing questions. Imagine a classroom in which students are working on different tasks, including some that utilize video to "clone" the teacher. Welcome to the *Learner-Active, Technology-Infused Classroom*.

A high school advanced placement (AP) environmental science teacher had her students exploring population pyramids to analyze the patterns of underdeveloped versus developed countries. She posed a problem to her students: select three countries around the world that are in different stages of development, study their population growth over a period of no fewer than 50 years, generate population pyramids, and offer suggestions as to how each country might stabilize its population. A visitor to the classroom sees students working in groups, pairs, and individually on a wide variety of tasks. Students are using spreadsheets to load data that will determine the shape of the population pyramid. Advanced students are using computer programs to create simulations that engage in "what if" analysis. Some are brainstorming possibilities; others are researching countries' backgrounds. The teacher has printed *how-to sheets* for students using computer programs. She posts a list of *small-group mini-lessons* on the board, such as "An In-Depth Look at Factors Affecting Population Growth" and "Analyzing Population Pyramids," for which students can sign up to attend. Students are eager to share their findings and insights with one another and move freely around the room doing so. When the bell rings, no one wants to leave class. Welcome to another *Learner-Active, Technology-Infused Classroom*.

A middle school Spanish teacher offered her students a "reality challenge" fashioned after *The Amazing Race*, offering each team the longitude and latitude of a location in a Spanish-speaking country to where they were transported. They had to write a narrative of how they would return home from there. Using Google Earth, they had to walk around the neighborhood and have conversations with at least three people they found, asking for directions and advice. Some students were using computers to familiarize themselves with the neighborhoods; pairs of students were using conversation starter cards, attempting to mirror conversations that might happen if they were in this situation; some were in a *small-group mini-lesson* with the teacher, learning about conjugating -ar verbs; some were individually writing portions of their narratives to share with their team members. One student needed help on verb conjugation and went to the *resource table* to find a *how-to sheet*; another wanted advice on subordinate clauses and put her name on the *help board* for the teacher. Welcome to yet another *Learner-Active, Technology-Infused Classroom*.

A Philosophy, Framework, and Solution

It is important to view the *Learner-Active, Technology-Infused Classroom* as a comprehensive framework for teaching and learning, not as one possible method among many that you may use. One cannot be *Learner-Active* in the morning but not in the afternoon. One cannot use this method for some students and something else for others. The *Learner-Active, Technology-Infused Classroom* is a complex framework of interdependent structures and strategies that, together, provide the best possible learning environment for all students, thus being differentiated in and of itself. Mastering the art of designing a *Learner-Active, Technology-Infused Classroom* requires certain paradigm shifts that will change your view of teaching and learning forever.

There is room for almost any method you may run across in the *Learner-Active, Technology-Infused Classroom*. As you read other books and articles, attend workshops and conferences, and complete coursework on various educational topics, consider how they align with this framework and how they can fit. Unless you're advocating for a totally lecture-based, teacher-centered classroom, most likely you'll find that most of the popular strategies for fostering learning will fit nicely into the *Learner-Active, Technology-Infused Classroom*. Just stay focused on the extent to which you are providing engagement, responsibility for learning, and academic rigor. Remember, though, that a lot of popular teaching strategies and programs today still presume the teacher is the information deliverer. So as you shift your paradigm, consider how these strategies and programs could be modified to work in your student-driven classroom.

This is not a framework that is meant to stand alone; it is meant to be a solution to many of the challenges facing schools today. The *Learner-Active, Technology-Infused Classroom* is the perfect solution for designing classrooms that offer Multi-Tiered System of Supports (MTSS), such as Response to Intervention (RTI). Relatedly, it is the perfect venue for implementing Universal Design for Learning (UDL). Schools are pursuing learning environments that provide a 1:1 ratio of student to computing device. The *Learner-Active, Technology-Infused Classroom* provides key structures for shifting from a more teacher-directed learning environment to one in which students engage in learning with significant access to a computer. Schools are looking to provide students with a STEM (science, technology, engineering, and math) or STEAM (add arts) focus. Design process is a natural component of the *Learner-Active, Technology-Infused Classroom* as students identify and solve real-world problems. Schools are looking to build twenty-first-century skills in students. The structures of the *Learner-Active, Technology-Infused Classroom* build all of the targeted skills and more. Schools are considering how to provide virtual learning experiences for students so that they may enroll in a course that they attend via computer. The principles of the *Learner-Active, Technology-Infused Classroom* apply in this venue, as well as in the more conventional physical classroom. Schools are challenged to design effective co-teaching (inclusion) classrooms to provide instruction for all students, including special needs students, in one inclusive learning environment. The *Learner-Active, Technology-Infused Classroom* is the solution to this challenge, providing a perfect venue for two adults to share a learning environment without one taking precedence over the other.

Ultimately, consider how the framework and related structures and strategies presented in this book address the needs of your students and of the world of education today. Apply the principles as you make decisions about instruction in the classroom.

What to Expect

Designing a *Learner-Active, Technology-Infused Classroom* requires adaptive change, and adaptive change takes time and mental energy. Embarking on this instructional design journey will take you through three distinct levels in the change process. The first is "dynamic disequilibrium." This occurs when you are implementing new strategies and structures for the first time. One moment you are excited and celebratory, and in the next you find yourself disappointed and in despair. One day you're thrilled that you found this book; the next day you're ready to toss it in the trash. (But please don't.) This is a really important time to keep a journal (written or digital) to track your experiences, successes, and challenges. The act of writing allows you to reflect on events and learn from them. A year from now, the journal will be a wonderful documentation of an amazing journey in instructional design. One teacher kept a journal in her first year of transformation. In her second year, she complained that her students were just not as good at the *Learner-Active, Technology-Infused Classroom* as her last year's class. Then one day she sat down and read her journal from the prior year. She realized that she spent much more time in the fall teaching them the structures. In fact, last year's students weren't all that good at this learning environment either, but she helped them understand it. This year, she just assumed she was going to have students who were starting the year as if they were last year's students at the end of the year. Keeping a journal can provide you with important insights, particularly in your first few years of designing a *Learner-Active,*

Technology-Infused Classroom. This first phase of the change process typically lasts a year or less. Once you begin to repeat the instructional design process with a new set of students, you tend to move to the next phase.

Human beings, by nature, seek stability. The early stages of the change process are often unnerving, so a natural inclination is to find those structures or strategies that appear to work the best and adopt them as the definitive solution. This causes you to enter the second phase: "contrived equilibrium." You'll design a rubric template, for example, to which students respond well; and you'll decide that all rubrics should always be written in this exact same way. This is a dangerous phase, because you meet with exciting, successful moments, but, to be honest, you don't know what you still don't know. Often teachers are asked to provide turnkey training and walk others down the exact path they have taken to designing the *Learner-Active, Technology-Infused Classroom.* I advise against any turnkey training until you've experienced your fourth year of implementing this framework. While you may enjoy the successful achievement of your goals, the journey is truly just beginning, and you have a lot more learning ahead of you. This phase can last a year, a few years, or, in some cases, the length of your career. The key is to push on to the third phase through continual reflective practice.

The third, and destination, phase of the change process in designing *Learner-Active, Technology-Infused Classrooms* is that of "reflective practitioner." Arriving at this phase means you are continually questioning the structures and strategies you employ and making adjustments along the way. Times change, society changes, students change; and masterful teachers adapt their classroom practices accordingly. Returning to the earlier example, you may find that different styles of rubrics work for different students under different circumstances. You may modify your rubrics based on the time of year, the type of problem students are solving, and so forth. Each time, you question whether or not this is the best possible implementation.

I met with a teacher to review her *Authentic Learning Unit (ALU)* and offered several suggestions for improving it. She exclaimed, "You know, *you* wrote this with me three years ago." I smiled and shouted, "I've evolved!" What was acceptable to me three years prior was no longer good enough. Reflective practitioners eagerly open their practice to their own critique and that of others.

Although you may think you can begin at phase three, the instructional design work that lies ahead takes time and is like learning any new skill. Let's face it, if you take up diving, you don't expect to enter the Olympics the following year. Only time will produce improved results. Malcolm Gladwell (2011) claims it takes 10,000 hours of practice to achieve mastery. Use a journal or other means to continually reflect on strategies and structures you are trying and how they worked out. When something does not appear to work, avoid the temptation to revert to former methods. Probe more deeply to consider what structure or strategy you could change to make it work. If you reflect on the situation, you will push yourself to find the key to success.

The Change Process in Action

If something is not working in your *Learner-Active, Technology-Infused Classroom*, it typically means that a structure or strategy is missing. I worked with two sixth-grade teachers who shared the teaching responsibility for two homeroom groups of students. Students would spend a half day with each teacher. The teachers reported that it was too confusing and time-consuming for students to schedule their own time and manage their folders. As we discussed the challenges, the teachers arrived at the solution to shift their perspective from their day to the students' day. They had each student manage one folder; when students left for lunch, the teachers swapped the stack of folders so students had them available when they returned from lunch to the other classroom. They decided, too, to have students schedule their time for the week, taking into account both teachers' classrooms, on Monday morning. These small adjustments produced great success.

The change process applies to students as well. I visited a high school *Learner-Active, Technology-Infused Classroom* in chemistry. I approached a group of students sitting at a round table and sat down to talk to them. I asked how they liked learning this way. They unanimously agreed they liked this better than classroom lectures, because they were more engaged, could talk to others about the work, and enjoyed solving real-world problems. Then one student added, "But she doesn't teach." I sympathized with their plight of having to teach themselves and asked what they were learning. "Nuclear fission and nuclear fusion." I asked how they are learning this. As they shared their stories, they included how the teacher offers some whole-group lessons to share ideas to get them thinking; they use an *activity list* the teacher prepared to locate ways to learn; there is a *help board* and when they put their name on it, the teacher comes over with a small whiteboard to explain things. As the conversation went on, one of the boys tapped a girl on the arm and said, "Hey, she does teach!" I advised the teacher to conduct a *benchmark lesson* on what teaching looks like in the *Learner-Active, Technology-Infused Classroom* as students, too, shift their paradigms as to what teaching and learning look like.

Imagine, Consider, Create

As you work to design your *Learner-Active, Technology-Infused Classroom*, take time to *imagine* the possibilities, *consider* the research and experience of others, and then *create* your classroom. When you reach the *create* sections,

I encourage you to stop and spend some time designing the materials being described. This book is not intended to be read straight through in one sitting. It is meant to guide you through rethinking your classroom and instructional design. You'll note that there will be some structures and strategies that you already use, some that you can easily envision adding to your repertoire, and some that you feel will absolutely not work in your classroom. Start by adding those that make the most sense to you; but never lose track of those seemingly impossible ideas. Keep them in your journal and return to them down the road.

Efficacy for your students is a worthy goal; outfitting them with the knowledge, structures, and strategies they need to accomplish their goals will help establish the trajectory of their lives. Several years from now, you'll look back on your classroom and find it hard to believe what you've accomplished. The key is to keep on innovating and reflecting. Enjoy the journey!

REFERENCES

Emdin, C. (2016). *For white folks who teach in the hood ... and the rest of y'all too: Reality pedagogy and urban education.* Boston: Beacon Press.

Gladwell, M. (2011). *Outliers: The story of success.* Boston: Little Brown and Company.

Glasser, W. (1998). *Choice theory: A new psychology of personal freedom.* New York: HarperCollins.

Heifetz, R. A., & Linsky, M. (2002). *Leadership on the line: Staying alive through the dangers of leading.* Boston: Harvard Business School.

Jukes, I., Schaaf, R. L., & Mohan, N. (2017). *Reinventing learning for the always-on generation: Strategies and apps that work.* Bloomington, IN: Solution Tree.

Sousa, David. (2017). *How the brain learns* (5th ed.). Thousand Oaks, CA: Corwin.

Sulla, N. (2015). *It's not what you teach but how: 7 insights to making the CCSS work for you.* New York: Routledge

Tapscott, D. (1998). *Growing up digital: The rise of the net generation.* New York: McGraw

Tapscott, D. (2009). *Grown up digital: How the net generation is changing your world.* New York: McGraw-Hill.

2

Engaging Students Through a Core Problem to Solve

It's Tuesday and a global history teacher is presenting her students with a lesson on the timeline of events during the new imperialism period in Africa's history. Why? Because this is where it falls in the curriculum. She's a dynamic teacher who presents the material with ease. She involves the class in the lesson, building the timeline as she goes. She gives them a map of Africa to fill in as the timeline progresses. As you watch, you wonder what her students are thinking, how interested they are in the topic, and whether they see the need for this information in their lives. Are they truly engaged in the meaning of the content or are they merely being compliant?

Next door, her colleague has just presented her students with an opportunity to select one of the seventeen goals from the U.N.'s 2030 Agenda for Sustainable Development that addresses needs in Africa and determine how youth in their local community might join in to make a difference. She shows short video clips that powerfully highlight some of the seventeen goals; she shares news from the most recent U.N. Youth Assembly and points out that they can apply to be delegates if they so choose. She and her students discuss how these issues affect them in their lives and why they should get involved. She shares that she put copies of "UN and SDGs: A Handbook for Youth" in the *resource area*, along with a narrative of this challenge and a guiding rubric. She stresses the importance of understanding the historical underpinnings of these topics in terms of the effects of the age of new imperialism and the more current neo-imperialism in order to substantiate their claims and solutions. Suddenly, you see the power of engagement. As students delve into the goals of the 2030 Agenda, they will have the need to learn more about the new imperialism that led to or exacerbated the current conditions in Africa and how it affects them. In order to develop their plan, they will need to build an argument, laying the historical foundation and addressing current actions of imperialistic countries that are affecting Africa. The teacher will provide a variety of ways for each student to learn and grapple with the concepts and content, including a *small-group mini-lesson* with her on the timeline progression of new imperialism.

The first teacher relies on her charismatic personality and interesting delivery to engage her students. It's hard to tell if students are driven by the subject matter or by her. In contrast, the second teacher develops an activity that will allow students to take charge of their learning, producing a need for her students to learn the desired content—not just a need she presents intellectually, but a need that her students *feel* because they cannot complete the task without this content. People learn best from a *felt need*.

The first step to engaging students' minds and getting them grappling with content is to ensure they have a *felt need* to learn. *Problem-based learning* provides an excellent venue for creating *felt need*. The more authentic the problem, and the more voice students have in deciding on a problem to solve, the more likely students will be to want to tackle it, learn, and then work tirelessly toward their goal.[1] At the start of designing your *Learner-Active,*

> **"The more authentic the problem, and the more voice students have in deciding on a problem to solve, the more likely students will be to want to tackle it, learn, and then work tirelessly toward their goal."**

Technology-Infused Classroom, you will design the problems for students to solve so that you build your own understanding of a powerful *problem-based task* and accompanying structures. As your comfort level increases, you can have students identify problems they wish to solve within a content topic. Eventually, consider allowing students to present problems they want to solve while you determine how you can weave the curriculum into their interests. For now, we'll address teacher-designed *problem-based tasks.*

---

1 The phrases "project based" and "problem based" are often used interchangeably. For the purposes of this book, project-based learning could involve closed-ended problems, such as creating a scale drawing of the school. *Problem-based learning* involves solving open-ended problems, such as creating a scale drawing of a proposed school that would be considered a geometric work of art. In this way, *problem-based learning* is a subset of project-based learning. Here, you will focus on *problem-based learning* to truly engage students in the process of grappling with content.

Three Pillars

The *Learner-Active, Technology-Infused Classroom* is a framework that includes problem-based *Authentic Learning Units* (*ALUs*), a collection of structures that put students in charge of their own learning, and powerful teacher facilitation of learning. The *ALU* engages students in learning; the structures empower students to take responsibility for their own learning; and the teacher's facilitation strategies build students' ability to put a plan into action to achieve success, thus, building efficacy. Essentially, you can't have one or two without the others, or you don't have a *Learner-Active, Technology-Infused Classroom*. All three pillars are needed to support your classroom and the eventual achievement of student efficacy.

You might find that all of the structures work well in empowering your students; however, without the *ALU*, students only compliantly work through lists of activities. You might like introducing each unit with a new *ALU*, but without the empowerment structures, your students will still be dependent on you for their next steps. You might find that, armed with an *ALU* and empowerment structures, your classroom can run without you; but it can't. Your students don't know what they don't know; they need you to push their academic thinking and help them learn to take control of their learning. Three pillars: that's what you need!

First, you (and eventually you and your students) will design the *ALU*; then you'll delve into the related structures and facilitation strategies to make it work. Think of it as a three-legged stool: you won't have stability unless all three legs are present (see Figure 2.1).

Figure 2.1. Three-Legged Stool

CONSIDER

Learning From a Felt Need

Think about all that you have learned in school, and all that you remember. Can you name the six noble gases? Can you state the cause of the French and Indian War? Can you explain the relationship between the length of the hypotenuse and the length of the legs of a right triangle? Can you define a chromatic scale? Can you factor a polynomial? Can you identify the number of lines and rhyming scheme of an English sonnet? Can you name three artists from the Renaissance period? Most likely, you learned *all* of that in school; yet for many, it is difficult to recall the answers to all of these questions.

Can you offer directions for how to get from your house to your place of work or school? Can you tell someone how to succeed at your favorite hobby? Can you explain how to make an appointment for a haircut? Can you recite the lyrics to a favorite song? Can you explain how to brush your teeth? Chances are, these questions are slightly less challenging than the previous. Why? In the case of this set of questions, you most likely, at some point, were motivated, compelled, driven, or inspired to learn this information; you built this knowledge in an authentic context: you had a *felt need* to learn. You may have learned the information in the former set of questions well enough to succeed on a test, but how much of that knowledge did you retain?

The fact that many teachers offer review before tests speaks to the reality that they don't believe their students can learn and retain information. As a teacher, it is sad to think that your students will never remember much of what you will teach them. That's a lot of time and energy on your part to reap little return on investment. Clearly, part of schooling, particularly in the secondary grades, is mastering the art and science of learning, so it may not be so important to remember some of the content. However, given that people learn best when they have a *felt need* to learn, teachers could improve students' retention if they positioned content to be presented within an authentic context.

My first memorable experience related to learning from a *felt need* was at age 12, when I decided to build a treehouse. I started nailing boards to trees, and my father stopped me, pointing out that I really should start with a blueprint. Together, we created a scale drawing of the proposed tree house. I had a *felt need* to learn ratio and proportion. We then framed out the house with studs, 16 inches on center, as they say in the building industry; we were doing this the right way! This treehouse wouldn't have any ordinary ladder;

we designed a staircase. I had a *felt need* to learn how to use a protractor. What an exciting project it was! I later became a math teacher.

Frank Smith, in *The Book of Learning and Forgetting* (1998), distinguishes between classic learning, which develops "inconspicuously and effortlessly" from a *felt need* in our everyday lives, and official learning, which is intended to develop from hard work and a structured, controlled teaching approach. He pointed out that by the time they enter school, children have learned about 10,000 words without any formal education, and that was before the advent of today's technology! Teachers complain the students can't learn the twenty vocabulary words on the weekly list; but Smith's research showed that, on average, young children are learning in excess of 2,000 words a year without formal training. Perhaps one of the differentiating factors is *felt need*. Note that this research was prior to the availability of digital devices and apps that provide independent learning experiences.

I was speaking with a ninth-grade teacher who was a thirty-year veteran teacher, beloved by his students. His passion for his craft was evident as he applied to run a *Learner-Active, Technology-Infused Classroom*—essentially, starting all over again to design a very different classroom. After his first year he told me that during a unit in May, he overheard his students talking and recalling information they'd learned in September. He said that in his thirty years of teaching, he never had his students recall and talk about what they learned in September. *Felt need* is a major factor for retention of information.

From Skills First to Application First

It's time to consider a necessary paradigm shift for your classroom (Figure 2.2). The conventional approach to instruction has been to teach lower-order skills first, and then to provide a scenario through which students can apply those skills, often known as the culminating project.

For example, the teacher presents lessons on the Pythagorean Theorem and how it is used in Metcalfe's Law to assess the strength of a

Figure 2.2. Paradigm Shift

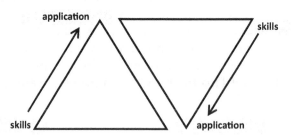

telecommunications network. Near the end of the unit, the students who have completed their work are presented with a project: assess the social network of an organization or person of their choice to make recommendations for improvement.

While this may seem like an interesting challenge to pursue, the problem lies in the teacher's approach. Students are expected to learn the Pythagorean Theorem absent of a meaningful reason why. The danger here is that students may not see the need for isolated skills and therefore not fully engage themselves in the learning process, such that some students may never, in the teacher's mind, excel to the point of the problem-solving phase and thus remain at the bottom of Bloom's taxonomy indefinitely!

Instead, in the *Learner-Active, Technology-Infused Classroom*, instruction begins with an authentic, open-ended problem that presents a context for learning. Opening a unit of study on the Pythagorean theorem with the "More Friends Good, Fewer Friends Bad?" problem (Appendix A), thus placing students in the position of social media advisor, creates "buy in," as students know their findings and recommendations could be useful to themselves or others. In this case, they may actually succeed in improving their own or an organization's social media network. I've seen high school students have their work and recommendations adopted by local businesses. The open-endedness inspires students to create, and therefore engage with, the subject matter. Once students possess a *felt need* for skills, teachers can provide opportunities through which students can learn. Learning becomes meaningful and interesting. This requires shifting an age-old paradigm of the teaching–learning process: from teacher as information deliverer to teacher as learning facilitator. This shift is made easier by the advent of computer technology in classrooms. Computer technology and Internet access provide educators with exceptional resources for both setting the context and building the skills.

Let's see how this might play out in the classroom. (Some of the vocabulary here may be new to you, but all of the terms will be introduced in subsequent chapters.) A teacher is about to start the unit on renewable energy that includes hydroelectric power. Consider how this teacher might build a scenario to set the context for learning:

The mention of waterfalls makes many people in the northeast United States, where I grew up, think of Niagara Falls. In addition to being a beautiful and inspirational tourist attraction, Niagara Falls has been one of the world's top producers of hydroelectric power since the early 1900s. Did you know, though, that Marmore's Falls in Italy is actually man-made? It soars more than three times the height of Niagara Falls. The most interesting part, however, is that it was constructed in approximately 271 BC! For greater electric power, perhaps we should tap into local water sources to locate or even propose the construction of a waterfall.

The teacher has set the stage for learning about hydroelectric power (Appendix B). He is attempting to create a *felt need* for the subject-area content. First, the teacher will "launch" the unit by presenting the scenario through facts, videos, pictures, and more. The intent is to energize the students around solving the problem. Next, he will share an *analytic rubric* with the class, asking students to carefully read the Practitioner column with their group and make a list of what they're going to need to learn. Then he will lead a class discussion on the task, what they will need to learn, and how they're going to find the information they need. From there, he will provide students with an activity list for the first week that offers them a variety of ways through which to learn. He will refer to the *scaffold for learning* he designed during unit planning in order to develop subsequent *activity lists* from which students will plan out their learning paths. This scaffold includes certain whole-class, *benchmark lessons*, such as the concept of renewable and non-renewable energy, the hydrological cycle and its impact on hydroelectric power, the environmental consequences of hydroelectric power, and so forth. It includes some *small-group mini-lessons* for those students who need help in certain concepts or skills, such as understanding the different types of hydro plants, calculating the amount of available power, the impact of damming on the regional ecosystem, and so forth. For some skills, a *how-to sheet* of instructions or a screencast will provide the direct instruction needed. *Peer experts*, various related assignments, quizzes, tests, websites, computer software, a waterfall simulation, and more will complete the *scaffold for learning*. The teacher will ask the groups to determine how they will tackle the problem. He'll be looking for a mix between individual and collaborative work. Individuals will be expected to observe, conduct information searches, keep a designer's log, draw diagrams, make calculations, and suggest a possible water source within the region or state. Group members will come together to share information, discuss similarities and differences in their findings, and develop the final plan.

Many of the activities that will take place in the class will be the kind of activities that take place in most good classrooms today, with four major exceptions:

1. The *problem-based task* is presented at the start of the unit to build a *felt need* for learning.

2. The *analytic rubric* is used to guide instruction, not assess a final project.

3. Not all students are doing the same thing at the same time. Students plan how they will use their time, thus providing for seamless differentiation, maximizing classroom resources, and building the kinds of project-management skills needed in 21st-century society.

4. The teacher actively facilitates learning by moving around the room and meeting with individuals and groups, with minimal time spent addressing the entire class.

Designing your instructional units to present students with the problem or challenge at the start of the unit will increase the likelihood that students will be driven by a *felt need* to learn. This engagement will increase the likelihood that students will retain their learning. Teachers are always surprised when they realize that students coming to them from well-run *Learner-Active, Technology-Infused Classrooms* do not experience "summer slide," retain what they learned the prior year.

What Makes a Problem?

The word "problem" can sound intimidating, as though there is something wrong that must be fixed. In the *Learner-Active, Technology-Infused Classroom*, a problem is an open-ended challenge, meaning that there is no one right answer. For years, students have been focusing on being able to raise their hands and have the one, right answer, focusing heavily on convergent thinking. Today's global citizens must be both divergent and convergent thinkers: able to generate questions and ideas, thinking widely, thus divergently, and able to synthesize information and test out ideas against known facts and data to determine the best idea or plan, thinking narrowly, thus convergently.

"Today's global citizens must be both divergent and convergent thinkers: able to generate questions and ideas, thinking widely, thus divergently, and able to synthesize information and test out ideas against known facts and data to determine the best idea or plan, thinking narrowly, thus convergently."

Years ago I was granted funding for a study to offer insights as to whether or not learning in a *Learner-Active, Technology-Infused Classroom* improved critical and creative thinking. (The results indicated that there is merit to that notion.) I conducted the study across two fourth-grade classrooms. One class (control group) studied in the more conventional ways of schooling. The other (experimental group) studied through a *Learner-Active, Technology-Infused Classroom* approach. Both groups studied their state, part of the social studies curriculum. At the end of the initial learning period, the two classes were presented with a related problem to solve in forty-five minutes, in groups of four. The problem was to consider where to construct another airport in the state. For each group of four students, I read and handed out the problem, pointed out that they had a wealth of resources in the classroom, including Internet access, and told them they had forty-five minutes to develop their recommendation. I then asked if there were any questions. Consistently, the experimental group students asked questions about process, resources, and expectations. Consistently, the control group students raised their hands to call out a geographic location as the answer; I had to remind them that they had forty-five minutes to research and discuss a solution. Throughout the period, I was not in the room, but the researcher observing the groups said that the experimental groups were engaged and focused. After I returned to give them the ten-minute warning, they were even more focused to complete the solution in the time allotted; whereas the control groups decided on an answer within the first few minutes and then became behavior problems. Ten minutes later, I returned to the room to hear each group's decision.

Again, consistently, the experimental groups offered thoughtful responses with evidence as to why their chosen location would be the best; consistently, the control groups presented an answer with little supporting reasons, even when prompted for more. This small, beginning study into the topic was profound for me. By fourth grade, and no doubt earlier, student have learned that school means there is one right answer and you should identify it quickly. Still, in what was probably less than a half year of learning in a different way, the students in the *Learner-Active, Technology-Infused Classroom* broke through that mold and became thoughtful, purposeful, solution finders. Engaging students in solving open-ended challenges makes the difference.

In the case of this airport problem, the challenge wasn't as much of a problem (there was nothing wrong with the existing airports) as a scenario: what if the state were to build another airport? The scenario has no one right answer, no teacher's-edition answer; it only has to satisfy a collection of criteria, such as being large enough, avoiding wetlands, and so on.

Designing an original poem, short story, piece of art, or performance are also open-ended problems with no one right answer, but, rather, criteria that must be satisfied. So don't let the word "problem" make you think something has to be wrong. Of course, there are a plethora of real-world situations with problems to solve that should be included in your collection as well; but every *problem-based task* does not have to be a problem to be fixed. Sometimes, the problem could be developing a new creation, work of art, recreational idea, or plan to enhance one's life.

The key is to ensure that, to address the *problem-based task*, it is not enough for students to simply learn information and present it in a new format. They must "grapple" with content to develop something new related to the content itself, as opposed to the presentation of content. More on this later. For now, just know that a problem is any open-ended situation in which students must create something original based on applying their understanding of the curricular content. In the *Learner-Active, Technology-Infused*

Classroom, the problem is further enhanced by reflecting authentic, real-world situations or possibilities.

The best problems have a balance between collaborative problem-solving and individual content mastery. The *problem-based task* is intended to be a small-group problem with two to four students engaged in offering a feasible solution. While the planning, brainstorming, solution discussion, and evaluation are best addressed as a team, activities related to building content mastery are largely accomplished individually. This ensures that students build individual content mastery, but also build the skills of collaborative problem solving.

How Many Problem-Based Tasks?

In the *Learner-Active, Technology-Infused Classroom*, a unit of study begins with an authentic *problem-based task* and includes myriad robust and varied opportunities to learn. The *ALU*, therefore, with a *problem-based task* at the core, serves as the cornerstone of the learning experience. Armed with a well-crafted *ALU*, students can identify what they know and what they need to learn, make decisions about activities in which they will engage, monitor their own progress, and take responsibility for their own learning. Therefore, all content should be addressed through an *ALU*.

Given that students learn best from a *felt need*, every curricular unit should be designed as a problem-based *ALU*, which means you'll need to design back-to-back *ALUs* across the year. A typical *ALU* lasts four to five weeks. The intent is to allow students enough time to engage with the problem and grapple with the content in order to build understanding and the ability to apply it to solve the problem. As the teacher, it takes time and mental energy to design an *ALU* with all of the support materials, so you would not want to have to design them on a weekly basis.

If designing multiple, back-to-back *ALUs* sounds daunting, take heart. Although learning to craft an exceptional *ALU* at first takes time and patience, the results in the classroom will make the investment worthwhile. The first *ALU* is the hardest to design. You'll find each successive design experience to be faster and easier. If you have other grade-level or subject-area colleagues with whom to design, you can divide and conquer!

CREATE

Optimally, students will become problem-finders and identify the problems they wish to solve. However, when getting started in designing your *Learner-Active, Technology-Infused Classroom*, it is important for you and your students to benefit from a careful application of the basics of unit design. As you become more familiar with problem design, you can involve your students in cocreating problems with you and, eventually, allow students to decide on problems they wish to solve independently or in groups. Students in *Learner-Active, Technology-Infused Classrooms* routinely generate lists of problems that need to be addressed in the school, community, state, nation, and world. They then decide on those they wish to solve. Move at your own pace, though: first learn to design a well-crafted *ALU*, and then you can move to increasing student voice in problem generation.

For starters, design the *problem-based task statement* of the *ALU* for an upcoming unit of study. Remember that the purpose of the *problem-based task* is to motivate students, giving them a purpose for their learning. Given that, think about your classroom and the content you need to teach. Your goal is to develop an authentic, open-ended task that will create a *felt need* for your students to learn the curricular content.

Here are some guiding steps to developing your task. If you find yourself having difficulty with any of the steps, return to the previous step and rethink your decisions:

Step 1: Keep the Standards in Mind

A well-crafted *ALU* addresses curricular standards and, even though it is focused on specific subject-area content, often addresses standards from across the year and across subject areas. The best design approach would be to simply consider your overall curriculum for the year; ask yourself what kind of problems or challenges students could address if they understood the year's content; brainstorm *problem-based task* ideas, and then, using scope and sequence charts, check off all of the concepts and skills that would be addressed by the *task*. After brainstorming a few different *problem-based tasks*, you will start to see the gaps and focus on designing additional *problem-based tasks* to address those gaps. However, in an effort to monitor teaching toward student achievement, some schools have put in place pacing guides that require specific curricula to be taught at specific times, which does not allow for a lot of flexibility in *ALU* design. If that is your situation, start with the curricular standards for the time period you need to address and brainstorm a *problem-based task* around that specific content.

Consider your curriculum and identify the general content, skills, and concepts you plan to teach over a four- to five-week period. Remember, units that run for longer than five weeks tend to become too complex, and students can lose focus on important content. Units that run for fewer than two weeks tend to be too labor intensive to design and don't allow students to explore content with much depth.

As you begin the process, make a list of the concepts and skills you plan to teach over the specified period of time. It's important that your unit not exceed the amount of time you would normally allocate for the content. If your content focus is too limited—for example, standard deviation —it may be difficult to identify an authentic problem to solve, and you will not cover enough content in the time period. If your focus is too broad—such as statistics — it may be difficult to identify an authentic problem to solve that covers all of the curricular skills. In this case, descriptive statistics might be a nice grouping of skills for which to generate an *ALU*.

You may also find that as you map out your concepts and skills, several that may have been originally slated for different times of the year will intertwine. Be open to cross-unit content connections when generating authentic problems. Sometimes, however, a *problem-based task* can seem so interesting that it takes on a life of its own, but veers off the course standards. Just be sure that you focus on standards your students need to master in the time allotted in the curriculum to cover it.

Step 2: Think Application

Suppose your students did, in fact, master all of that content. What could they do with it? What problems could they solve? What challenges could they address? What could they create? Why do students need the information? With what audience could they share their ideas and solutions? If you have trouble identifying a *problem-based task*, you might be looking at too narrow a topic. Try combining topics. In the earlier example of "More Friends Good, Fewer Friends Bad?" (Appendix A), you would be hard-pressed to come up with a task for learning about the relationship between the length of the sides and the length of the hypotenuse of a right triangle; it's much easier to design a task around the broader topic of application of the Pythagorean theorem. That challenge will build a *felt need* for students to learn the more basic skills related to right triangles and relationship between the length of the sides and the length of the hypotenuse.

Start by asking yourself, "When would someone use this knowledge?" After you respond, once again, ask yourself, "So what?" That will drive you to consider how important that application of the knowledge is. Once you defend your answer, ask, "But why?" As you continually apply the "Why?" and "So what?" questions, you will hone in on an interesting problem. Below is an internal dialogue from those who have developed *ALUs*.

> Students need to know how the United States became a country because it's important to understand the history of our country.
>
> *Why?* Because history often repeats itself.
>
> *So what?* Well, the history of our country's emergence may repeat itself in the world today.
>
> *Why?* Well, ultimately human beings seek independence and control over their lives.

Ahhhh, so perhaps students should consider a territory today that the United Nations has identified as being under colonial rule, with the goal of decolonization, and study the American Revolutionary War through the lens of deciding what lessons can be applied to this other country's situation.

In this case, the students would not be expected to spend an inordinate amount of time studying the other country, as that would represent too much of a departure from the curriculum. They might, however, research a country for homework to set the context for studying the American Revolution. Throughout their study, they would keep track of similarities and differences in the histories of the two countries.

This problem-based challenge covers myriad concepts and skills in the areas of colonization, cause-and-effect, timelines, research, writing, citations, claims and counterclaims, and more. Students could send their ideas to the U.N.

Another strategy for identifying a strong problem is to use "The Tree of Whys." You can access a video on IDE Corp.'s YouTube Channel (www.youtube.com/user/LATIClassroom). You begin by brainstorming three reasons the content is important. From each of those, you draw three lines and develop three reasons why that reason is important. You then find the ones that are really compelling and, then, from each of those you begin to draw three lines and develop further reasons, although at some point in the process you will hone in on a strong problem (see Figure 2.3).

Figure 2.3. Tree of Whys

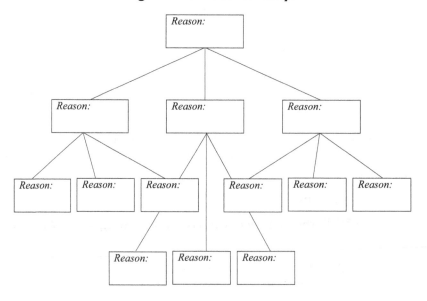

Given that today's Internet-savvy students are aware of and interested in the real world, problems derived from reality are often very motivating. A great source of real-world problems is the news. Peruse newspapers, news shows, and the Internet, and you are likely to find a wealth of ideas from which to write your authentic problems. Problem-focused organizations include www.un.org, www.weforum.org, www.peacecorps.gov, www.wri.org, www.worldwatercouncil.org, www.who.int, and others.

Your objective is to arrive at an authentic, open-ended problem that will intrigue and motivate students and build a *felt need* to learn the content. Most *problem-based tasks* should be addressed by a group of students so that they are collaborative in nature. (Note, however: individual content mastery and responsibility are the key to success. Your *ALU* should never set up a situation where one student does all the work or, conversely, a student fails to learn the necessary content.) As you brainstorm, generate as many different ideas as you can before you commit to one. It is often tempting to take the first idea that comes to mind; but the best idea generally emerges a little farther into the brainstorming process.

Step 3: Think Authenticity and Relevance

Remember, brain research (Sousa, 2017) tells us that for information to settle into long-term memory, it must make sense and have meaning. Consider this exercise from James Adams' book *Conceptual Blockbusting* (1990). For best results, cover the rest of the page and only uncover the text as you read it. Take a look at the list of words below for about eight seconds and try to memorize them.

> **saw, when, panicked, Jim, ripped, haystack, the, relaxed, when, cloth, the, but, he**

Chances are, you can remember about seven of the thirteen words, the typical number of disconnected pieces of information the human brain can remember at once. Now look at the same words below for a few seconds to see if it's easier to remember them.

> **Jim panicked when the cloth ripped, but relaxed when he saw the haystack.**

Most people find it easier to remember the words once they are presented in a sentence, because arranged into the known grammatical structure of a sentence, *they make sense*. Can you remember the sentence? Most people still have difficulty. What if I told you that Jim was jumping out of a plane using a parachute? Look at the sentence one more time. Now the sentence is even easier to remember. The context provides *meaning*. When you present content to your students in the absence of sense and meaning, it appears like those thirteeen disconnected words.

Ensuring that content is presented with sense and meaning can be accomplished by providing students with authentic contexts for learning the content. Authenticity means that a problem is realistic, could happen, or could fall into the realm of science fiction.

Relevance means that the problem could actually occur in a student's life at that time. Thus, relevant tasks are a subset of authentic tasks. Designing a scale model of a hotel suite to pitch to a hotel is authentic and, depending on the students' interest in pitching to a hotel owner, it could be relevant. However, it might be more relevant to design a skateboarding park that could be pitched to the principal and school board or to the town government.

Sometimes relevance emerges through the existence of an audience. For example, should voting in national elections be required by law? Engaging in a debate would be authentic, in that this is a question often pondered. Developing a position and contacting members of government who would be involved in this decision makes it more relevant as the student is actually communicating with an audience that can propose legislation. Analyzing poetry and writing an original poem is authentic, and, depending on the student's view and subject area, may be relevant. Submitting poems to www. teenink.com for possible publication makes the task even more relevant, since the intent is to have the student's work widely shared.

Secondary school students typically thrive on relevant tasks, so, where possible, make the *problem-based task* both authentic and relevant. At the high school level, students should be engaging in high levels of reasoning, as in a debate, building mathematical proofs, or literary analysis. It is important to resist feeling compelled to fabricate some contrived scenario for your ALU. Sometimes the problem itself is being able to think at the level of writing a literary analysis; however, identify the "why" behind it so students have a reason to engage in literary analysis. Throughout life, students will read fiction and non-fiction with authors attempting to convey both obvious and subtle messages; life relationships will depend on a student's ability to understand the deeper meaning in a communicative setting, and to be able to communicate in writing as well. Literary analysis represents the difference between saying, "nice story," and "wow!" Thus, literary analysis prepares one for more effective communication in life. That's a worthy, relevant reason to engage in literary analysis.

In the *Learner-Active, Technology-Infused Classroom*, learning is driven by a real-world, authentic, open-ended, application-oriented problem to solve. The *problem-based task* for your *ALU* must be authentic. If the problem is also relevant, then that's a bonus. It is most likely not feasible to develop a curriculum of entirely relevant problems; but some of the *ALUs* you present to students should be relevant. All should be authentic.

Step 4: Think Open-Endedness

In the world of content, there is the known and the unknown. In 1940s America, people worked largely in factories, on farms, or in service areas. Their success rested upon following specific rules and protocols. In today's creative economy (Howkins, 2013), the most successful workers solve problems, generate ideas, and create. All of the latter require being immersed in the unknown and its possibilities. School curricula today still focus on mastering the *known*, with some expectation that applying that content to the unknown will magically follow.

An *ALU* should focus students both on the known and the unknown. It is in the realm of the *unknown* that the best, open-ended, authentic problems emerge. If students are to learn about the plate tectonics, they could certainly create a 3D representation of the Earth's plates. Such a project exists in the realm of the known. The student researches plate tectonics and references maps and models in order to create a replica. It may be a fun and interesting project, but it is not open-ended, thus, it's not a problem.

Asking a student to predict future changes to the Earth based on these moving plates now moves to the "unknown," as does asking students to consider changes and threats to where they currently live, the land of their recent ancestors, or destinations they may want to live in the future makes it more relevant, in addition to being open-ended.

No one right answer exists, as the "right" answer is yet unknown. Open-ended problems do not have one right answer. At best, students can propose a plausible answer. In their quest for this answer, however, they grapple with content; that is, they think deeply about it, question it, and think about it through various perspectives. Open-ended problems produce a *felt need* to learn and allow students to grapple with content.

The next time you consider asking a student to write a report or create a model, ask yourself if the task moves beyond students simply capturing and reporting on the known. How can you move it to the realm of the unknown? What can they *do* with that information to create new information, recommendations, or solutions?

Engagement in learning is less about what students are doing with their bodies and more about what students are doing with their minds. Some tend to think that if students are working in groups, talking with one another, using computers, and exploring content through hands-on situations, they are engaged. They may be engaging their bodies, but not necessarily their minds. Reciting the outcomes of the U.S. Civil War as a result of students working in groups, playing matching games, and the like might engage bodies and mouths, but not minds. Asking students to propose how life today might be different if the South won the war engages their minds. They have to think; they have to apply the *known* to determine the *unknown*.

As you brainstorm task ideas, continue to refine them to make them sufficiently open-ended, thus promoting engagement in curricular content. Decide how they might apply all of the *known* content to propose a solution to a problem for which the solution is yet *unknown*.

Step 5: Think Audience

Once the students arrive at their solutions, with whom will they share that information? As David Geurin (2017) says, "avoid the trash can finish" (p. 89). Audience is important as it connects students to a more authentic reason to solve the problem than handing in an assignment to the teacher for approval. Audience could include school-based personnel, as in the case of pitching the idea for a new elective to the principal, or making recommendations to the food services director for new menu items based on student surveys and nutritional analysis. An audience for an *ALU* could be a local business or organization, a friend or family member, a government official, an author, a newspaper or magazine, a company, or a national or international organization! Might the task have global implications, promoting global citizenship? Might it have national or local implications? How can students feel like they are really making a difference by developing this solution? How can you use audience to expand students' thinking about their place in the world? "The sense of audience is an opportunity to practice empathy, to picture the project through the end user's eyes" (Geurin, 2017, p. 89).

Step 6: Think Product

What will students *do* to present their solution to the problem? What will the final product look like? Avoid thinking along the lines of a project, with "glue and glitter flying." A product could be a poem, op-ed article, webpage, poster, song, prototype, storyboard, series of graphs, infographic, skit, work of art, or multimedia presentation.

Consider offering choices based on learning styles and multiple intelligences. If the presentation of the content is not the curricular goal of the *ALU*, might you give students options for presentation? Clearly, if your curricular goal is an argumentative essay, then that's what it is! However, if your curricular goal is preventing the extinction of a species, does it matter whether students create a video, an infographic, or a letter? Universal Design for Learning (UDL—www.cast.org) presents guidelines for ensuring that all students have access to quality instruction, thus maximizing their learning potential. One of the three tenets is to "Provide Multiple Means of Action and Expression." To what extent can you allow students to choose the product?

You must first decide what you are looking for students to demonstrate in terms of content. Then you can decide what options to offer students in terms of their delivery of that demonstration of knowledge. Students will appreciate the choice of final product. Students may even suggest viable products other than those you have in mind.

Design your *ALU* as a collaborative problem-solving experience for pairs, triads, or a group of four. Think about how many students should be involved in tackling the task, and design the task statement so that all students have a powerful learning experience. Some *ALUs* or aspects of *ALUs* lend themselves better to pairs than groups of three or four. You could also design a collaborative task in which there are parts that you want each student to tackle individually. For example, students might engage in problem-solving and brainstorming as a group, but then individually write their argumentative essay, if that is the skill you are teaching.

Step 7: Think Content

It is important to engage students in grappling with targeted content that aligns with curricular standards. One common pitfall of employing a more authentic, open-ended approach to learning is to allow the product and/or media to overwhelm the content. Students who are asked to create a multimedia presentation on encouraging people to vote may spend a significant amount of time searching the Web for pictures and sound bites; they may work hard to learn new slide transitions and interesting ways to present the information. All of these are worthy skills, but they have little to do with civics. This is not to say that you should not have students make multimedia presentations; rather, that you should have them use class time engaging with critical subject-area content and develop the multimedia aspects on one particular class period or for homework.

When designing an authentic, open-ended, *problem-based task* statement, continually assess how much of students' time will be spent focusing on the primary content of the unit. Figure 2.4 represents a graphic organizer that can be used to assess content focus in a task statement. The center bull's-eye represents the concepts and skills included in solving the authentic, open-ended tasks that are most closely aligned to the curricular content. Concepts and skills that are related to the content or other grade-level skills, perhaps covered in other units or subject areas across the school year, reside in the second ring from the center. Finally, concepts and skills that have little to do with the course content or related content, no matter how worthy they might be, reside in the outermost ring, representing peripheral content.

In "A Place for Robots" (Appendix C), students are designing a robot that could help NASA in their quest for exploring Europa, one of Saturn's icy moons. While it might prove interesting for students to research other planets and moons that might have evidence of water, and it might be

Figure 2.4. Bullseye Graphic Organizer

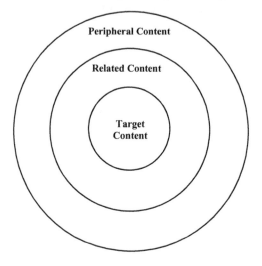

helpful to building students' science knowledge, if science is not your target content, you'll want to minimize the amount of class time spent on this in favor of the targeted content, which in this case is robotics. You could allow students to research alternate sites for NASA to explore outside of class as an optional activity. You could connect with the science teacher to see if there could be a connection between science class and robotics class for this unit.

When designing an *ALU*, strive for the bulk of the content and the bulk of the students' in-class time to be focused on targeted content, with some time spent on related content, and little or no class time spent on peripheral content. Peripheral content may be tolerated based on other school goals. For example, if using a design process is a goal of a STEM/STEAM school, it would make sense to engage students in applying design process strategies even when writing an original poem.

Students will need to develop a final product that demonstrates their mastery of the content, and, in some cases, the skills involved in that physical product development are neither in the center nor second ring of Figure 2.3. For example, developing an argument might be the content; however, creating a multimedia presentation to portray it may not be course content. To ensure that the product does not overwhelm the content, establish clear timelines as to when your students can work on the product. For example, have them gather up the information they plan to present and then give them one block of time to develop the presentation.

Another pitfall is to design an authentic, open-ended problem around a real-world event that is exciting, such as the Olympics or a presidential election, where the content isn't in the curriculum. Students are engaged and excited, but they are not grappling with the content of the course or grade level. It is often possible, however, to creatively connect your content to a critical news event by focusing on one aspect of the event or from the perspective of the subject area.

Take a moment to reconsider and refine your task ideas to ensure that your students will focus most of their time on the target content of your curriculum standards.

A Look at a Sample Task Statement

Read through the following task statement, designed for high school students:

> It's easy to take the water we drink for granted—turn on a tap and it's always there. But the water we drink every day has traveled for many miles through rivers and pipes to get to the tap for that convenient drink. In some countries, people (including children!) spend days travelling miles to and from their nearest water supply. Both here and abroad, these precious water supplies are continually threatened by pollution and development, which can make the water undrinkable and even cause our rivers and wells to dry up when rainwater no longer accumulates in these sources.
>
> In this we see the seeds of a global problem. In towns and cities across the United States, water supplies are under threat; beyond our borders, people in developing countries have to battle against large industries to get access to drinking water. Countries on the same river are worried about those upstream polluting their water, and if there will even be any clean water left for them. There is no alternative for water, and it is essential for life. Territory, religion, and energy resources have always been at the root of large-scale wars. Could the next global conflict be over water?
>
> Here in New Jersey, we can see the effects of using local water as a dump for industrial, agricultural, and residential waste. The Passaic River has suffered for centuries as a dumping ground for all kinds of pollutants, from raw sewage to cancer-causing dioxins. As well as being under threat from pollution, the river itself is at risk of disappearing as more and more of its basin is being built upon—reducing the amount of water that gets into the river.

At every level—individuals, communities, and governments—people can take action. American Water (the largest water utility company in New Jersey, and supplier for Paterson) is offering grants of up to $10,000 for community projects that can help to protect the future water supply of New Jersey. How can the Passaic River be cleaned and protected for the future? Some project ideas are listed below:

♦ Watershed Cleanup

♦ Reforestation Efforts

♦ Biodiversity Projects (habitat restoration, wildlife protection)

♦ Streamside Buffer Restoration Projects

♦ Wellhead Protection Initiatives

♦ Hazardous Waste Collection Efforts

♦ Surface or Groundwater Protection Education

Your task is to develop a proposal for American Water that will address concerns about the Passaic River and show how we can preserve our local water resources for future generations. But cleaning up one river is only part of the solution. You will then take your project plan beyond your local area and look for other areas around the world where similar problems exist. You will publish your project proposal as a plan of action for local communities in the global village.

Let's take a look at how the task designer purposefully and deliberately designed this task:

1. The task statement immediately connects the students' personal experience to the content through the statement "turn on the tap water and it's always there." Students can relate to that experience.

2. Next, the task statement deepens the students' understanding of the situation with "the water we drink every day has traveled many miles through rivers and pipes." Students may not have thought of that.

3. Pointing out that even children walk for days and miles to retrieve water elicits an emotional response from the students, and emotional responses increase the likelihood of learning.

4. To challenge the students to engage with the problem, the task statement presents the severity of the problem with "water supplies are continually threatened by pollution and development, which can make the water undrinkable and even cause our rivers and wells to dry up."

5. The second paragraph expands upon the students' knowledge base and presents some enduring understandings: "There is no alternative for water," "water is essential for life," "territory, religion, and energy resources have always been at the root of large-scale wars."

6. The paragraph also presents an interesting higher-order, global question to drive home the importance of the topic: "Could the next global conflict be over water?"

7. The third paragraph moves from a more global perspective to a local problem, in this case the polluted state of a local river.

8. Next, the task presents an actual grant opportunity that exists, making the task authentic *and* relevant. (Remember, relevancy is important to high school students.)

9. The task statement then presents an authentic demonstration of knowledge: "How can the Passaic River be cleaned up and protected for the future?"

10. The bulleted list offers students choices of content focus, allowing them to specialize based on interest.

Finally, the task statement lays out the product to be developed: a proposal to clean up a local problem while making connections to other similar situations around the world.

Slow Start, Quick Finish

When designing *ALUs*, you'll most likely spend a significant amount of time designing the *problem-based task* statement. This might make you anxious at first. After all, if you spend too much time on the task statement, how will you finish designing the unit? The reality is that unit design is not an incremental process. *ALU* design is heavily front-loaded, requiring a significant amount of time to arrive at a worthy task statement. The *problem-based task* is so crucial to the success of the *ALU* that it is worth the time invested. The remaining support pieces will flow from this and take considerably less time to complete. The up-front investment in time and energy to develop a strong task will pay off in the end.

RECAP

At this point, you should have at least one task statement that you think is your best. See how it matches up to the key points covered in this chapter. Use this list to ensure that your task statement:

♦ Is standards based;

♦ Applies learning to an authentic situation;

♦ Asks students to provide a solution to an open-ended problem;

♦ Includes an audience other than the teacher and classmates;

♦ Focuses primarily on the curricular content;

♦ Connects the content to students' lives;

♦ Elicits an emotional response, where possible;

♦ Introduces vocabulary or concepts to deepen students' understanding of the content;

♦ Presents a choice of product for the students to complete.

REFERENCES

Adams, J. (1990). *Conceptual blockbusting: A guide to better ideas* (3rd ed.). Reading, PA: Addison-Wesley.

Geurin, D. (2017). *Future driven: Will your students thrive in an unpredictable world?* Bolivar, MO: David Geurin.

Howkins, J. (2013). *The creative economy: How people make money from ideas.* London: Penguin.

Smith, F. (1998). *The book of learning and forgetting.* New York: Teachers College Press.

Sousa, D. A. (2017). *How the brain learns* (5th ed.). Thousand Oaks, CA: Corwin Press.

3

Engaging Students Through Clearly Articulated Expectations

Sixth-grade students meet as a class to read through an *analytic rubric* at the launch of a unit of study. They circle everything they need to learn to accomplish the *problem-based task*. The teacher asks the students to share what they circled, making notes on the board. Together, they plan for the lessons to come: identifying skills and concepts that are new to all and those that have already been mastered by some. He uses this data to plan out *activity lists* for his students.

Eighth-grade students are studying modern-day slavery to consider the concept of slavery, its effects, and the changing landscape from the Civil War through today. Their task is to design a powerful media piece to build people's awareness of modern-day slavery and what causes a person to want to enslave another person, with the intent of motivating people to take action. As individual students decide on specific topics on which to focus and on the medium through which they will address the public, the students are designing two rows in the rubric customized to meet their needs. The teacher will then approve these rows for each student.

A ninth-grade teacher provides students with a compelling introduction to the next unit, using video clips and news stories. He asks them to then meet in their *home groups*, have one person retrieve copies of the *analytic rubric* from the *resource area*, and individually read down the Practitioner column, writing down questions they have about what is expected of them. He then asks them to discuss their questions with their *home group* members. After several minutes, he asks if there are any remaining questions. A student asks a question and, rather than answering it himself, the teacher asks if anyone in the class can answer the question. He is teaching his students how to read an *analytic rubric* and be clear on what is expected of them.

Twelfth-grade students come to class having watched the teacher's launch video for homework. They access the digital site the teacher created for them that includes a text version of the *task statement* and the *analytic rubric*. Students review the rubric first individually and then as a team. They click on links from the rubric to get a better understanding of what is expected of them.

Sixth-grade science students are considering the global impact of dust from the Sahara desert that is being transported to the Caribbean through the trade winds and causing the death of coral. They have three rubrics associated with the task: one for developing a causal map (see Figure 3.1), one for their solution statement, and one for the "pitch" to advocate for their solution. (See Appendix D for the task and rubrics.) As students work they refer to the rubric to determine what they have to accomplish; they then refer to an activity list that offers them learning activities to build their understanding of concepts and skills. As the teacher facilitates, she asks students to indicate where they are on the rubrics and discusses their work with them, seeking to build greater understanding and challenge them with questions to probe their thinking. She then initials certain boxes on the rubric, indicating that she agrees with the progress thus far. By the time students hand in their final plans, she'll pretty much know their level of success, as she's worked with them all along to help them to achieve at the higher levels. The rubric drives students' action and the teacher's facilitation.

A team of seventh-grade teachers is designing a themed unit around the magic in Harry Potter and lessons for adulthood. Students will engage in experiences from the novels throughout the unit across their classrooms. The science and social studies teachers have related *ALUs* for the students while the English and math teachers will incorporate their subject-area content into those *ALUs*. They will use *nested rubrics* to support students in understanding what is expected of them. That is, an *ALU* might reference scoring in the *Practitioner* column of the argumentative writing rubric; the English language arts (ELA) teacher will design the argumentative writing rubric and support students in building their writing skills.

A group of middle school students is exploring the idea that today's cloud-based technology may be setting up a new feudal system in which the currency of land is replaced by cloud ownership; essentially, are we becoming "digital serfs"? (See Appendix E.) They notice that to be in the *Expert* column, they must develop cause-and-effect chains that map Feudalism to today's cloud-based society. They decide they are definitely going for the expert level.

Figure 3.1. Rubric: Deadly Encounters—Causal Map

	Novice	Apprentice	Practitioner	Expert
Number of Events	fewer than five different events/situations	five to seven different events/situations	eight to ten different events/situations	more than ten different events/situations
Content	events beginning with the Sahara desert leading to the damage to coral reefs	♦ comprehensive chain of events detailing cause-and-effect chain from dust in the Sahara to damage to the coral reefs ♦ includes events with multiple effects	♦ comprehensive chain of events detailing cause-and-effect relationships ♦ includes events with multiple effects, with chains continuing from each ♦ includes predictions as to the effects of the death of the coral reefs to the environment and people	all of *Practitioner* plus includes other contributing factors at various points in the chain
Arrows	arrows point from cause to effect	♦ arrows point from cause to effect ♦ comments on arrows to describe relationships	♦ arrows point from cause to effect ♦ comments on arrows to describe relationships ♦ arrows are differentiated by color according to strength of relationship, e.g., major cause vs. contributing cause (includes key)	all of *Practitioner* plus arrows showing introduction of other contributing factors
Story-Telling	diagram tells a partial story of the events surrounding the problem	diagram tells a story of the events surrounding the problem, from dust in the Sahara to compromised coral reefs in the Caribbean	diagram: ♦ is easy to read and follow ♦ tells a clear story of the events leading to the problem	all of *Practitioner* plus images used to enhance the message

CONSIDER

Years ago, a principal with whom I consulted shared an idea he used in a faculty meeting, and we at IDE Corp. have used it with success ever since in training teachers to design *Learner-Active, Technology-Infused Classrooms.* In conducting workshops, we'll group teachers into fours and hand them a bag of gumdrops and a box of toothpicks. The instructions are to build your dream house using only gumdrops and toothpicks within the next fifteen minutes and then be prepared to offer a two-minute presentation on your creation.

Consistently, teachers get right to work, creating some amazing dream houses. At the end of the time period, each group of teachers shares its creation. Everyone is proud; applause is loud.

Unbeknownst to the teachers, we are carrying an *analytic rubric* that has criteria such as "includes five different geometric shapes." Most groups' creations include squares, rectangles, and triangles; some use an additional shape; few use five. Another criteria has to do with color-coding areas of the house; another with including interior and exterior walls. As we grade these marvelous creations, the scores, based on the rubric, are typically quite low.

I recall one workshop in which I was announcing the scores as I was handing out the scored rubrics. "Team A achieved a 29 percent; Team B achieved a 42 percent; Team C achieved a 36 percent, and so forth." As I read each score, I dropped the scored rubric on the table. Teachers quickly reached for the rubric to see how they were scored. The anger welled up and they indicated that they were treated unfairly. Soon someone called out, "Well if we had the rubric ahead of time, we could have gotten an A!" I didn't say a word but just waited. A hush fell across the room and then, with a sigh, someone said, "I get it." I cannot tell you how consistently this happens with groups of teachers. The teachers' own emotional response to the unfairness of judging them without first clearly articulating the expectations leads to the connection that that's what teachers do to students every day. In our consulting work, we often have teachers tell us they will never teach again without first handing out an *analytic rubric*.

In one workshop, the scores of four teams were below 50 percent; the fifth team received a 56 percent. The latter started cheering and exchanging high-fives for their success. When all quieted down, I pointed out they were cheering for an F. They stopped, admitting that they hadn't even thought of that; they were just so happy to have achieved the highest score. When you neglect to give students clearly articulated expectations up front, you set them up to accept and justify failure.

One of my colleagues was in a classroom decorated with Native American masks. She commented on how beautiful they were, to which a student responded, "Oh sure, I got a B. But I could've gotten an A if we had a rubric for *that* project. Who knew you'd get extra points if you laminated it?" Without clearly articulated expectations up front, students are left to read your mind; and if they repeatedly fall short of doing that, they stop trying.

"Without clearly articulated expectations up front, students are left to read your mind; and if they repeatedly fall short of doing that, they stop trying."

The Task–Rubric Partnership

While the *problem-based task* statement is intended to be motivational, creating a *felt need* to build content mastery, the *analytic rubric* details the targeted curricular content and provides students with clearly articulated expectations for their work. It should drive student action in the classroom. That means that students should regularly review the rubric and, based on what they need to accomplish next, take action to learn that content (Figure 3.2.).

Rubrics were originally designed as a way to assess performances on standardized tests. The goal was to have multiple people assess a piece of

Figure 3.2. The Task–Rubric Partnership

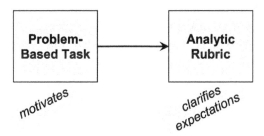

student work and arrive at the same grade, producing interrater reliability. In an *Authentic Learning Unit (ALU)*, you are going to use an *analytic rubric* to drive instruction at the start and throughout the completion of the student's work on the *problem-based task*. In this case, the *analytic rubric* offers clearly articulated expectations for the finished piece of work and a "roadmap" for getting there. Students will use the rubric before beginning any work, to gain a better understanding of their goals. They will use it throughout the unit to self-assess and set intermediate goals. As the teacher, you will use it to facilitate learning: to confer with the students regarding their current progress and guide them with further instruction and resources to achieve their goals. Essentially, the *analytic rubric* should be visible or easily accessible to students at all times; it should provide enough, specific information regarding expectations for the final product to make it useful.

Using Analytic Rubrics to Drive Instruction

The rubric describes the solution that you're expecting students to develop. That final product might be a prototype, model, article, performance, presentation, and so forth. The rubric should reflect mastery of content standards as they would be evident in the final product, the outcome of the unit of study. While the rubric offers increasingly high-quality descriptions of performance as you read across, it should not be used as a list of activities for the student to complete. It is important for the *analytic rubric* to describe what students will hand in at the end of the unit to demonstrate their understanding and application of the content.

As just mentioned, holistic rubrics were designed for large-scale assessments in which multiple raters would be grading work. The rater refers to a rubric, typically of six columns, to determine which column in its entirety best describes the work. With an *analytic rubric*, each row can be assessed independent of the other rows, thus allowing the scorer to select a different column score for each row of the rubric.

Holistic rubrics are often difficult for students to use as a guide for their work because students have to be able to assess all of the components at once, as a whole. With students being able to focus on just one aspect of the work at a time, *analytic rubrics* are particularly effective tools for driving instruction. The student assesses progress and then determines the steps to take to move to the next level.

The structure, therefore, of the *analytic rubric* is a collection of rows that represent components of the final product, and columns that represent levels of performance quality. Each cell in the rubric offers criteria for completing one component at a specific level, offering clarity for students. Given that the rubric is used by the student throughout the unit to drive learning and action, when designing an *analytic rubric*, you—and your students when you eventually engage them in cocreating—should be mindful of six important considerations:

1. *Titling Performance Levels:* Consider headings that describe developmental levels of increasing mastery that serve as a path to increasingly greater success, such as Novice, Apprentice, Practitioner, and Expert. When you are a novice at a skill, you push on to become more masterful. Avoid labeling the columns (levels of quality) as grades: A, B, C, D, and F. That is more reflective of a final grade and not conducive to using a rubric to engage students in the learning process. The message should be that it is okay to be a novice when you're first tackling a new concept or skill; in fact, it is to be expected. An *analytic rubric* with developmental headings encourages students to celebrate their progress and keep going.

2. *Creating a Progression of Success:* To create a progression of increasingly higher quality performance criteria related to a row component, label the columns with the performance levels (e.g., Novice, Apprentice, Practitioner, Expert) from left to right, with the highest-quality performance level being on the right. We read from left to right; therefore, increasing performance levels as one reads across the page sends a message that learning is a progressive journey. This allows students to first succeed at the Novice level, then move to the Apprentice level and so on.

3. *Titling Row Content:* Label the rows with the various components of the final product. For example, an informative/explanatory writing rubric might have row titles of: topic introduction, topic development, cohesion, formal writing style, and conclusion. Each row should represent a focused aspect of the final product such that you can describe it well enough for the student to succeed in performing to your level of expectation.

4. *Ordering Criteria:* Arrange the rows to mirror a reasonable order of components in building to the final product. This will help students envision how to tackle the challenge. In the informative/explanatory writing rubric example, you would label the first row

"Topic Introduction" rather than labeling it "Conclusion." Keep those components that are most connected to the target content near the top, and use the lower rows for related components. For example, if students are creating a multimedia presentation of their solution to the challenge of encouraging people to vote in elections, your curricular content is understanding government and civic responsibilities, so those rows should be near the top. The look of the presentation, while important, is secondary to the curricular content; thus, that row should be near the bottom so as to not draw too much attention to the presentation at the start.

5. *Keeping Rubric Language Positive:* Given the purpose of the rubric is to guide learning, as opposed to evaluating an already-completed assignment, use language that describes positive steps toward the goal. Avoid using negative criteria, pointing out what's missing. Instead, use positive descriptions as to what *does* exist. If you want students to represent data in a graph, the *Novice* column might read "creates a graph of the data." The *Apprentice* column might then read, "includes an appropriate graph for the data, with data accurately represented." The *Practitioner* column might then read, "includes an appropriate graph for the data with labelled axes and keys, and data accurately represented." Note that the descriptions build on one another in terms of understanding and complexity; no description represents a negative aspect of what was not included or executed properly. The student masters one developmental level and then considers what must be accomplished to master the next.

6. Build on a description of increasingly higher-quality performance as you move from left to right. Keep the criteria focused on describing the performance as opposed to activities to accomplish. Be sure that each column focuses on improving on the performance directly to the left of it.

It may be difficult to take all of this in at this point. As you review rubrics in the Appendices and then write your own, return to this list so that you gain a better understanding.

The Balance Between Quantitative and Qualitative Criteria

It is tempting to design an *analytic rubric* solely from quantitative criteria; however, it will fall far short of your academic goals for your students. Consider the (not recommended) *analytic rubric* in Figure 3.3 for writing a paragraph for admittance to a STEAM academy.

Figure 3.3. Quantitative Criteria

	Novice	Apprentice	Practitioner	Expert
Sentences	one to two sentences	three to four sentences	at least five sentences	more than five sentences
Spelling	some words are spelled correctly	no more than two errors	no more than one error	no spelling errors
Grammar	some correct grammar is evident	no more than two errors	no more than one error	no grammatical errors
Punctuation	some correct punctuation is evident	no more than two errors	no more than one error	no punctuation errors
Content	at least two criteria from expert level	three of five criteria from expert level	four of five criteria from expert level	includes name, personality adjective, reason for wanting to attend the STEAM academy

Using the rubric in Figure 3.3 for foundational writing skills, assess the following two paragraphs:

Paragraph 1: May name is Ashley Shine. I am a curious person. I like to learn about things. I like to build things. I like STEAM. I want to join the STEAM academy so I can build things.

Paragraph 2: Call me curious! (Some call me Ahsa Rodan.) A British playwright once wrote, "Curiosity killed the cat," so I'm glad I'm not a cat. Still, I have always been curious about everything around me; I have strong desire to know how things work. From as far back as I can remember, I was taking apart my toys to figure out how they worked. By fourth grade, I was assembling all of the disassembled pieces to create new inventions that would help me. I created a machine to drive my empty dish across the counter and place it in the sink. While my mom wasn't enthusiastic about that invention, she did encourage me to create and build other things. After all these years as a budding inventor, I am hoping to learn more about how I can help people with my inventions. That's why I want to attend the STEAM magnet school in the fall.

Figure 3.4. Qualitative Criteria

	Novice	Apprentice	Practitioner	Expert
Content	includes name and a reason for wanting to attend the STEAM academy	includes • full name • descriptive adjective for personality • a reason for wanting to attend the STEAM academy	includes • full name • descriptive adjective for personality that fits with a STEAM program • background on interests that would lead to admittance into a STEAM magnet • a reason for wanting to attend the STEAM academy	all of *Practitioner* column plus more detailed information about at least two of the criteria listed
Sentence Quality	sentences include a simple subject and simple predicate	sentences follow a similar structure but include descriptive words	• some variation in sentence structure • use of descriptive words • proper use of clauses and phrases	all of *Practitioner* plus use of one or more other writing strategies
Sentence Flow	each sentence focuses on topic	some sentences relate to one another	use of transition words and phrases to enhance paragraph flow	sentences follow one another with smooth transitions based on content and writing strategies
Mechanics	includes correct spelling of grade-level words, and correct end punctuation	includes correct spelling, verb tenses, and end punctuation	includes correct spelling, grammar, and punctuation throughout	all of *Practitioner* plus includes spelling, grammar, and punctuation challenges

Using this rubric, both students would be considered expert writers; however, clearly, the second paragraph was written by a student who possesses a greater command of the written language. This level of writing must be described qualitatively. Consider the modification of the rubric, presented in Figure 3.4.

The second *analytic rubric* successfully differentiates between the two writing samples. Compare the criteria in the rubrics in Figures 3.3 and 3.4. The former contains solely quantitative criteria, whereas the latter offers descriptive criteria to capture the quality of writing beyond sheer quantity. While it is easy to become fixated on filling in the grid, be sure to read through your rubric criteria carefully to ensure that they describe the quality of the performance.

CREATE

The first step in designing your *ALU* was to develop a *problem-based task* challenging students to create a solution or "product" (article, prototype, performance, presentation, etc.). Now, use the steps below to design your analytic rubric, keeping in mind that you want your students to use the rubric to drive their actions. Your goal is to describe a final product or performance so that your students can assess their progress and plan to get to the next column. As you begin designing your *Learner-Active, Technology-Infused Classroom*, you will design an *analytic rubric* for the *problem-based task* you designed in Chapter 2. As your students gain familiarity with rubrics and begin to identify their own problems to solve, involve them in the *analytic rubric* design. Eventually, students will be able to present you with a rubric for you to review and advise them on enhancing to meet curricular goals.

Step 1: Determine the Structure of the *ALU* Solution

Given the *problem-based task* you developed for your *ALU*, think about what that final product would look like, as the job of the rubric is to describe the final product. Will it be a prototype? Article? Drawing? Public Service Announcement? Essentially, what will students hand in at the end of the unit? Will you be able to assess student mastery simply by considering that product? Sometimes the product itself won't tell you enough about the student's abilities: the reason for the "show your work" approach on a math exam. In that case, you can have a portion of the final product be a log or design journal. Students would hand in the log or journal with specific aspects of their work that led to the final product, much as an actual scientist, writer, engineer, artist, and other professionals would keep. Sometimes a final product is a collection of multiple sub-products, for example: a product prototype, a designer's notebook, and a letter to pitch the product to a company. Your rubric can be divided into sections to accommodate each of these, or you can design separate rubrics for each. Decide on the various aspects of the *ALU* solution for which you will need performance criteria so you can structure the rubric in one or more sections.

Step 2: Identify What Grade-Level Performance Would Look Like

Given that the purpose of the *analytic rubric* is to offer clearly articulated expectations, begin rubric design by asking yourself what you would consider to be a strong, grade-level performance. For each product, or sub-product, to be developed by the student, write down a list of descriptive phrases, focusing more, at first, on the curricular content demonstrated in the product than on the product appearance. If you allow students to choose their final product form, some may create multimedia presentations while others offer oral presentations, and still others written work; but the same subject-area content should be evident in all. What would a strong, content-rich solution look like?

In the *ALU*, "Teachers, Schools, and Pop Culture" (see Appendix F for task and rubric), students evaluate current depictions of teachers and schools in the media and make recommendations to a specific organization, individual, or company for how to more realistically represent the educational world. What would the "pitch" look like? You might want the students to conduct surveys of peers regarding the media piece; present a clear claim as to the realistic depiction of teachers and schools in the media piece; support that claim through evidence; and offer two to three realistic suggestions for better representation of teachers and schools in the media piece in question.

In the *ALU*, "More Friends Good, Fewer Friends Bad?" (see Appendix A for task and rubric), the students will use the Pythagorean theorem and Metcalfe's law to evaluate the power of social media networks. What would that look like? You might want to see them use the Pythagorean theorem to compare the social networks of an organization and its competition, then use it to compare at least three qualities of a social network; and you might want to see recommendations based on network characteristics for possible improvements, with mathematical evidence for their solutions.

As you think through the final product and imagine looking at high-quality examples, identify what you would expect to see. At this point, don't attempt to categorize the criteria. Just create a list of what the final product and subproducts would look like. Be as specific and descriptive as possible.

Step 3: Define the Rubric Categories

Next, group the criteria into categories. In the *ALU* example, "Deadly Encounters" (see Appendix D for the task and rubric), for the causal map, you might find some criteria dealing with cause-and-effect pairs, some with illustrating the chain reactions with arrows, and others with the story-telling aspect of the map. For the *ALU*, "Digital Serfs" (see Appendix E for the task and rubric), you might find some criteria dealing with demonstrating an understanding of the feudal system, some with comparing and contrasting the feudal system and cloud-based society, and others for presentation format.

A strong *analytic rubric* generally has four to seven categories, or rows. If you have too few categories, you may not be asking for a rigorous enough demonstration of learning. If you have too many, the rubric may appear overwhelming. However, when you have multiple subproducts, you can consider each to have a set of rows, so you would most likely exceed seven categories overall. In that case, I'd recommend each subproduct have its own rubric page, as in the case of "Deadly Encounters" (Appendix D). Review your categories to ensure that they are heavily oriented toward the desired subject-area content. If your content is not presentation, avoid dedicating more than one row to that. Better yet, let the students make the presentation in any format they like; your rubric, then, can just be focused on your content.

If you teach on a team of different content teachers, mixing content in one rubric can work, as long as students know which teacher to depend on for support and evaluation of which criteria. Often it is better to have an *analytic rubric* for each subject area addressed through the *ALU*.

Step 4: Define the Rubric Columns

Your rubric should have four columns. The third column should represent grade-level mastery and the right-most column should provide a reach to challenge your academically advanced students. That leaves the first two columns to represent steps toward grade-level expectations. The purpose of the columns is not for students to first complete the first column before moving on to the second. It is so that when they look at the grade-level column, if it seems overwhelming, they can take a step back to get started. It also increases the likelihood that, as they are working, they will find themselves somewhere on the rubric so they can celebrate progress toward the end goal.

Step 5: Write a Developmental Progression for Each Row Across the Columns

The next step is to write an individual row or category. You should form your Practitioner column from your brainstormed list of expectations. Based on each row category, fill the Practitioner column with a description of what you expect. Be sure to review your state or district curriculum standards to ensure that you reflect them in the description. Figure 3.5 offers the Practitioner column of a rubric on developing a man-made solution for hydroelectric power.

Once the Practitioner column is written, consider the developmental levels of quality students would follow to arrive at that level of performance. Where might they start? What naturally follows? Use this line of thinking to develop the Novice and Apprentice columns. Keep in mind that as you read from Novice to Apprentice to Practitioner, you want to see a natural progression of learning, the way you would instruct students. Review the Practitioner column to ensure that all of your expectations are included. If you expect it, it must be articulated in the rubric.

Figure 3.5. Hydroelectric Power: Practitioner Column

	Novice	Apprentice	Practitioner	Expert
Solution Design			♦ includes a solution to a complex real-world problem, based on a wide variety of scientific knowledge ♦ demonstrates effective use of the design process and scientific method ♦ includes a wide variety of student-generated sources of evidence, including competing ideas and evidence ♦ includes prioritization of criteria and tradeoff considerations	
Explanation			♦ detailed proposal with maps, images, data tables, and/or other illustrative examples ♦ ample, relevant, cited textual evidence to support the need for both the waterfall and the hydroelectric power source ♦ includes proposal evaluation that considers a range of constraints, including cost, safety, reliability, and aesthetics, and to consider social, cultural, and environmental impacts	
STEM Connections			♦ includes scientific knowledge through sources and experiments to support both the need and the solution ♦ includes use of technology for modeling and exploring "what if?" scenarios ♦ includes engineered 3-D prototype of solution ♦ includes a mathematical analysis of costs and benefits as a critical aspect of decision-making	
Human Impacts on Earth Systems			♦ details the sustainability of human societies and the biodiversity that supports them through the responsible management of natural resources ♦ highlights the contribution the proposal makes to society by producing less pollution and waste and precluding ecosystem degradation	

Also note that the progression across the columns should not represent different activities. For example, you would not have one column indicate the student makes a graphic organizer, the next an outline, and the next a rough draft. These are different stages in the overall product development; as such they would each have a row dedicated to that subproduct. Within a row dedicated to counterclaims, you might indicate, as depicted in Figure 3.6, the beginning level would be that the student identifies a counterclaim. The next level includes the evidence to refute it. A single citing of evidence to refute the counterclaim might be weak, however, so rather than simply adding the next component, you'll note that at the next level the student must use multiple valid sources to refute each counterclaim. At this level, too, the expectation is that the student will identify more than one counterclaim to the proposal. The expert column has students identify the reasoning behind the counterclaims, demonstrating a higher level of academic rigor. Each successive column should describe a higher quality of performance.

Figure 3.6. Rubric Criteria Progression

	Novice	Apprentice	Practitioner	Expert
Opposing Claims	includes one counterclaim	includes one counterclaim and evidence to refute it	includes: ♦ at least two counterclaims ♦ evidence to refute all counterclaims introduced ♦ use of multiple, valid sources to refute counterclaims	all of *Practitioner* plus offers reasoning behind counterclaims

Step 6: Write the Expert Column

Writing the Expert column is slightly different from writing the others, as you're looking to inspire students to achieve at levels that are higher than grade-level expectations. Essentially, there are four ways to move from the Practitioner column to the Expert column:

1. The first, and least powerful, is to make a quantitative leap; that is, have students produce more. If the Practitioner column asks for four facts supporting the proposal, the Expert asks for more than four. If the Practitioner column asks for varied sources, including books, journals, and the Internet, the Expert column asks for two of each. Sometimes, asking for more is the appropriate approach; however, always challenge yourself to make a qualitative leap, modifying the quality rather than quantity of response.

2. The second option is to make a qualitative leap of *extended content*; that is, content that may not typically be introduced at the grade level or at all. If students are asked to construct a ski slope as a series of line segments, the Expert column might require them to use parabolas for moguls. If the Practitioner column of a world language rubric asks students to use present and past tenses in their writing, the Expert column might ask them to use future tenses as well. If music students are asked to analyze a song based on meter, tempo, and rhythm, the Expert column might require them to also consider tonality, intervals, and key signature.

3. A third option is to make a qualitative leap of *higher cognitive level*; that is, requiring a more sophisticated level of thinking. If students are asked to list cause-and-effect relationships of an event, the Expert column might require them to include primary,

Figure 3.7. Hydroelectric Power: Practitioner Column

	Novice	Apprentice	Practitioner	Expert
Solution Design			♦ includes a solution to a complex real-world problem, based on a wide variety of scientific knowledge ♦ demonstrates effective use of the design process and scientific method ♦ includes a wide variety of student-generated sources of evidence, including competing ideas and evidence ♦ includes prioritization of criteria and tradeoff considerations	all of *Practitioner*, plus the solution offers alternative options to increase the persuasive value of the proposal
Explanation			♦ detailed proposal with maps, images, data tables, and/or other illustrative examples ♦ ample, relevant, cited textual evidence to support the need for both the waterfall and the hydroelectric power source ♦ includes proposal evaluation that considers a range of constraints, including cost, safety, reliability, and aesthetics, and to consider social, cultural, and environmental impacts	all of *Practitioner*, plus includes evaluation of competing design solutions (such as dams) based on scientific ideas and principles, empirical evidence, and logical arguments regarding relevant factors (e.g., economic, societal, environmental, ethical considerations)
STEM Connections			♦ includes scientific knowledge through sources and experiments to support both the need and the solution ♦ includes use of technology for modeling and exploring "what if?" scenarios ♦ includes engineered 3-D prototype of solution ♦ includes a mathematical analysis of costs and benefits as a critical aspect of decision-making	all of *Practitioner*, plus explains how STEM thinking helped in the development of the solution
Human Impacts on Earth Systems			♦ details the sustainability of human societies and the biodiversity that supports them through the responsible management of natural resources ♦ highlights the contribution the proposal makes to society by producing less pollution and waste and precluding ecosystem degradation	all of *Practitioner*, plus describes various predictions, positive and/or negative, based on scientific evidence or empirical data for the long-term impact on the primary community that would profit from the proposal, as well as any secondary or tertiary community impacts

secondary, and tertiary effects. For example, if students are to identify cause-and-effect relationships of the increase in water temperature on Caribbean coral reefs, an obvious response from some research might be the death of the microscopic plants that feed the coral reefs. A secondary effect would be the death of the coral reefs. A tertiary effect would be the loss of the fish that thrive among the coral reefs. A quaternary effect would be the devastation of the economies of the Caribbean nations. Thinking through related levels of events, including projecting future effects, requires higher cognitive skills. In "Hydroelectric Power" (Appendix B), students must include an evaluation of their proposal. At the expert level, they evaluate competing designs as well to strengthen their argument. This requires a higher level of thinking, comparing and contrasting multiple options as opposed to simply supporting one.

4. A fourth option is to make a qualitative, *metacognitive leap*; that is, asking students to reflect on their own thinking process. This usually takes the form of asking students to talk or write about how they went about solving a problem, explaining a process to others, or reflecting on their plan to manage a project. If the Practitioner column requires the students to use at least three geometric figures to make a new shape, the Expert column might ask them to describe how they went about making the design.

A common misconception when addressing the needs of gifted learners is that because they are so capable, they should produce more. Quantitative and extended content leaps from the Practitioner column to the Expert column do not challenge gifted learners as do higher cognitive and metacognitive leaps. A well-crafted rubric will present varied ways to move from the Practitioner column to the Expert column throughout the rubric.

Figure 3.7 presents two columns from the rubric on developing a hydroelectric power solution. Note how in each row the student is challenged to a higher cognitive level, asked to tackle skills beyond the expected grade level, or asked to reflect on the thinking process involved.

Step 7: Foster High Academic Standards

Review the rubric you have just designed. As previously detailed, you'll want to make the Practitioner column grade-level performance and fill the Expert column with a description of truly exemplary work. Use these two columns to foster high academic standards. Refer to your state standards to ensure you're using the language and including the nuances of the standards. Consider what understanding and application of content would look like and include that criteria in the rubric. If it is too easy for students to achieve at the Expert level, there will be little or nothing to challenge those who are able to move beyond the norm, and average students will be satisfied with their performance rather than pushing themselves to achieve more. Be comfortable knowing that few, if any, of your students will be able to score completely in the Expert column.

Step 8: Ensure Objectivity

It is important to write the criteria in as objective a manner as possible so that student and teacher alike will assign the same performance level. "Neat" means something different to everyone. "All lines drawn with a ruler or straight edge" means the same thing to everyone. This aspect can be a challenge. However, taking the time to define a performance allows you to raise academic standards. Read through your rubric to ensure that you have clearly defined all criteria. Where space is an issue, use a checklist or a nested rubric. For example, if you use the term "neat" in your rubric, provide a separate checklist that describes what neat looks like. If the unit content is physics, but you are asking students to write an argumentative essay to promote their solution, keep your rubric focused on physics content and include a reference to a rubric for writing an argumentative essay that is a separate rubric unto itself, preferably designed in partnership with the English teacher. When students encounter the reference to the nested rubric, they retrieve that *analytic rubric* for further guidance. This is particularly helpful when offering students options for the final product. You may write an algebra unit task that allows students to create a multimedia presentation, three-dimensional model, or written report. Focus on the algebra content in the rubric and refer students to a separate *analytic rubric* for the type of final product. You can utilize those rubrics throughout the year as students design various products.

Step 9: Include Executive Function Skills

You can promote executive function skills throughout any unit. Consider your *ALU* task and include rubric criteria that will build executive function skills. While there are forty executive function skills that are important for students (Sulla, 2018), here are some that will fit almost any unit:

- **Cause-and-effect relationships:** Have students identify primary, secondary, tertiary, quaternary, and quinary cause-and-effect relationships. As an example, consider how supply and demand affect product availability and pricing. A strong marketing campaign causes an increase in demand for the product (primary) which, when available inventory is low, can cause an increase in the price (secondary) and an increase in production (secondary). The increase in price can cause a reduction in demand (tertiary). Paired with an increase in production, this can cause an increase in stored inventory (quaternary) and can lead to a reduction in price (quinary). You can have students identify existing cause-and-effect chains and project future effects.

- **Seeing multiple sides to a situation:** Have students consider different points of view related to the *ALU* task. It might be of those affected by the problem; it might be those to whom students will advocate for their solution.

♦ **Categorizing information:** Have students categorize information related to the *ALU* task. Rather than giving them the categories, have them decide on categories to use.

♦ **Predicting outcomes:** Have students engage in predicting outcomes to experiments and thinking through future events related to the *ALU* task.

♦ **Considering future consequences in light of current action:** Have students consider unintended consequences of their or others' decisions.

A Closer Look at the Complete Rubric

Let's recap some of the important features of a high-quality rubric. Consider the rubric for "Justice for All" (Appendix G) shown in Figure 3.8. (Note: The choice of this rubric is for illustrative purposes; you'll want to think through the points made here as they relate to your grade level and subject area.) Students are considering the U.S. Civil Rights movement and school desegregation, past and present, and proposing a plan of action for achieving further levels of justice in education. Read down the Practitioner column; it is full of criteria related to these topics, such as "multiple, recent examples of how/where segregation is still an issue in education" and "the short-term and long-term implications of these examples on society." It includes language from the standards, such as, "includes precise claim, distinguished from alternate or opposing claims" and "includes clear relationships among claims, counterclaims, reasons, and evidence." The first step in assessing the quality of your rubric is to read down the Practitioner column to ensure that it details the curricular content being studied. If there are any curricular skills you want students to tackle, they belong in the rubric.

Next, look at the developmental movement from Novice to Apprentice to Practitioner. In the first row, the Novice is acknowledged for defining civil rights. The Apprentice must expand the definition to include the purpose behind these rights. The Practitioner column introduces a level of perspective, asking students to note the evolution of civil rights over the years.

For the row "Commendation or Call to Action," the first level of achievement includes stating and supporting an opinion regarding a segregation issue in education. At the Apprentice level the student must include cited evidence and recommended next steps. At the Practitioner level, the student must, among other things, list reasons for putting the proposal into action and provide short-term and long-term implications of the proposal. At the Expert level, the student must share the plan with person(s) of power and ability to make a difference.

Figure 3.8. Rubric: Justice for All

	Novice	Apprentice	Practitioner	Expert
Exploration of Past Events	♦ defines civil rights ♦ includes one example of past segregation ♦ includes one example of past desegregation efforts	♦ defines civil rights and the purpose behind them ♦ includes three examples of segregation and desegregation in the past ♦ provides detail of the events and their implications on society	♦ defines civil rights, the purpose behind them, and their evolution over the years ♦ includes at least five examples of segregation and desegregation in the past, including in education ♦ provides detail of the events and their implications on society ♦ correlates how segregation and desegregation efforts relate to the U.S. Constitution and civil rights	all of *Practitioner* plus: ♦ reflection on the importance of diversity, and equity and one's duty as a U.S. citizen
Current Examples	includes ♦ one recent example of how/where segregation is still an issue ♦ one recent example of a desegregation effort	includes ♦ more than one recent example of how/where segregation is still an issue in education ♦ the implications of these examples on society ♦ recent examples of efforts to desegregate education	includes ♦ multiple, recent examples of how/where segregation is still an issue in education ♦ the short-term and long-term implications of these examples on society ♦ recent examples of efforts to desegregate education, both through laws and by choice ♦ varied and credible digital and print sources	all of *Practitioner* plus: ♦ examples of segregation and desegregation in education in at least one first-, second-, and third-world country
Commendation or "Call to Action"	includes ♦ opinion regarding a segregation issue in education ♦ support of opinion with several pieces of evidence	includes ♦ solution to a segregation issue in education ♦ support of opinion with several cited pieces of evidence ♦ recommendations for "next steps"	includes ♦ solution to a segregation issue in education, supported by evidence, including data and statistics ♦ list of reasons for putting this proposal into action that relate to civil rights ♦ multiple perspectives and sources ♦ detailed "next steps" to ensure justice for all ♦ implications for the short-term and long-term, based on plan for action ♦ counterclaims to the solution ♦ ramifications of dismissing the call to action	all of *Practitioner* plus: ♦ shares solution and action plan with person(s) of power and ability to make a difference
Writing Style	includes ♦ claim ♦ supporting evidence for claim ♦ concluding section that follows from the argument	♦ includes precise claim ♦ includes claims, counterclaims, reasons, and evidence ♦ includes supporting evidence for claim and counterclaims ♦ includes precise words and phrases, telling details to convey the significance of ideas ♦ creates clear and cohesive ideas using varied sentence structures ♦ includes concluding section that follows from and supports the argument presented	♦ includes precise claim, distinguished from alternate or opposing claims ♦ includes clear relationships among claims, counterclaims, reasons, and evidence ♦ includes supporting evidence for claim and counterclaims ♦ includes strengths and limitations of claim and counterclaims ♦ demonstrates anticipation of audience's knowledge level and concerns ♦ demonstrates cohesion among major sections ♦ includes precise words and phrases, telling details to convey the significance of ideas ♦ creates clear and cohesive ideas using varied sentence structures ♦ includes concluding section that follows from and supports the argument presented	all of *Practitioner* plus: ♦ demonstrates anticipation of and addresses challenges that may be faced in pursuing this call to action

In each row, the rubric designer is considering how one would go about achieving the goal of designing a worthy final product, breaking it down into progressive steps. Note that the steps would not be the assignments:

♦ Fill out a graphic organizer

♦ Write a rough draft

♦ Write a final draft

While those are steps in a process, they describe student action more than a final product. Instead, you could have a rubric row for graphic organizer to be submitted with the final product that might look like Figure 3.9.

Figure 3.9. Sample Rubric Row

	Novice	Apprentice	Practitioner	Expert
Graphic Organizer	includes at least two topics on the subject	includes at least two topics on the subject with at least two detail points off each	includes at least four key topics on the subject with at least three different detail points off each, including some details that are not widely known	all of *Practitioner* plus includes a third level of detail

Given that you'll be using the rubric to drive instruction and guide your students, keep in mind that they will read each column and decide what they have to do to achieve at that level. Essentially, you are mapping out the path to success for them. Note the developmental progression in each row.

The Grading Dilemma

The key to teaching through an *ALU* is realizing that your role as the teacher is to ensure that *all* students achieve at the Practitioner level. Your job is to provide high-quality, varied learning experiences so that all students succeed; consequently, grading students on the final product is more like grading your own performance. The unit rubric is not intended to produce a grade as much as it is to drive instruction. If you do grade the performance, and if you succeeded in your role in the classroom, it should earn an A or a B; essentially, you are grading yourself as a teacher. If the authentic, open-ended unit task is compelling, students will engage for that reason alone and not for the grade. After all, when students engage after school in various sports and online activities, they're not doing so for a grade.

Throughout the unit, the students will engage in a number of activities, both collaboratively and individually. You should grade individual assignments and individual contributions to the final product. Intermediate deadlines for various stages of the final product will help students manage the project more successfully, and related individual assignments should also be graded. You should additionally administer quizzes and even tests across the course of the unit. All of these grades will allow you to see how each student is progressing with individual content mastery.

You will know whether or not *you* have achieved your goals as a teacher by the success rate of your students in achieving at the Practitioner column.

Some teachers make the mistake of handing out the *problem-based task* and *analytic rubric* and then expecting students to achieve success on their own. Given that at the start of the *ALU* you will have offered your students no prior instruction, they would be hard-pressed to succeed. The purpose of the *problem-based task* and *analytic rubric* is to offer an instructional roadmap as to what lies ahead on the learning front for your students. As the teacher, your job is to provide students with nearly limitless opportunities to learn, such that, in the end, all of your students succeed.

Once the students have fulfilled the requirements of the Practitioner column of the *analytic rubric* and have met with success, however, what assurance do you have that the students have mastered the content? After all, you provided ongoing instruction and guidance so that students *would* succeed; but what happens in the absence of that level of support?

Assessment Through the Transfer Task

Wiggins and McTighe (2005) used the term "transfer task" to describe an end-of-unit assessment. In the *Learner-Active, Technology-Infused Classroom,* the transfer task would be a focused, performance-based task that can be accomplished by an individual student in a short period of time, typically one or two class periods. The intent is to assess how well the student can transfer the knowledge learned to a new situation. The *problem-based task* introduced to launch the unit is intended to build a *felt need* to study the unit content. The students then spend two to five weeks, depending on the length of the unit, delving into subject-area content, with your guidance. At the end of the unit, they should be able to complete a transfer task in a shorter period of time, now possessing the knowledge they need to solve the problem.

The transfer task should be authentic and cause students to apply their learning, thus demonstrating understanding of the content. It should not require a significant amount of time. As an example, you could use "Digital Serfs" (Appendix E), in which students decide if today's "cloud-based" society is a reflection of feudalism, as both a *problem-based task* and as a transfer task. When used as a transfer task, the student is asked to develop and support a position and a way to educate others. Given that students have already studied feudalism using a different *problem-based task*, it will not take them long to develop their solution. When used as a *problem-based task* for learning content, it takes approximately four to five weeks, as the students are learning about the concept, history, and effects of feudalism across that time period.

You will want to consider what resources (e.g. charts, maps, tables), if any, to make available to your students while solving the problem. The transfer task should be assessed by a rubric or a scaled checklist. In the case of pure evaluation, you could use a holistic rubric or an *analytic rubric*. The rubric should focus heavily on curricular content more than the presentation of information. Typically, the end-of-unit transfer task asks students to simply offer a solution rather than create a multimedia presentation or other time-consuming product.

RECAP

The *analytic rubric* presents students with clearly articulated expectations so that they can take responsibility for their own learning; it drives instruction. Use this list to ensure that your *analytic rubric* includes these points:

- ♦ The Practitioner column accurately and completely represents the content that is the focus of the unit.

- ♦ The Novice and Apprentice columns offer a developmental progression toward the Practitioner column.

- ♦ The Novice column captures what a beginning performance might look like without using negative language.

- ♦ The rubric is mostly written with qualitative as opposed to quantitative criteria.

- ♦ Criteria are written to be objective, with little or no room for subjective assessments.

- ♦ The progression from Practitioner to Expert utilizes a combination of approaches (extended content, higher cognitive level, metacognitive) where possible.

- ♦ The rubric includes related executive function skills.

REFERENCES

Sulla, N. (2018). *Building executive function: The missing link to student achievement.* New York: Routledge.
Wiggins, W., & McTighe, J. (2005). *Understanding by design.* Alexandria, VA: ASCD.

4

Engaging Students Through Differentiated Learning Activities

Seventh-grade students are working on various aspects of their "Leaders for Peace" project. They are reading novels that they individually chose related to various types of conflict. As a group, they are developing a campaign to promote peaceful resolution of conflicts; they can choose to focus on personal, school, community, state, national, or global conflict. They are selecting a medium for sharing how people today can make a difference in advocating for peaceful conflict resolution. Some are designing videos, others websites, and others printed materials. They are also developing and printing 3-D logos for their group's campaign in conjunction with the art teacher. According to the *analytic rubric*, they have to analyze how an author develops and contrasts the points of view of different characters or narrators in a text. Justine isn't sure she knows what this means so she looks at her *activity list* and chooses a video to watch to help her out.

Ninth-grade Spanish students are making plans to celebrate Hispanic Heritage Month with a series of events promoting the idea of a country being a "tossed salad" more than a "melting pot," in this case, honoring the historical and cultural heritage of Hispanic countries. Isabella engaged in an extensive search over the weekend on pastimes and developed a slideshow as a vocabulary reference. Her teacher commended her and added it to the digital *resource area* and *activity list* as an *optional activity* for her peers.

High school chemistry students are engaging in problem-finding projects of interest related to greenhouse gases. Asha, Bryan, Mai, and Melvon decided to investigate different types of lighting to make recommendations to the principal to rethink lighting in the school. The teacher is offering a *small-group mini-lesson* at 2:00 for those interested in exploring Greenhouse Gas Equivalencies Calculator on the US Environmental Protection Agency's website. Bryan and Asha decide to sign up so they can utilize this resource in their argument.

Middle school students are designing robot prototypes to address various problems in their community. One group of students is designing a robot that will navigate house gutters to clear out leaves and debris, allowing water to move through freely. They are having difficulty figuring out how to effectively use the sensors to recognize a change in vertical direction as the robot climbs the downpipes. One of the group members adds his name to the *help board* so that the teacher will come over to help them when she is available. They then refer to their *analytic rubric* to decide what they should tackle while they wait for help in that area.

CONSIDER

Beyond the *Problem-Based Task* and *Analytic Rubric*

A well-constructed *problem-based task* builds a *felt need* for students to learn; it motivates them. The corresponding *analytic rubric* provides clearly articulated expectations so that students can set and pursue goals. The next step is to consider how students will learn the concepts, skills, and content needed to complete the task. In a conventional setting, teachers spend much of class time presenting information to students, feeling comfort in knowing they covered the curriculum. In the *Learner-Active, Technology-Infused Classroom*, the students spend much of the time engaging in *learning activities* that they've chosen or found, thus taking charge of their own learning. These might include *how-to sheets, videos, screencasts, learning centers, peer experts, small-group mini-lessons,* and more. Masterful teachers focus less on teaching to the whole class and more on identifying and developing appropriate *learning activities* and empowering students to take charge of their own learning, thus ensuring that instruction is appropriate for individual students' needs. Students remain engaged in learning when they receive instruction in skills and concepts they need in order to solve a bigger problem and when that instruction is matched to their ability level and learning style strengths. The educational Twitter chats in the spring fill up with questions about how teachers are going to keep students engaged until the last day of school; my response is always: in the *Learner-Active, Technology-Infused Classroom*, the last day of school arrives and students exclaim, "It's over already?"

Teachers don't engage students; purpose, autonomy, and mastery do (Pink, 2011). As Einstein believed, teachers create the conditions through which students learn.

Learning Activities Versus *Practice Activities*

As you move away from providing instruction from the front of the room in order to design a more differentiated learning environment, you will have to consider other ways through which students will learn concepts and skills. Oftentimes in a classroom, the teacher presents the content while students attend, follow along, and, sometimes, take notes. Students then engage in independent activities aimed at practicing what they learned. The problem is that not all students are at the same cognitive level and are, thus, not necessarily ready to learn that whole-group lesson at the time and in the way the teacher is presenting it. This leaves some students bored and others frustrated. In the *Learner-Active, Technology-Infused Classroom*, students continually engage in instructional activities that are just above their ability level, thus maximizing the probability of success and building momentum toward achieving the standards. Through this learning environment, all students can succeed at high levels in one classroom, including special education students, new language learners, and gifted students. This level of differentiation requires a variety of independent activities that provide students with direct instruction, thus mirroring what the teacher would, in the past, have presented to the whole class. It is, therefore, important to realize that the former practice activities used after the lesson cannot serve as learning activities, as students would have to discover answers and teach themselves, neither of which are goals of the *Learner-Active, Technology-Infused Classroom*. This is why it is important to ensure you provide *learning activities* before *practice activities*.

"Learning activities have three components: a specific content focus, directions, and feedback" (Sulla, 2015, p. 113). They may be videos, printed directions, learning centers, interactive websites, and more. The key is to ensure that students are being offered explicit instruction in the target concept or skill, just not from the front of the room in a whole-class setting.

Vygotsky's Zone of Proximal Development

As stated earlier, but worth repeating, it is ineffective to attempt to teach skills from the front of the room via a whole-class lesson. The diversity of students' cognitive readiness, even in homogeneously grouped classrooms, is too great. Cognitive psychologist Lev Vygotsky (1978) introduced the term "Zone of Proximal Development" (ZPD) in the early twentieth century. Vygotsky claimed that everyone has a current body of knowledge. Based on your own body of knowledge, you have a proximal zone: that which you are cognitively ready to learn. Outside of that is your distal zone: that which you are not yet ready to learn. Consider a student who understands the concept and process of multiplication. The skill of division lies in her proximal zone because, based on her current body of knowledge, she is ready to learn that skill. Quadratic equations are in her distal zone because she does not possess the cognitive readiness to understand them.

Figure 4.1 offers a summary graphic for ZPD. When you consider standing in the front of your class of students, ready to present a skill, for some that skill is in their proximal zone, the middle ring, so they will gain from your lesson. For others, that skill already lies in their current body of knowledge, the center circle, so they will be bored and feel like their time is being wasted, or they will feign attention and daydream about other things. For others who do not possess the prerequisite skills to tackle what you are about to teach, that skill lies in their distal zone, the outermost ring, so they will be lost and frustrated, and potentially become behavior problems. So at any point when you are teaching skills to an entire group of students, chances are, you are reaching roughly a third of the class. Consequently, whole-class, *benchmark lessons* are best used to introduce concepts, not skills, that relate to the *Authentic Learning Unit* (*ALU*). *Benchmark lessons* should build students' awareness of what they need to learn and why, related to developing a solution to the problem-based task. In the *Learner-Active, Technology-Infused Classroom*, whole-class lessons are not intended to be used for skill instruction.

Mihaly Csikszentmihalyi (1990) found that people learn best when they are in a state of flow—when they are so engaged in an activity that they lose track of everything else around them. (See Figure 4.2.) Building on

Figure 4.1. Zone of Proximal Development

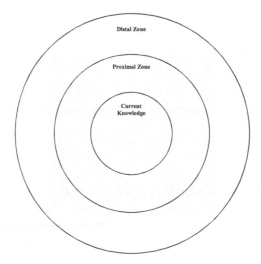

Figure 4.2. Csikszentmihalyi's "Flow"

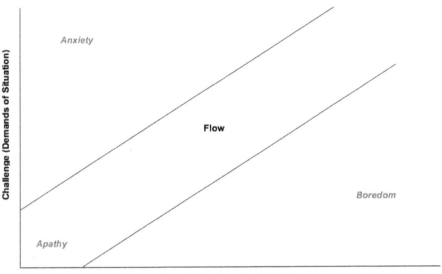

Vygotsky's work, he points out that for every task in which we engage, we have an ability level that determines how successful we will be. When tasks are just above our ability level, allowing us to be challenged but also achieve success, we are more likely to experience a state of flow. That state of flow, however, is very individual. A set of activities that evokes flow in one student will not necessarily evoke flow in the next, presenting the need for differentiation.

Marc Prensky (2006) draws a parallel between Vygotsky's and Csikszentmihalyi's work and video gaming. Teachers may report that students cannot maintain their attention throughout a lesson. When considering the hours that students engage with a video or computer game, one cannot assume today's students have a minimal attention span. Prensky concludes that video and computer games are successful, in part, because they use a "leveling up" approach to skill building. When the student starts playing the game, she is at a particular level. She may have to replay the level several times until she masters it, at which point she advances to a slightly more challenging, and thus motivating, level. Video game designers have a vested interest in maintaining the attention of their players. If the game were too difficult, their players would abandon it with frustration. If it were too easy, their players would become bored and opt to play something else. Leveling up ensures that as the players meet with success at each level, they are compelled to attain the next. Teachers would do well to apply this leveling up concept to their classrooms, which again presents an argument for purposeful differentiation.

Over the years, most of the regular education teachers I've interviewed have reported some level of frustration in not being able to meet the needs of all of their students. When I ask if they only had one student, could they ensure success, they respond affirmatively. When I suggest that if they had two students, they could ensure success, they also agree. As I continue to add to the number, generally the numbers four or five seems to be the cutoff for feeling successful in ensuring that all students achieve. If, as a teacher, you feel strongly that you could succeed with one student, teaching to that student's proximal zone, then you already have the keys to success for each student! What you need in order to differentiate instruction are "teacher-cloning tools"—ways through which students can learn other than through an in-person encounter with you.

As you prepare to introduce a curricular skill to your class, plot your students on a graphic like the one in Figure 4.1 so you can see who already knows the skill (center), who is ready to learn it (next ring out), and who doesn't have the prerequisite knowledge to learn the skill right now (outermost ring). Make sure you have enough differentiated *learning activities* to teach to the middle, challenge the center group, and support the outer group in being ready to learn the skill.

The *Learning Map*

You're about to develop a set of *learning activities* through which students will achieve the level of demonstration of knowledge outlined on the *analytic rubric*. The best way to start the process is with a *learning map*, which is essentially a roadmap to producing the solution for the *problem-based task*.

Start with a piece of blank paper or digital canvas. Visualize your students tackling the *problem-based task* that's at the core of your *ALU*. Write down what your students might "do" first to provide a solution to the problem. Be very specific. For example, in "More Friends Good, Fewer Friends Bad?" (Appendix A), to get started, students must first explore the Pythagorean theorem and Metcalfe's law to ensure they have the mathematical tools to address the problem. Then they must identify an organization to analyze and gather data on all of their social media as well as that of some of their competitors. Next they must apply their mathematical tools to complete the analysis, and finally they must make recommendations based on their mathematical analysis. The problem-based task now breaks down into four distinctly different work phases (Figure 4.3).

Once you have your *learning map* for a portion of the *ALU*, at each step, decide what concepts or skills students will need and the ways in which they could learn them. To explore the Pythagorean theorem and Metcalfe's law

Figure 4.3. Learning Map: More Friends Good, Fewer Friends Bad?

> Explore Pythagorean theorem & Metcalfe's law

> Identify organization to analyze and gather social media data

> Apply Pythagorean theorem & Metcalfe's law to organization

> Make evidence-based recommendations to organization

they might refer to a text explanation, use *how-to sheets*, watch videos, use a learning center, engage with peer experts, and so on. Once they understand these mathematical tools, they need to identify an organization to analyze. To ensure they gather all the data they need, they might refer to a *how-to sheet* or the *quality work board* to see prior years' examples. They might watch a screencast produced by their teacher or a prior student in the course. They might attend a *small-group mini-lesson* with the teacher.

As they move on to apply these mathematical tools to their organizations, they might watch a video produced by the teacher, follow a *direction sheet* for steps to take, utilize a *peer expert* and more. Remember that the *learning map* focuses on what students will need to accomplish in steps to achieve the overall *problem-based task*. The *learning map* is not a list of skills, but a breakdown of the solution and ways in which students will learn the skills to accomplish each step (Figure 4.3). The intent is to help you, as the teacher, think through the steps students will have to take to achieve the solution to the problem, so that you can be a powerful resource and support person in that process. In the *ALU* "Teachers, Schools, and Pop Culture" (Appendix F), first students must explore pop culture depictions of teachers and schools; then they must conduct surveys and interviews to see how these are received; next they select and research one organization to attempt to persuade to change their depiction; finally they develop a pitch to change this depiction. These would be included on the *learning map* (Figure 4.4).

To accomplish these steps on the *learning map*, students will need specific skills, which will be included as *learning activities* on your *scaffold for learning*, and, ultimately, on their *activity lists*. Note that teacher-given *small-group mini-lessons* are not included here; you will most likely offer them for almost every skill. The *learning map* focuses on ways to learn independent from the teacher. Note, too, that while you may see a lot of repetition, there are nuances. For example, in "More Friends Good, Fewer Friends Bad?" (Appendix A), I do not want a *peer expert* helping to analyze the data to make recommendations as that's a complex skill and I fear the *peer expert* may do more of the work than I want. However, for considering how to pitch the recommendations to the organization, a *peer expert* might have some great ideas. The more deliberate and purposeful you are in determining how students will learn, the greater success your students will have.

A *learning map* can also give you a sense of where you will need *benchmark lessons*. In this example, you would offer an early *benchmark lesson* on the power of social media for an organization in which you introduce Metcalfe's law and build a *felt need* for the Pythagorean theorem. You might then have *learning activities* on exploring Metcalfe's law, proving the Pythagorean theorem, and Pythagorean triples. You might run a *benchmark*

Figure 4.4. Learning Map: Teachers, Schools, and Pop Culture

Identify and explore pop culture depictions of teachers/schools

Survey and interview peers from around the world and analyze data

Explore the organization promoting one of the media pieces

Develop a pitch to convince the organization to change

lesson on using the Pythagorean theorem to analyze data, in which you discuss the various qualities of a social network that could be analyzed. At some point, students would need to analyze the data on their organization's social media presence. The *learning map* should make you think through the learning process and map out the skills students will need to learn.

You will not end up building a *learning map* for every aspect of every *ALU*, but to provide for purposeful differentiation, as you begin this journey of instructional redesign, it's a great way to truly visualize the path your students may take. Even though different students will approach the problem from different angles, begin with one path that you can imagine. You can then teach students to develop *learning maps* as well, having them then identify possible resources at each step.

Lesson-Level Differentiation

Sixth-grade students are developing scale drawings of an obstacle course they are building for a STEM project. They need to include a variety of angles and triangles and, as such, need to know how to construct triangles using a protractor. The teacher has given the class a 3×3 grid of *learning activities* for constructing triangles. Each successive column provides more difficult experiences; the rows represent visual, auditory, and hands-on activities. (Figure 4.5 is an example of IDE Corp's "Learning Styles and Readiness Grid," also referred to here as a differentiation grid.) Earlier in the year, students completed assessments to identify their learning style strengths, and the teacher encouraged the class to pay attention to their strengths, but to also challenge themselves to strengthen other modes. One student who is unsure of how to use a protractor decides to follow the hands-on activity in the first column, using an app to explore angle measurement using a protractor. Another already knows how to use a protractor and chooses an auditory offering of a video to learn to construct triangles.

Differentiation is a natural process; we all tend to gravitate toward that which suits our interest level, skill set, and learning style. A person may not know how to videoconference using a phone, but when that person's loved ones are away traveling, or off at college, she has a *felt need* to learn. Armed with a *felt need*, she pursues the way in which she knows she will learn best. She may look for an app to download and follow the directions, search the Internet, or ask a friend to show her.

In the early 1980s, I was offering beginning computer instruction to teachers who claimed that word processing seemed useless as it took much more time than handwriting (clearly based on their lack of technology skills). Instead, I introduced how the computer could allow them to shop and email their college-aged children. Before I knew it, everyone was engaged in using the computer in ways that were purposeful for them. After that, they saw word processing as

Figure 4.5. Constructing Triangles

	Need Some Help	Ready for This	I Know This Already
Visual	Follow the "Measuring Angles" *how-to sheet* to learn to measure angles using a protractor. Then draw ten different types of angles and use the protractor to measure each.	Follow the "Constructing Triangles" *how-to sheet* to learn how to construct triangles using a protractor. Then construct six types of triangles (equilateral, isosceles, scalene, right, acute, and obtuse.)	Follow the "What? No Protractor?" *how-to sheet* to learn how to construct an equilateral triangle using only a protractor and straightedge. Then design three similar triangles.
Auditory	Listen to and watch the "How Big is the Angle?" video to learn to measure angles using a protractor. Then draw ten different types of angles and use the protractor to measure each.	Watch and listen to the "From Protractor to Triangle" video to learn how to construct triangles using a protractor. Then construct six types of triangles (equilateral, isosceles, scalene, right, acute, and obtuse.)	View the "What? No Protractor?" video to learn how to construct an equilateral triangle using only a protractor and straightedge. Then design three similar triangles.
Kinesthetic/Tactile	Use the "Angle Explorer" *learning center* app to explore various angles and how to measure them with a protractor. Then draw ten different types of angles and use the protractor to measure each.	Using the "Constructing Triangles" *learning center*, follow the direction sheet to learn how to construct triangles using a protractor. Then construct six types of triangles (equilateral, isosceles, scalene, right, acute, and obtuse.)	Attend the "Compass-Constructed Triangles" *small-group mini-lesson* to learn how to construct an equilateral triangle using only a protractor and straightedge. Then design three similar triangles.

"It is contrary to human nature to ask a group of diverse individuals to all sit and listen to instruction on a concept or skill they may or may not need and in a way that may or may not address individual learning styles. Yet, this is what occurs in classrooms every day."

a more powerful tool. It is contrary to human nature to ask a group of diverse individuals to all sit and listen to instruction on a concept or skill they may or may not need and in a way that may or may not address individual learning styles. Yet this is what occurs in classrooms every day.

Whole-class instruction may seem easier for the teacher and may appear to give the teacher a sense of control, but the only control in place is over physical bodies, if even that, not minds. A student can sit and pretend to be listening while thinking about something totally different from the lesson. A teacher might assume a lesson is going well because five students are asking and answering questions and are excited about the skill; but videotape the next lesson you offer and you'll see the reality of your audience.

Differentiation is a combination of providing a variety of activities through which students can engage in learning, teaching students to self-assess and make appropriate decisions about their learning, and allowing students to make choices and have some control over their learning. I once had a group of students tell me that they felt that when teachers just present the same lesson to everyone it is disrespectful of them. That's a powerful sentiment! For differentiating instruction for a particular skill, plan out learning choices using a "Learning Styles and Readiness Grid" (Figure 4.5).

The *Scaffold for Learning*

To achieve a high level of student engagement in learning through differentiation, you'll want to ensure you offer students a variety of possible *learning activities* and *practice activities* across *participatory structures*: different ways to participate in learning. Students may engage in whole-class lessons, small-group lessons, pairs work, individual work, hands-on activities, technology activities, and so forth. Your *analytic rubric* defines what your students need to learn to accomplish the task at hand. You're now going to consider all the ways in which they can participate in the learning process; I refer to this as a *scaffold for learning* (Figure 4.6). It becomes the foundation for

Figure 4.6. Scaffold for Learning

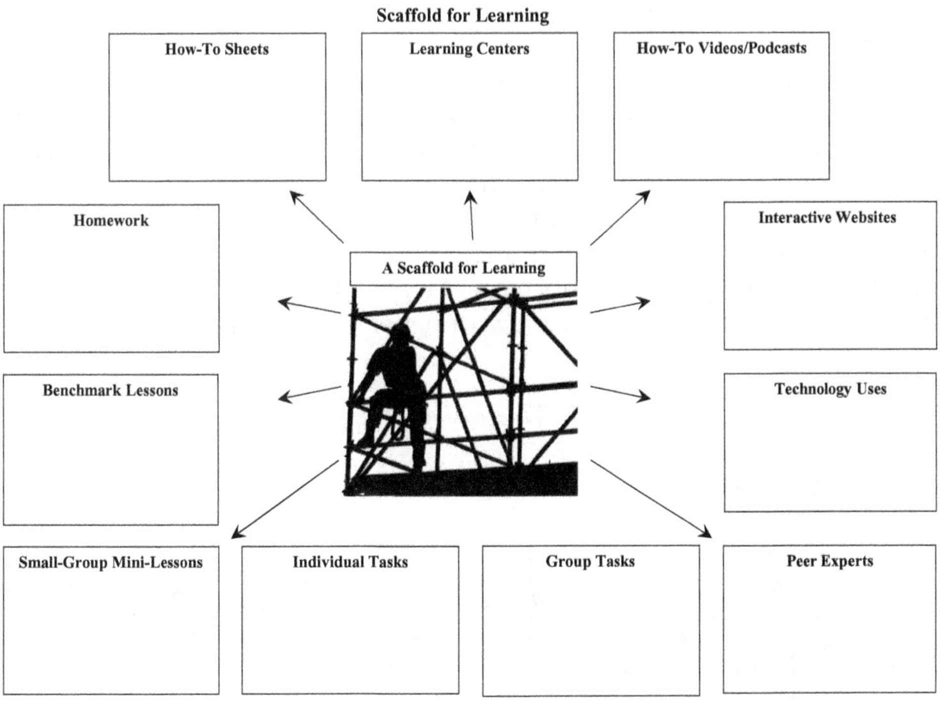

Scaffold for Learning

| How-To Sheets | Learning Centers | How-To Videos/Podcasts |

Homework

Interactive Websites

A Scaffold for Learning

Benchmark Lessons

Technology Uses

| Small-Group Mini-Lessons | Individual Tasks | Group Tasks | Peer Experts |

providing students with myriad opportunities to learn, thus differentiating learning to ensure success for each student. As you design your *ALU*, use the *scaffold for learning* to brainstorm various ways in which students could build content mastery. You don't typically share the *scaffold for learning* with your students. It serves as a planning tool for you.

CREATE

The learning process is not set in stone; it's different for each learner and varies with the content, which is what makes teaching such a complex craft. As the teacher, you'll want to decide on the best approach to introducing a topic, the goal being to make students aware of new learning they will want to pursue. In some cases, an inspirational kickoff *benchmark lesson* is the best. In others, having students grapple with the content in advance of the *benchmark lesson* allows the teacher to then synthesize those experiences for students during the *benchmark lesson*. Loosely, Figure 4.7 offers an instructional path that relates to the *scaffold for learning*.

For example, when starting students on exploring the concept of tessellations and the additive nature of angles, you might present a *benchmark lesson*, to inspire and intrigue them. You would show them tessellated items from nature: a honeycomb, a turtle shell, tessellated windows on a building, tessellated tiles in a walkway, and pieces of art. You would then engage students in a discussion of what is similar about these images, drawing their attention to the faraway look and the close-up look. Once you've triggered students' awareness (Gattegno, 1987) of this special type of pattern in nature, architecture, and art, you can have them engage in a variety of *learning activities* around understanding and designing tessellations.

Alternatively, you might start with an individual, pairs, or small-group activity that allows students to grapple with the content before you introduce it. You would give students bags of tessellation pieces and ask them to assemble them to fit on a larger piece of paper with no open space showing

Figure 4.7. The Path to Learning

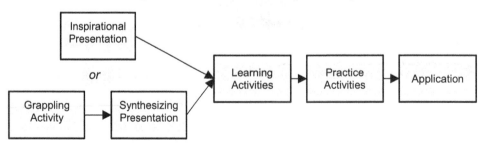

inside the design. This could range from triangles to more complex geometric configurations. After students explore, you would offer a *benchmark lesson* to synthesize what they discovered and introduce them to the structure of tessellations. You would then have them engage in a variety of *learning activities* around exploring tessellations and the additive nature of angles.

Regardless of the entry point to skill acquisition, students should be able to engage in a variety of *learning activities* and *practice activities* related to the content, as are represented on the *scaffold for learning*. As you work through each section of *participatory structures* below, stop and add to a *scaffold for learning* for your *ALU* by considering how each mode of engagement can support student learning. Note that the *scaffold for learning* examples shown in this book each address a portion of a unit. Over the course of a three- or four-week unit, you would need several pages to capture all of the possibilities. This is like your new *Learner-Active, Technology-Infused Classroom* planbook: ways through which students will learn the content you are responsible for teaching.

The *Benchmark Lesson*

One way students participate in learning is through a *benchmark lesson*—a whole-class lesson focused on triggering awareness of what students need to learn at different points (benchmarks) throughout the *ALU*. Whole-class instruction is not an effective venue for engaging students in learning specific skills, no matter how talented and engaging the teacher. It can, however, be a powerful venue for inspiring students and making them aware of the skills they need to learn to accomplish the *problem-based task* at hand. Thus, in the *Learner-Active, Technology-Infused Classroom*, teachers are challenged to think differently about that whole-class lesson. Just because you're presenting content to the whole class does not mean you're conducting a *benchmark lesson*. The intent of the *benchmark lesson* is to "trigger awareness" (Gattegno, 1987) of what skills and concepts students need to accomplish their *problem-based task*.

Consider a *problem-based task* in which students are using a mythology structure to build awareness of the importance of a healthy body image and self-esteem. Students will write modern-day myths teaching relevant lessons. The teacher may offer a *benchmark lesson* to the class to introduce them to the concept of myths as venues for teaching life lessons. The teacher wouldn't begin the unit with how to write a myth, as students have not yet read and studied myths, nor have they researched their topic on which to write a myth.

Consider a *problem-based task* in which students are working to submit an original still-life oil painting to a juried student art exhibit. At the start, the teacher might present paintings from various artists, discussing the unique nature of oil painting, along with the importance of first drawing the objects to gain a familiarity with them. A few days later, the teacher might follow up with a *benchmark lesson* on the power of underpainting. As the *problem-based task* unfolds, there are learning "benchmarks" along the way.

Introducing concepts to the class at key developmental checkpoints in the unit, or benchmarks, is accomplished through the *benchmark lesson*: a ten- to fifteen-minute whole-class lesson to introduce students to a concept that is essential to the problem-based task. As teachers, we have a tendency to think that we must directly "teach" content or students will not learn it. Often, that teaching is presented to the whole class from the front of the room, which may be more efficient for teachers, but it is not effective for student learning. Students' brains must construct knowledge. This is accomplished by having students grapple with content, often individually or in a pair or triad. The *benchmark lesson* is not the venue for having students learn and retain content; it is not the place to check for understanding. It is, however, a perfect venue for providing inspiration, whetting appetites, and piquing interest. The best *benchmark lessons* produce "aha" moments for students that drive them to want more information and learning. This is a very different approach to whole-class instruction with which *Learner-Active, Technology-Infused Classroom* teachers must grapple.

Conducting the *Benchmark Lesson*

To maximize the brain's potential to learn, keep your *benchmark lessons* to ten to fifteen minutes. As teachers, we are notorious for being able to stand in the front of the room and talk about a subject to our seemingly captive audience. It is critical to remember that while you may be enjoying your own presentation, your students most likely will not be absorbing all the content you think they are. The key is to make your lesson count!

Start with a clear, focused, and narrow objective. Avoid covering too much in one *benchmark lesson*. It's better to offer several *benchmark lessons* to build on the concept. During a lesson, the first couple of minutes involve getting the brain engaged. The next ten to twelve minutes are prime brain activity time: students are most likely to absorb what you are teaching. Then the brain begins to enter into a lull (Sousa, 2017). Stop talking!

Be mindful as well of the primacy-recency effect: a "phenomenon whereby, during a learning episode, we tend to remember best that which comes first (prime-time 1), second best that which comes last (prime-time 2), and least that which comes just past the middle (down-time)" (Sousa, 2017, p. 139). If you think about it, that means the first point you make and the last will be remembered; everything in the middle may be lost. That is why it is so important to begin your *benchmark lesson* with a compelling point you want to make, build it, and then repeat it at the end.

When offering a *benchmark lesson*, use the first minute or so to focus your students' attention through some sort of personal reflection. Your students have come to this lesson from other activities and, most likely, their minds are still focused on those, whether walking through the hall, finding a piece of paper, or working on another assignment. When you begin talking, your students' brains may not be focused on you. As students are settling into their seats for the lesson, have them reflect on a life experience or existing knowledge they have regarding the concept you are about to teach. If you're going to introduce the concept of electromagnetic energy, you might ask students to think about what tuning their radio, watching television, microwaving popcorn, and sending a text message have in common. If you are going to introduce the concept of globalization, you might ask students to think about five items they use in everyday life and where they think they were made. If you're going to introduce a unit on Shakespeare and his themes that are still current among teens today, you might start by asking students to write down what they know about Shakespeare, or what are some of the top angst-causing problems among teens today. The purpose of the personal reflection is to get the students focused on the topic at hand as their brains are engaging, so that when you begin to speak, they will be ready to hear.

Make your objective known; write or project it on the board. Use your lesson to create connections among the concept, real life, and students' experiences. Where possible, utilize technology; for example, find a compelling video clip or image. Make your point, write it, restate it. Do not assume that saying something once ensures that all students will remember it.

As an example, students in French class who are writing directions to design their own adventure games must understand the power of the preposition: how just one word changes the meaning of a sentence. As students assemble for the lesson, have the following questions projected: "Where is the floor in relation to your feet?" "Where is the ceiling in relation to your head?" (Note: you would write the sentences and conduct this lesson in French, however, for the purpose of this book, let's look at it in English.) After allowing students to consider the two reflection questions, project several incomplete sentences on the board involving two objects with the preposition missing (see Figure 4.8).

Note: in this example, you'll need to have a desk handy that has an inside compartment for the sentence "The book is in the desk." Obviously, you can change the two objects to work for your classroom.

Tell your students to watch what you do with the book as you place it on the desk. Then ask them where the book is. Once students answer, fill in the blank in the first sentence with the word "on." Then tell them to watch again and place the book under the desk, asking students where it is. Fill in the blank in the second sentence with "under." Next, place the book inside the desk and continue filling in blanks. Next, hold it hovering over the desk.

Figure 4.8. Benchmark Lesson on Prepositions

The book is _____ the desk.

The book is _____ the desk.

The book is _____ the desk.

The book is _____ the desk.

Based on the items you choose, see how many different sentences you can complete with different prepositions. Then draw students' attention to those now filled blank lines. Discuss what the words tell the reader and how changing just that one word changes the meaning of the whole sentence and clarifies exactly where the book is in relation to the desk. Introduce the term "preposition" as a powerful word that describes the relationship between two items. Often, students learn parts of speech and grammar through studying a world language; so while they should know what a preposition is, they may not truly grasp the power of it until they are navigating their way through a non-native language. Offer an example from the *ALU* task to show how different their adventure game directions would be if they simply used a different preposition, and how the success of their game is going to depend on how well they use prepositions to offer clear directions. That's it! *Benchmark lesson* is over. You introduced a concept, you demonstrated it in a visual way, as well as through your words, and you related it back to the *ALU*. Students will now have access to a variety of *learning activities* through which they can learn to recognize and use prepositions (the skill part of the process) based on their ability level. For students who are just grasping the concept, they'll engage in *learning activities* focusing on the most common prepositions; those who already understand the concept may engage in *learning activities* requiring them to determine the six types of prepositions (time, place, direction, agent, instruments, and phrases.)

As you offer a *benchmark lesson*, make sure your students are in a position to pay attention. That may include scanning the room to make sure all are seated or standing so that they can see you and whatever props you might have, asking students to close their laptop computers, and asking them to close any notebooks, and put down any writing instruments. During a *benchmark lesson*, all that students should be doing is listening, watching, and participating. *Benchmark lessons* are not designed for note-taking except in the case where you deliberately want to build note-taking skills. (Note-taking can occur in *small-group mini-lessons*.)

Given that you have set a time for the *benchmark lesson*, set your expectation that students will be ready at the appointed time. Avoid having to remind students and call them to the lesson, building dependence on you; this would mean other students have to wait for their peers to get ready. Make your expectations clear from the beginning of the school year that they are to watch the time and be ready.

During the *benchmark lesson*, make sure your students are following along by using a thumbs-up, thumbs-down signal in response to a question; small whiteboards where students hold up a quick response; or a technology app that allows students to enter a quick response digitally. An exit card would allow students to answer a question on an index card and hand it in before leaving the *benchmark lesson* and returning to their work. It's a good idea, too, to then offer a targeted, *small-group mini-lesson* (more on that *participatory structure* next) so that those who did not feel they understood the lesson can receive more instruction from you.

Keep in mind that the purpose of the *benchmark lesson* is to offer well-timed introductions to concepts through short segments of whole-class instruction. Timing should coincide with students' *felt need* to accomplish the next phase of the *ALU*. Imagine students who are designing a roller coaster and are at the initial stages of exploring how a marble runs along rails (physically or virtually on a computer). As they are grappling with how to keep the marble on the rails, how to ensure it can climb the next hill, and how it can avoid falling off a loop, you have the perfect opportunity for a *benchmark lesson* on the physics behind a rollercoaster. You can introduce concepts such as kinetic and potential energy, acceleration and deceleration, and the influence of gravity and friction.

You will most likely offer one to three *benchmark lessons* across the week. Avoid setting a prescribed time for your *benchmark lessons*. Think through the week and plan the number and times for the *benchmark lessons*, being mindful of the flow of work taking place in the *ALU*. At the start of a school year, with students who are not used to *Learner-Active, Technology-Infused Classrooms*, you may want to conduct a daily *benchmark lesson* (not always at the same time), focusing on both academics and process, so that students feel they are getting the direction they need. As students become familiar with all of the ways in which they can learn and all of the ways in which they can engage with you, they will be more capable of independently using longer periods of time well. If you decide to conduct a *benchmark lesson* early in the class period, leave at least fifteen minutes before the start. This way, students can use the time meaningfully for their work. If you start a *benchmark lesson*, say, five minutes after the start of the class period, students can't delve into any other work; you end up causing them to waste precious time waiting for the *benchmark lesson*. Encourage your students, too, to schedule around the *benchmark lesson*, if need be, rather than trying to fit activities into tight time slots. For example, if they need thirty minutes to work on some aspect of an *ALU*, they can start it, attend to the *benchmark lesson*, and return to it. Their schedules do not have to perfectly fit in a way that causes them to finish all activities before the *benchmark lesson*.

Given that you are looking to inspire students and introduce them to a new concept, showing the connections to the *problem-based task* they are working to solve, you or another teacher are the best people to offer it. On rare occasions, you might have a student who understands the concept and wants to create a presentation on it, with your guidance, of course, and offer a *benchmark lesson*. However, *benchmark lessons* are not intended to be offered by students to their peers. This is where the teachers' knowledge of the students and learning process, expertise, and inspirational ability are needed.

Using the *ALU* task you've designed, consider various points along the way at which you should introduce certain key concepts, based on the majority of students reaching a benchmark point in the overall *ALU*. How will you launch the *ALU* to build student interest and intrigue? What might you introduce a few days into the unit? The second week? And so forth. Figure 4.6 provides you with a *scaffold for learning* image to cue your thinking. All of your actual *ALU* activities will not fit in the boxes; you may wish to use a page for each box or some other document layout that works for you. Make a list of all of the *benchmark lessons* you plan to offer. Use the Rubric to Assess a Benchmark Lesson (Appendix H) to guide the development and delivery of your *benchmark lessons*.

Opting Out of a Benchmark Lesson

At times, though rare, you may find that you have a student or two who do not need the *benchmark lesson* you are about to present. Offer those students the option of opting out of the lesson if they wish. They may decide to attend anyway, and that would be their choice. Otherwise, they should move to an area outside the rest of the group and work quietly on another activity they scheduled. This approach honors your students and the use of their time. While *benchmark lessons* should be focused on concept introduction such that any level of student can benefit, the student who, for example, already fully understands the power of claims, counterclaims, reason, and evidence and already uses them in writing should be allowed to opt out of that *benchmark lesson*.

Presenting Skills to Your Students

The *benchmark lesson* is aimed at teaching concepts and triggering students' awareness as to content that will help them in accomplishing the *problem-based task*. Students, however, also need skill instruction! So many of the other structures on the *scaffold for learning* are aimed at skill and content acquisition. Introducing skills requires three essential elements:

1. Activating prior knowledge by focusing students first on the prerequisite skills they've already mastered to succeed in mastering the skill being introduced.

2. Creating a connection to students' lives and the real world to ensure that the skill being presented has meaning and makes sense (Sousa, 2017).

3. Providing a variety of ways through which students can learn and practice the skill, including those geared toward learning styles, cognitive progression (Sulla, 2015), disabilities, advanced learners, and giftedness.

While you can present skills to your students in small groups, and that will be one of the topics that follows, consider the many other ways in which you can provide students with learning opportunities in which they can engage independent of you. Videos, printed directions, picture directions, learning centers, and peers are just some of the ways through which students can learn independent of a teacher. In the *Learner-Active, Technology-Infused Classroom*, the teacher becomes the masterful "bridge builder" who creates varied opportunities through which students can learn, building toward greater student efficacy.

Designing *Learning Activities* Versus *Practice Activities*

As mentioned earlier, the key is to identify and design *learning activities* (Sulla, 2015) as differentiated from *practice activities*. A *learning activity* has three distinct characteristics from other classroom activities and assignments:

1. **It is focused on one targeted, discrete skill or concept**; it is not too broad in content. In math, a *learning activity* might focus on factoring a quadratic equation; a *learning activity* on quadratic equations would be too broad. Watercolor painting techniques would be too broad a topic; however, dry brush technique and flat wash technique would make two focused *learning activity* topics.

2. **It includes directions**. A *learning activity* offers the student directions for completing the skill or grasping the concept. It may offer a demonstration or modeling, as in the case of a video, or step by step directions with images, as in the case of printed directions or a learning center.

3. Where possible, **it includes feedback**. It may include sample scenarios with answers. It may offer a visual. In the case of a *learning activity* on recognizing antecedents in a sentence, the last part could offer some practice that the student would have to complete, followed by the answers. In the case of a video on using coil clay technique to create a small pot, the feedback would be in the successful completion of the pot, perhaps guided by some questions to assess the final product.

As you move beyond the *benchmark lesson*, you have to ensure you have a broad collection of *learning activities*. In the past, you may have presented content to the whole class and then given them activities to practice what they learned. *Practice activities* presume learning has already taken place; they cannot be used in place of *learning activities*. Without well-crafted *learning activities*, you will be leaving student learning to chance. The following sections offer more detailed descriptions of structures for providing *learning activities*.

How-To Sheets

You can provide your students with direct instruction in skill development using a printed *how-to sheet*. Students who are visual learners and enjoy independent learning may actually prefer a *how-to sheet* to listening to a teacher's lesson. Students can follow the directions at their own pace, re-read as necessary, and refer to diagrams and examples you've included.

A *how-to sheet* should focus on a particular skill, such as balancing a chemical equation, calculating percentage of increase, conjugating verbs in Latin, and so on. *How-to sheets* are also useful for teaching students how to use various technologies, such as calculators, apps, microscopes, and 3-D printers; and they can be used for instructing students in the structures of the *Learner-Active, Technology-Infused Classroom*, such as how to schedule time.

How-to sheets should have clearly numbered steps, with the student taking one action per step. Include screenshots, diagrams, or images to help the student understand the step. For young students or those who have difficulty staying focused, add small boxes to the left of each step for them to check off as they complete the step.

How-to sheets provide "just-in-time-learning." At the point the student has a "felt need" to learn a skill, he or she can retrieve the *how-to sheet* from the *resource area* and follow the written directions.

How-To Podcasts, Screencasts, and Videos

Computer technology makes it easy to create your own personalized audio and video files to provide your students with direct instruction in a skill or concept. Podcasts generally consist of audio, while screencasts include images from a computer. Screencasts are easily created using one of a number of apps that capture what is happening on your computer screen or interactive whiteboard while you narrate it. For videos, use a video camera, tablet, or cell phone to capture the video and audio of a lesson or performance offered by you, students, or other adults. Using readily available technology, you create podcasts recording your voice presenting information to your students. Students can listen to or watch these as needed to build a particular skill. Many teachers will use QR codes (though newer technology will soon replace the QR code) either posted on a wall with an accompanying image or as a link on an activity list to bring up podcasts, screencasts, and videos.

Plan out your lesson, focusing on a narrow objective. In creating a screencast, for example, capture the action on the computer or interactive whiteboard using one of a variety of available screen capture programs. Then add your voice-over to narrate the screencast. The key to recording your voice is to speak slowly. Keep in mind that after the human brain hears words, it has to process them. Sometimes, when you're recording familiar information, it's natural to speak quickly, because your brain has already processed it. When recording your voice for your students, be mindful of their need to process information. Chunk the words so that you pause for your students to process what you just said. In other words, the point is not to speak each word slowly, but to speak in phrases followed by pauses. Here is an excerpt from an audio script for a podcast or screencast on identifying themes in novels:

> The theme of a novel *(pause)*, identifies the author's point *(pause)* in writing it *(pause)*. What message is the author trying to convey? *(pause)* In a novel, *(pause)* the theme often lies *(pause)* beneath the surface *(pause)* so you have to read more deeply *(pause)* and analyze more carefully. *(pause)* In *The Great Gatsby (pause)* what message *(pause)* did F. Scott Fitzgerald want to convey? *(pause)* On the surface, *(pause)* the novel is about an ill-fated romance. *(pause)* However, at the core, *(pause) The Great Gatsby is* about the demise *(pause)* of the American Dream. The author drives home the point, *(pause)* throughout the book, *(pause)* that the pursuit of social status *(pause)* and material gain *(pause)* destroyed the American Dream *(pause)* on which the country was founded.

Note that the pauses are at points that will allow the listener's brain to process key information that was just stated. Use voice inflection and intonation to capture and maintain the attention of the listener. Carefully pronounce words, and avoid colloquialisms. This will enhance the listener's experience.

Podcasts, screencasts, and videos, like *how-to sheets*, focus on a single skill or narrow set of skills so that each does not require too much time to complete. You might have a corresponding printed sheet to which students refer while listening and/or watching. You might have a sheet for students to complete that demonstrates to you that they understood the skill or concept. For example, after viewing a screencast on balancing chemical equations, you might offer several examples for the student to tackle.

If the topic is somewhat abstract, such as in the case of identifying the theme of a text, you might offer students a transcript, which would be particularly helpful for your more visual learners. Your students who are strong auditory learners may lean towards listening to podcasts and screencasts for skill development over following a printed *how-to sheet*. Your students who are fast visual processors may find podcast and screencast explanations too long and opt for the printed *how-to sheet*.

Consider recording *benchmark lessons* or *small-group mini-lessons* for students' later review. This is particularly useful for students who were absent at the time of the lesson. I presented this idea to a science teacher years ago, before the advent of digital video cameras. I walked into his classroom one day to find him working with some students, asking probing questions about an experiment in progress. Other students were looking up information on a computer; still others were meeting in groups to discuss their findings from an experiment. I then heard the teacher's voice on the other side of the room. I walked over to find a group of three students watching a video of the teacher. The screen revealed just his hands folding a paper airplane as he gave verbal directions. He was taking his students outside at the end of the week to learn about the physics behind flight. I later found out that he had set up a video camera in his basement and was filming short clips of demonstrations for his students. He told me that he realized that standing in the front of the room giving an entire class directions for folding a paper airplane was a poor use of his and his students' time. By creating the video, small groups of students could work on preparing for the flight lesson while he focused on pushing other students' thinking on other experiments. I asked the students how they liked learning this way and they unanimously agreed it was better than listening to the teacher in the front of the room.

Using podcasts, screencasts, and videos, you can capture skill lessons and demonstrations for students to use when they need them. This style of information dissemination will appeal to your digital generation of students. Plus, you will free yourself from repeating skills lessons in favor of using your time to engage in higher-order questioning and thinking with those students who are ready. Technology provides many opportunities to "clone" the teacher.

Start small: create key videos. Then have students create some, adding to your repertoire; teaching others solidifies one's own learning. Work on expanding your collection to various cognitive levels, including for advanced students who can be given the next challenge.

Note: I strongly recommend checking whether your school has a specific policy and perhaps a permission form for parents to complete if you decide to film their children. All schools handle this differently, but essentially, if you are videotaping someone and plan to use the video with others, you should secure permission in advance, and avoid using any student's last name.

Small-Group Mini-Lessons

You can provide skill instruction to a small group of like-ability or like-interest students through a short lesson on a particular skill. Students sign up to participate in the lesson in advance (more on the structures to support *small-group mini-lessons* in Chapter 5). A *small-group mini-lesson* should last approximately seven to ten minutes, after which time you may want to have the students stay together to practice the skill with you checking in later. *Small-group mini-lessons* are effective for students who benefit from in-person, direct instruction from you, and they appeal to auditory learners. There are four main reasons to conduct academically focused *small-group mini-lessons*:

♦ As a follow-up to a *benchmark lesson,* for those who may continue to have difficulty grasping the concept or have questions that were not answered during the lesson;

♦ To provide an introduction to a skill for those students who may be auditory learners or who benefit from working with the teacher for skill development;

♦ To provide reinforcement for students who may need help in a skill; and

♦ To provide an advanced skill for those students who have mastered the current content.

Also conduct process-oriented *small-group mini-lessons* to help students master the structures of the *Learner-Active, Technology-Infused Classroom,* such as scheduling, which is covered in more detail in Chapter 5.

Structuring *Small-Group Mini-Lessons*

Create an area in the room that is conducive to meeting with a small group. You might set up a table in a corner of the room, for example. Consider whether or not you want the table near an easel, whiteboard, or interactive whiteboard. It's important to be considerate of the students who are not working with you by keeping your voice to a volume that is loud enough for just those students sitting with you to hear. Be mindful of this when you designate your area. I worked with teachers who created the *small-group mini-lesson* area in the middle of the room. They soon realized that the conversations from that area were disturbing students all around them and relocated the area to a corner of the room to minimize the distraction to the rest of the class.

Drawing on brain research, keep the following in mind as you design *small-group mini-lessons*:

♦ Structure each *small-group mini-lesson* so that it has a very narrow focus on a very specific skill that you can present in a short period of time, which not everyone will need at the same time. Keep your group size to no more than six students, with options for overflow students who also wanted to sign up. If you find too many students are signing up, you may need to focus the topic better. For example, the topic "Factoring Trinomial Equations" is too broad. Instead, offer *small-group mini-lessons* on "Review of Factoring Binomials," "Identifying Common Factors in Factoring Trinomials," "Factoring Trinomials with Negative Terms," and "Factoring Challenging Trinomials." You would also have *how-to sheets* and *how-to videos* on these topics so that students could decide how they learn best. While students will have to tackle all of these topics, they may, for example, select the *small-group mini-lesson* if they are struggling or if they are addressing a more advanced and, thus, challenging topic and, in both cases, want the live interaction with the teacher.

♦ Make your instruction count! You have a short period of time while your students' brains are highly activated to have them build new skills. The *small-group mini-lesson* must be very tightly structured. Let the students know the objective up front. Ask questions to activate their prior knowledge. Use visual aids and demonstrate what is appropriate. Make every sentence purposeful and deliberate. Have students take notes and repeat back to you certain steps of key points. At the end, summarize, and, potentially, allow students to stay in the *small-group mini-lesson* area to practice. While you may know a skill, crafting the best way to convey that skill to others is the goal of *small-group mini-lessons*.

♦ Throughout the lesson, check for understanding. Unlike the *benchmark lesson*, the *small-group mini-lesson* is designed to offer direct instruction in a skill or concept. Ensure that the students are understanding what you are presenting.

- Take into account that some students may choose to attend the *small-group mini-lesson* because they are confused, but as you start, the content solidifies for them and they no longer need to participate. In this case, allow students to leave the area when they feel they have the information they need. You can provide "opt-out" points at which this happens so as not to disturb the flow of your presentation. One student exclaimed to his teacher, "Wow, you really must respect me that you trust me to know when I can go."

Other Considerations

While they may seem like a simple structure, there are several nuances to *small-group mini-lessons* that will make them a powerful learning opportunity in your *Learner-Active, Technology-Infused Classroom*.

- Stick to your time slots. Begin and end *small-group mini-lessons* on time. Otherwise, student scheduling becomes compromised and your class will not run as smoothly. If you find a topic warrants more time, schedule a follow-up lesson.

- **After conducting a *small-group mini-lesson*,** return to facilitating learning in the classroom. Therefore, avoid scheduling back-to-back *small-group mini-lessons*. Given that the rest of your students are most likely working independently, often on *learning activities*, you want to ensure you are offering the necessary facilitation. You want to be careful not to spend too much time with a small number of students off in a corner of the room.

- **Let students know the schedule for *small-group mini-lessons* in advance,** so that they can plan to attend. In the *Learner-Active, Technology-Infused Classroom*, students take charge of scheduling how they will use their time. Consequently, it is important to give them responsibility for planning to attend a *small-group mini-lesson*. Avoid suddenly announcing one and asking students to attend at that moment, as it interferes with student control of their own schedules. Based on your facilitation and student requests, you may decide on the need for a *small-group mini-lesson* to be offered in the more immediate future. In that case, you can add it to the list of scheduled *small-group mini-lessons* and alert students in your daily announcement notes. Students would need to then revise their schedules to attend, which is not a problem, as the need to change plans along the way is an important life skill.

- **Sometimes you may need to invite students to a *small-group mini-lesson*.** As your students come to understand the

Learner-Active, Technology-Infused Classroom, they will learn to self-assess and to determine whether or not they need to attend a *small-group mini-lesson*. There will be times, even then, when you have to let students know that they must attend a lesson. Depending on the structures you have in place for communicating with your students, you might email them or include a comment in their personal folder.

♦ It's important to keep in mind that *small-group mini-lessons* are not only for those students who need help; they also can be **an effective way to address your high-achieving and gifted learners**. In fact, a well-timed, advanced *small-group mini-lesson* can be used to motivate average students to raise their level of achievement. If you announce an upcoming advanced *small-group mini-lesson* and indicate a prerequisite assignment or quiz to receive an entrance ticket or gain admission to the lesson, you might find that more of your students will step up to the challenge.

♦ **Offer a variety of ways to learn a skill beyond the** *small-group mini-lesson* so that students have more options than just attending the lesson to learn the skill. The Web offers a wide range of websites, videos, simulations, how-to pages, and interactive websites that you can use as *learning activities*. You can add a few that you design. As stated earlier, over time, you will enhance your collection with ideas and *learning activities* designed by students and your colleagues.

♦ **Let go of the notion that students must hear something from you in order to learn it.** Otherwise, you will be inclined to offer repeated *small-group mini-lessons* when students could learn through other structures. *Small-group mini-lessons* are one important component of the *Learner-Active, Technology-Infused Classroom*. While there is no one right number of *small-group mini-lessons* to offer each day, over the course of the entire day, you will want to offer approximately three *small-group mini-lessons,* or three across the course of the week if you teach in a departmentalized situation.

♦ **Position** *peer experts* **to offer some** *small-group mini-lessons.* It's possible for peer experts to conduct some *small-group mini-lessons*; however, it is very hard to unlearn that which was incorrectly taught. So you will want to ensure that they are able to offer the lesson and answer related questions. This is covered in more detail in the *peer expert* section later in this chapter.

Learning Centers

The term *learning center* tends to be associated with the primary grades, but, used correctly, they can serve as an effective opportunity for students to learn at all grade levels. It is important to use them as independent *learning activities* and not as stations in a timed rotation, as the latter would make you a "ferry master" and not a "bridge builder." When teachers move students from center to center in rotations based on an allotted time, they are not allowing students to take charge of their own learning, nor are they differentiating instruction. Rather, students should sign up for *learning centers*, as they are typically a limited resource only able to accommodate a certain number of students at a time. (*Learning centers* often involve some sort of kinesthetic, hands-on activity that requires keeping all the pieces in one place.) *Learning centers* fall into three categories:

♦ Those that require limited resources, such as primary sources, a fish tank, the sole microscope in the room, or a specialized computer;

♦ Those that involve a hands-on experience, such as working with clay, a pre-set science experiment, math manipulatives, and STEM kits, and;

♦ Those that involve materials that are best kept together, such as molecular model kits, map puzzle pieces, and photographs.

You can design *learning centers* for individuals, pairs, or groups. Essentially, students go to the *learning center* or retrieve a container or packet with materials to be taken to a desk, table, or other space.

You might set up an area of the classroom with an experiment, a model, or other resources that are best left stationary. Alternatively, you might place a set of manipulatives or other objects in a container for students to take to their location. If the materials are flat, such as cardboard or paper pieces, you could store them in a packet or folder. Students sign up for a period of time in the *learning center* and add it to their personal schedules.

When teachers rely primarily on whole-class instruction, they need class sets of materials for all activities. In the *Learner-Active, Technology-Infused Classroom*, class sets of materials are not necessary. Instead, students schedule their time to share resources. This allows teachers to make better use of budget funds by providing more varied resources, using them as *learning centers*.

In designing a *learning center*, realize that you will not be there to offer directions. Your printed or videotaped directions must be clear and, as in the case of *how-to sheets*, presented in such a way that each direction asks the student to take one action. Suppose you want students to dissect an owl pellet. A direction such as "separate the bones" leaves too much up to the imagination of the student. Instead, you might provide a direction sheet that offers clear steps. For example:

1. Look at the outside of the owl pellet to identify any pieces of bones sticking out.

2. Using a toothpick, carefully pull off the fur and feathers in search of a bone.

3. Once you find a bone, do not pull on it, as it may break.

4. Using a toothpick, continue to pull off the fur and feathers around the bone, being careful to identify other bones that might be overlapping.

5. Once you have uncovered a bone, place it on the tray for later identification.

6. Continue to pull off more fur and feathers in search of your next bone.

Note that each direction requires the student to take one action. This level of detail helps ensure students will meet with success and decreases the need for students to ask for help. You could include a podcast or video to offer an even greater explanation of the directions.

To build writing skills, you might create several *learning centers* in which students retrieve a packet that includes an activity and directions. In art, you might create a *learning center* in which students study a painting and respond to questions. For physical education, you might create a *learning center* in which students video and view themselves practicing a particular skill in a sport. For chemistry, you might create a *learning center* in which students use molecular kits to construct molecules. A computer could be designated as a *learning center* with a specific piece of software or website to be used.

Keep a *sign-up sheet* next to each *learning center* or in the *resource area* with enough time for students to retrieve, use, and replace the *learning center* before another student needs it. Students will learn to sign up in advance and coordinate the use of the resource with others. The *limited resource sign-up sheet* will be discussed, along with other critical structures, in Chapter 5.

Interactive Websites and Applications

Today's digital world is filled with apps that run on smartphones, tablets, Chromebooks, and computers. They are typically interactive, focused, and visually appealing. You can find apps to explore the laws of physics, learn grammar skills in a world language, interact with an online version of a magnetic poetry board, play music on a keyboard, explore timelines in history, learn the color wheel, explore maps, learn to read music, and more. The interactive nature allows students to manipulate objects, make predictions, experience cause-and-effect relationships, and create. To locate apps, use your Internet search engine and type the word app followed by the subject of interest, for example, "app poetry."

If you have access to handheld-computing devices, be sure to search out and load apps related to your curriculum and then make those apps part of your *scaffold for learning*. You may need to create a direction sheet for using an app.

Individual Versus Group Tasks

Learning is social; students learn well from one another. Today's students thrive on social interaction, both in person and through the Internet. Collaborative learning can be a powerful tool in the classroom; however, you must be purposeful in your assignment of group versus individual activities. Students must eventually perform independently, both on standardized tests as well as in life. It is your responsibility to ensure that all students have achieved personal content mastery. Consequently, it is important to provide students with individual *learning activities* that allow them to acquire and practice skills.

The best use of collaboration is when the activity is related to *higher-order, open-ended, problem solving*. Not unlike the collaborative world of work, students should independently gain a certain amount of content mastery and then come together to collaborate. When work teams come together, each person brings some level of personal expertise. Brainstorming ideas, analyzing problem solutions, and generating questions are some of the types of activities in which learning is enhanced through collaboration.

Computer technology can provide powerful opportunities for collaboration through networked software and web-based tools. Students can collaboratively build databanks, building on one another's knowledge, and even join with students around the world in this effort. They can collaboratively work on documents, spreadsheets, and other products. Students are no longer limited to working with others in the classroom; email and videoconferencing can expand the student body beyond the walls of the classroom or school.

A key skill to learn in collaborating is reaching decisions through consensus (Sulla, 2018). Instead of students voting and using a majority-rules approach, have them discuss a solution, offering pros and cons, until they can all at least live with, if not fully support, an idea.

Peer Experts

Peer experts provide an effective learning experience for both the student offering the instruction and the one being instructed. First, one of the best ways to ensure retention of learning is to teach someone else. Second, people learn best from those who are hierarchically similar; children learn more readily from other children than from adults. *Peer experts* are designated by the teacher as having mastered a specific skill and having the ability to share the skill with others. Make sure that the student designated as a *peer expert* is adequately equipped to teach others. Simply scoring high on a test is not an indication that the student can explain the concept or skill in an effective way. It is good practice to have the potential *peer expert* walk you through the explanation before showing others. It is also good to train your students, all of whom should be designated as a *peer expert* at some times across the year, that it's important to not simply take over the work. Being a *peer expert* is not about doing the work for others; it's about talking them through it in a way that they understand.

Once you have identified a *peer expert*, have them put their name on the *peer expert board* with their skill of expertise (see Chapter 5 for more on this structure). Students who are having difficulty with the skill can go to the *peer expert* for help. *Peer experts* also tend to check the *help board* in case they have expertise to share to meet another student's need. Avoid having that one student spend an inordinate amount of time teaching others. Students will solidify their own learning after they've explained a concept or skill to others two or three times. Once they present more than that, they run the risk of becoming bored with the topic or not having the time to complete their other work. Have them recommend another student to you as a *peer expert* for that skill so you can rotate students through areas of expertise.

Peer Experts Conducting Small-Group Mini-Lessons

Direct instruction must be offered by someone who understands the skill and knows how to present it to others, and that is usually a teacher. However, given that learning is social and students learn well from one another, students can offer *small-group mini-lessons* if they are well vetted by the teacher.

Create a process for students to opt to offer *small-group mini-lessons*. For example, you might require them to complete a quiz on the topic that demonstrates not only the ability to obtain the correct answer but to explain how to arrive at a correct answer and identify common mistakes. Then have the student offer up a lesson plan, of sorts, that has the student consider how to introduce the skill, points to make, ways to check for understanding and mastery, and ways to engage students in practice. While it may be tempting to suggest a student show others how to build a particular skill, it is important first to ensure that the student has sufficient mastery to share the approach with others.

Homework

Homework should be meaningful and purposeful. There is a cognitive benefit to providing students with homework. During the class period, students learn a new skill, and they spend time practicing it. Once time passes after the initial learning and practice session, and the students are home after school, a related homework assignment should require the students to recall the classroom experience. This further solidifies the learning. Consider designating homework for certain skills so that students assign it to themselves when they tackle them. For this reason, I do not recommend that students be allowed to complete homework in class. Doing so eliminates the cognitive benefit of returning to the content after the passage of time.

It is tempting in the *Learner-Active, Technology-Infused Classroom* to allow students to complete unfinished class work for homework. This, however, risks the danger of students engaging in *learning activities* at home that require greater teacher participation. In the *Learner-Active, Technology-Infused Classroom*, you are not delivering information from the front of the classroom. Rather, you are designing a variety of *learning activities* through which students will build content mastery, and you are facilitating learning by working closely with students to monitor their progress and pose probing questions to promote higher-order thinking. Clearly, some, or many, of these activities should be accomplished only in class with your facilitation. If you allow students to complete these *learning activities* at home, they may lose out on the richness of the experience.

Design unique activities to be completed at home, as a follow-up or extension to classroom activities. This may mean providing multiple activities from which students will choose, based on their progress in classroom activities. If students are writing narratives, some may be learning to use dialogue effectively while others are learning to use multiple plot lines. The homework should be aligned with their cognitive progress. You might want to include *practice activities* throughout the unit that can serve as homework assignments. By labeling activities on the *activity list* as LA (*learning activity*) or PA (*practice activity*), students can then assign themselves the appropriate homework based on their progress and available *practice activities*.

Often, *ALUs* have content that is not directly related to the core curricular content (see Figure 4.1). The outer-ring, peripheral content could be a perfect homework assignment. Often, students will be very interested in this aspect of the *ALU*, but it does not address your content and, thus, they need not be learning it with you nearby.

Homework should never be assigned as busy work to fill up students' time. It should satisfy a specific purpose and be meaningful. The purpose for homework might be to:

- **Activate prior knowledge** before introducing new content. Prior to introducing students to the concept of ocean garbage gyres, you might ask students to reflect on plastic bags and bottles they may see on the road that will eventually enter a storm drain and end up in the ocean, having them write about what they think happens to them. Just prior to introducing students to the concept of a sonnet, you might ask students to identify a poem they like or to write an original poem to bring to class, and explain what makes it a poem. Offer a question or task that enables students to draw upon personal experience to connect to a new concept or skill.

- **Grapple with new content** to create a healthy cognitive dissonance. Before introducing the concept of social justice, have students view a collection of photographs that depict issues related to social justice, such as identity, racism, homelessness, poverty, activism, and so on, and ask students to describe what they think is happening in the photo. Before introducing linear equations, give students a grid with several lines on it and ask them to devise unique names for each line that would guarantee someone else would place it in the exact same place on the grid. In grappling with new content, the student is asked to actually attempt to solve a problem that you will then address in class. They will be able to relate to the usefulness of the content and share their own ideas.

- **Reinforce content**. It is reasonable to ask students to practice that which they are learning in class. However, ensure that the reinforcement is necessary and not merely "busy work." Also, ensure that the student will have ample directions to rely on if needed. Where possible, have one aspect of the assignment move the performance to a higher cognitive level to offer a challenge after the practice.

- **Generate ideas**. Often in *problem-based tasks*, students need to generate ideas that they can then share with their peers and collaboratively evaluate. Students can be instructed to gather some information from books, articles, the Internet, or interviews and brainstorm ideas to share the next day with their groups.

- **Assemble final presentations**. At times, it will be more advantageous to use class time to focus on the subject-area content required to produce the ALU product rather than on the final presentation. For example, if students in science class are designing a new ride for a theme park, building an understanding of the laws of physics and the related cause-and-effect relationships should be content studied in class, with the teacher's expertise on hand. If part of the *ALU* is for the students to make a pitch to a theme park to include their ride, *and* writing skills are not a part of the teacher's content, then the brainstorming of points to make in the pitch should be developed in class, but drafting ideas for that final pitch could be assigned for homework. If the skills of presentation development are not part of the target curriculum, relegate the development of aspects of the *ALU* presentation to homework time. I say aspects because *ALUs* are designed to be collaborative, so you do not want to place on parents the burden of getting two to four students together after school.

Back to the *Learning Map*

Consider the *learning map* you designed earlier in this chapter. Now that you have been introduced to various *participatory structures* for learning in the *scaffold for learning*, you can begin to map out the various *learning activities* you'll need to provide for the unit. Referring to your *learning map* (see examples in Figures 4.3 and 4.4). At each step, decide what concepts or skills students will need and how they might learn them. Although it may be tempting to "teach" every concept and skill either from the front of the room or in small-group sessions, think about how you can "clone" yourself and provide direct instruction in other ways. A carefully designed *how-to sheet* offers written directions the student can follow. A screencast is great for capturing steps you would take to use a particular app. The student can watch the screen animation and hear your narration while you're explaining how to accomplish the task. They might then follow the printed *how-to sheet* and try it for themselves. Some skills are going to be too difficult for some students to tackle independently. You might film a video using a digital camera and walk students through the steps; however, you also might want to schedule a *small-group mini-lesson* for students who are going to require more personalized assistance.

Add to your *learning map* a column for how students will learn the skills needed to accomplish what you wrote on the left side (see Figures 4.9 and 4.10). The left side should be described in the *analytic rubric*; the right side is the foundation for developing your *scaffold for learning*. If you want to capture specific skills required, list them on the line, moving from what

Figure 4.9. Learning Map 2: More Friends Good, Fewer Friends Bad?

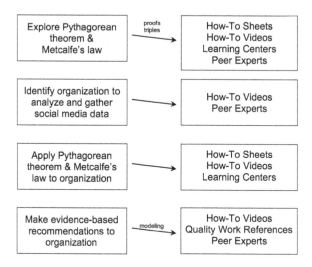

students need to accomplish (left side) and how they will learn, (right side) the necessary skills (middle), if not self-explanatory.

Once you complete the second column you can begin to identify or design actual *learning activities* to put on your *scaffold for learning*. Use a *learning map* to think through the steps students would take to accomplish the *problem-based task*; to consider how your curricular standards relate to your *ALU*; and to plan *learning activities* for your *scaffold for learning*.

Figure 4.10. Learning Map 2: Teachers, Schools, and Pop Culture

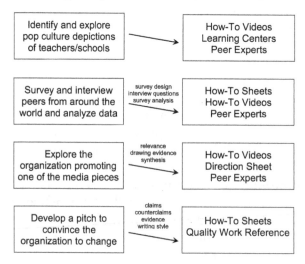

Back to the Learning Styles and Readiness Grid

As you consider the *learning map* you've just created, identify a skill that is a key part of the curriculum for this unit. For example, in science, such a skill might be how to create a food chain (Figure 4.11). It's probably easy to visualize yourself teaching students the skill you selected; but for the moment, let's assume you must create a set of instructional activities for the student to use to build a skill independent of you. Although concepts are often appropriately introduced to the whole class through a *benchmark lesson*, with questions, answers, and discussion, skills are best addressed on a more individual basis when students can personally grapple with the content based on activities that match their cognitive levels and learning styles.

Let's assume that some students are ready to learn the skill, in this case creating a food chain. According to Vygotsky, that skill would be in their proximal zone. Consider that some of your students may learn best through visual means, others through auditory cues, and still others through a more tactile approach. Figure 4.11 offers three different ways to learn the same skill, based on the designated learning styles. A *how-to sheet* allows you to turn your skill lesson into step-by-step directions for students to access again and again as needed. It's easy to record an enhanced podcast that includes

Figure 4.11. Differentiation Grid for Proximal Zone

Skill: Creating a Food Chain			
	Distal Zone A student who will be challenged to learn this skill/concept or lacks the prerequisite skills needed	**Proximal Zone** A student who is ready to learn this or is on grade level	**Current Knowledge** A student who is ready to move beyond this or is above grade level
Visual		Follow a printed *how-to sheet* with diagrams to match predator and prey in a four-item food chain.	
Auditory		Watch and listen to a video that describes several food chains existing in the natural world.	
Kinesthetic/ Tactile		Use a set of prey and predator cards with an answer key to create food chains.	

audio and still images. Keep a list of videos that would help your students; then sit down and record all of them. You will have created those "teacher-cloning tools" to which I referred earlier in the chapter. Designing kinesthetic and tactile activities can be more challenging and require additional resources, but be creative, ask colleagues, and search the Internet for ideas.

What about the students who are not yet ready to learn the skill you've identified? In this case, if a student is not familiar with identifying predators and prey, spending some time understanding the concept will make the subsequent skill development easier. Figure 4.12 offers the same grid with the left column filled in for those students who require some prerequisite work before tackling the skill of creating a food chain. You can offer videos of lessons you've offered in the past or create video segments to explain a concept or skill. Small cameras, tablet PCs, and phones can be used to focus on a desktop or paper so you can demonstrate a skill while narrating.

What about the students who have already mastered this skill? It may have been introduced to them in another class or by older siblings; or maybe they discovered it themselves while pursuing other interests. Although it may make the teacher feel better to think that additional practice is always useful, the reality is that asking students to sit through lessons or activities to learn that which they already know will most likely lead to boredom,

Figure 4.12. Differentiation Grid for Proximal and Distal Zones

Skill: Creating a Food Chain			
	Distal Zone A student who will be challenged to learn this skill/concept or lacks the prerequisite skills needed	**Proximal Zone** A student who is ready to learn this or is on grade level	**Current Knowledge** A student who is ready to move beyond this or is above grade level
Visual	Read a book on predators and prey.	Follow a printed *how-to sheet* with diagrams to match predator and prey in a four-item food chain.	
Auditory	Watch and listen to a video that describes various predators and prey.	Watch and listen to a video that describes several food chains existing in the natural world.	
Kinesthetic/ Tactile	Cut out pictures of predators and prey and glue them to a category board for predator and prey.	Use a set of prey and predator cards with an answer key to create food chains.	

frustration, and daydreaming. Fundamentally, it's disrespectful toward students. Instead, consider what they could do next. You may or may not wish to allow them to move ahead with curricular content; you could have them apply the learning to another situation, deepen their knowledge of the nuances of the skill, pursue some specific area of personal interest, or even design materials to present the learning to others in a creative way. Figure 4.13 offers the complete grid, now with the right column filled in that provides activities for the students who have already mastered the skill. In this case, the students will move on to explore food webs and the effect of the extinction of a species on the ecosystem. You've just explored a *learning styles and readiness grid* (also called a *differentiation grid*), a key tool for lesson-level differentiated instruction (see Appendix I).

The purpose of designing this *learning styles and readiness grid*, like the *learning map*, is to build your skills in designing truly differentiated activities. You've brainstormed nine activities that address a curricular skill. It would be extremely time-consuming to attempt to develop a grid for each skill or concept you teach. As you begin designing your *Learner-Active, Technology-Infused Classroom*, develop grids for key skills to expand your thinking on skill presentation in ways other than whole-class instruction. Over time, you'll brainstorm a variety of activities naturally to address the needs of

Figure 4.13. Differentiation Grid

Skill: Creating a Food Chain			
	Distal Zone A student who will be challenged to learn this skill/concept or lacks the prerequisite skills needed	**Proximal Zone** A student who is ready to learn this or is on grade level	**Current Knowledge** A student who is ready to move beyond this or is above grade level
Visual	Read a book on predators and prey.	Follow a printed *how-to sheet* with diagrams to match predator and prey in a four-item food chain.	Read a book or web page on food webs.
Auditory	Watch and listen to a video that describes various predators and prey.	Watch and listen to a video that describes several food chains existing in the natural world.	Watch and listen to a video that explains food webs.
Kinesthetic/ Tactile	Cut out pictures of predators and prey and glue them to a category board for predator and prey.	Use a set of prey and predator cards with an answer key to create food chains.	Play an online food web game to exploring placing species in the correct trophic level and spot in a food web.

your students. If you have ample computer technology available and can locate a variety of computer-based *learning activities* for a particular skill, create the grid as a word-processing document with hyperlinks of the web site URLs. Students can then click on a link and access a *learning activity*. In the case of student use, you might want to change the column headings to "Just Learning," "Ready to Dive In," and "I've Got This," or other similarly descriptive headings.

RECAP

Designing a *problem-based task* and *analytic rubric* is just the beginning of an *Authentic Learning Unit* (*ALU*). Implementing the unit requires a carefully constructed plan that provides students with a variety of ways to participate in learning. While short, whole-class *benchmark lessons* can be used to introduce concepts, most of students' classroom time will be spent engaging in activities to learn and build skills and concepts. Review your *scaffold for learning* to ensure that you've included a variety of ways for your students to learn the concepts and skills they will need to succeed at the *problem-based task*. Use this list as you review to ensure that you've included:

♦ *Benchmark lessons* to present unit concepts at key points in the unit;

♦ *Benchmark lessons* that focus on presenting concepts and not skills;

♦ A comprehensive list of printed *how-to sheets* to be designed to teach key skills throughout the unit;

♦ A list of podcasts, screencasts, and videos to be located or designed to offer instruction in skills and concepts;

♦ *Small-group mini-lessons* for focused skill instruction, being careful not to include too much content for any one session;

♦ *Learning centers* for students to explore concepts and skills in a hands-on manner;

♦ Individual *learning activities* and *practice activities* for building core content mastery;

♦ Group activities for planning, brainstorming, sharing, designing, and evaluating ideas;

♦ *Peer expert* opportunities for students to share their learning with and learn from one another;

- Apps to build concepts and skills;

- Homework that is structured to activate prior knowledge, allowing students to grapple with new content, reinforcing content, and encouraging students to generate new ideas.

REFERENCES

Csikszentmihalyi, M. (1990). *Flow: The psychology of optimal experience.* New York: Harper & Row.

Gattegno (C). (1987). *The science of education part I: Theoretical considerations.* New York: Educational Solutions.

Pink, Daniel H. (2011). *Drive: The surprising truth about what motivates us.* New York: Riverhead Books.

Prensky, M. (2006). *Don't bother me, Mom—I'm learning.* St. Paul, MN: Paragon House.

Sousa, David. (2017). *How the brain learns* (5th ed.). Thousand Oaks, CA: Corwin.

Sulla, N. (2015). *It's not what you teach but how: 7 insights to making the CCSS work for you.* New York: Routledge.

Sulla, N. (2018). *Building executive function: The missing link to student achievement.* New York: Routledge.

Vygotsky, L. S. (1978). *Mind and society: The development of higher psychological processes.* Cambridge, MA: Harvard University Press.

5

Empowering Students to Take Responsibility for Their Learning

IMAGINE

High school English students are reading J. D. Salinger's *A Catcher in the Rye*, as well as self-selected Salinger short stories, and working on developing a plan to convince Salinger's heirs with their ideas as to how his still unpublished writings should be handled. They are also responsible for a series of other tasks, including SAT preparation work. Upon arriving in class, students retrieve individual *student work folders*. Based on a pre-assessment that she completed yesterday, one student knows that she needs to attend the *small-group mini-lesson* on the writer's craft of using varied syntax. She includes that on her schedule for how she will spend her time over this week's two eighty-minute blocks. She notes, too, that there is a draft literary analysis due at the end of the week and realizes that she has not yet had her draft peer edited. She goes to the *peer edit scheduling board* to find a partner who also needs to peer edit today and signs up to work with a peer for the twenty minutes that the task will take. She also has a question about one of the notes her teacher left in her *student work folder*, so she adds her name to the *help board*. Another student who has already read several of the Salinger short stories on his own has scheduled time to create a podcast of his reviews of them so that his fellow students can use them in making decisions about which texts to select and read. He has never created his own podcast before, so he picks up a *how-to sheet* from the *resource table*. He also plans to spend a few minutes using the class's self-designed "excellent writing checklist" to review the quality of his written reviews before he records them.

On the first day of a new *Authentic Learning Unit* (*ALU*), sixth-grade students read their *problem-based task* and *analytic rubric* and make the list of what they will need to learn to complete the task. The teacher distributes a unit calendar with intermediate due dates, as well as quiz and test dates. Students use the calendar and *activity list* to schedule the next week on Friday.

Eighth-grade students are creating a watercolor mural to promote Earth Day, each depicting a solution they designed to an environmental problem they identified in science class. Four students submitted a small, original watercolor study demonstrating basic painting techniques in order to gain entrance to an advanced small-group mini-lesson offered by the teacher in texture techniques.

CONSIDER

Most schools have "lifelong learning" in their mission statements, yet few engage students in learning environments that actually create lifelong learners. A lifelong learner must break down goals into attainable steps, be resourceful, self-assess, manage time, manage a project, generate ideas, reflect,

> **"Most schools have "lifelong learning" in their mission statements; yet few engage students in learning environments that actually create lifelong learners."**

and more. Yet in most classrooms, despite a great emphasis on hands-on, collaborative learning over the past decades, teachers still overtly control much of the activity of students, telling them what to do and when to do it; when to speak and when to be quiet; and what resources to use. Creating lifelong learners means allowing students take charge of their own learning process and teaching them how to accomplish that.

William Glasser (1998) first wrote a book entitled *Control Theory*, and, in a later edition, renamed it *Choice Theory*, but his message was the same: you cannot control students' learning; students must choose to learn. Glasser presents his theory that, after survival needs are met, students choose to learn based on a sense of belonging, freedom, power, and fun (engagement.)

Students will not necessarily come to school with the skills required to take responsibility for learning. Teachers need to reach beyond content instruction to include instruction in these skills. That doesn't mean ignoring content instruction! It means taking advantage of opportunities to also teach the skills needed to build *student responsibility for learning*.

If you were to use a stopwatch and clock the amount of time you spend giving directions and waiting for your students to follow them and be ready for the next direction, you'd most likely be amazed. How much time do you spend on administrative tasks, transitioning students from one activity to another, addressing behavioral issues? If you could regain that time, you'd have more time for students to spend learning content. The time invested at the beginning of the year to teach students the structures and strategies to take responsibility for their own learning will prove to be well worth it as the year progresses.

The following metaphor presents a key paradigm shift for the *Learner-Active, Technology-Infused Classroom*: moving the teacher from being disseminator of information to the architect of a powerful learning environment that gives students responsibility for learning.

Teacher as Ferry or Teacher as Bridge?[1]

Did you ever stop to consider the differences between taking a ferry or traveling a bridge to cross a river? Taking a ferry leaves the traveler in the hands of the boat operator and releases the traveler from most responsibility. The ferry operator tells you where to park your car, decides when the boat will leave and how fast it will move, and takes all of the travelers across at the same time and speed. Your only responsibility is to show up on time. Taking a bridge puts the traveler in control and in the seat of responsibility. Different drivers use different lanes and drive at different speeds. All who cross the start of the bridge at one time do not necessarily end up on the other side at the same time. The journey is largely in the hands of the driver. But think about the magic of a bridge: a mass of steel suspended over a large expanse, being held in place almost miraculously, through the laws of physics. And yet probably few travelers hold that bridge in awe as they use it to move from one land mass to another, taking control of their travel, taking the bridge for granted.

As a teacher, are you a ferry or a bridge? Do you carry your students through the week, telling them when to do what tasks and how to do them? Do you present lessons to your entire class, deciding on a pace that seems appropriate? Do you have a "do now" to direct their actions as they walk into the classroom? Or do you create the structures for your students to take responsibility for their own learning? Do you offer expectations and pathways to success? Do you create structures that allow all of your students to achieve based on their differences? Becoming a bridge builder is a key paradigm shift of the *Learner-Active, Technology-Infused Classroom*. Think about your role in your classroom and, as you work through this book, decide on how you can become more of a bridge builder than a ferry master.

---

1 Reprinted from the IDEportal (www.ideportal.com) with permission.

IDE Corp. consultants work with teachers who wish to shift their paradigms to being bridge builders rather than ferry masters. These teachers design *problem-based tasks* with *analytic rubrics* that allow students to self-assess and set goals. They create *activity lists* that guide students through the day or week, listing the teacher's required *benchmark lessons*, optional *small-group mini-lessons*, group activities, and individual activities. Students begin the week by designing a personalized schedule for their work. They monitor their progress and reflect on their work habits in journals. *How-to sheets, screencasts,* and *videos* are available for students to use as they need to master a particular skill. They each keep their work in a two-pocket or digital *student work folder* that holds completed and in-progress activities. Teachers become facilitators, moving around the classroom, meeting with individual students and groups to guide learning. They carry grids or handheld computing devices to keep notes on student progress and skill mastery. They review *student work folders* and make comments. Based on the data they glean, they set *small-group mini-lessons* to teach skills and set whole-class *benchmark lessons* to build awareness of concepts and skills yet to be learned.

Masterful *Learner-Active, Technology-Infused Classroom* teachers create a complex system of interdependent structures to put students in charge of their own learning. To see it in action in a classroom is to realize that the students take this system for granted, feeling totally empowered to pursue their education and proud to take control, never realizing the incredible feat their teachers have accomplished in building it. Here's a story that bears repeating from chapter one. I visited a classroom and sat with a group of students. I asked them how they liked learning in this type of classroom. They responded that it was great, but "she doesn't teach." I asked what they were learning: nuclear fission and fusion. I asked them how they were learning the content. They described how the teacher offered a *benchmark lesson* to introduce the problem they had to solve, how she gave them a *rubric* to follow and *activity lists* with options for learning. They described how when they are stuck, they put their names on the *help board* and she comes over with her portable whiteboard. As one student continued to describe the classroom, another slapped yet another on the arm and said, "Hey, she does teach!" While it's important to educate students as to the new look of teaching, the fact that students think they are learning on their own may be a sign that the teacher has succeeded in designing a powerful system of structures.

> "To see it in action in a classroom is to realize that the students take this system for granted, feeling totally empowered to pursue their education and proud to take control, never realizing the incredible feat their teachers have accomplished in building it."

CREATE

You've designed a compelling *problem-based task statement*, standards-rich *analytic rubric*, and robust *scaffold for learning*. It's time to think about how that will play out in the classroom. As you read, keep a paper or digital journal of ideas you will want to implement. Take time to develop student materials to use in your classroom to build *student responsibility for learning*. This chapter will introduce you to the critical structures that should be in place in every *Learner-Active, Technology-Infused Classroom*.

The Home Group

One structure for providing students with a sense of belonging is to assign them to a *home group*. Assign a *home group* for each *ALU*, which should be approximately four weeks. I recommend groups of three or four. If your students are new to the *Learner-Active, Technology-Infused Classroom* of if you have a high number of English-language learners or students with disabilities, start with *home groups* of two and build from there. Never exceed a group size of four as the ability to collaborate and work together becomes increasingly compromised with a larger group size.

Although the students will have collaborative responsibility for the final product, much of concept and skill building will take place on an individual basis. Students will work in their *home groups* for brainstorming, planning, reviewing, and making some decisions for the final solution; however, much of the learning will take place individually and with other like-ability students. Consequently, it is unnecessary, and often unproductive, to establish groups of like-ability students as the *home group*. You do not want to create the academically challenged group and the gifted group. That being said, I would not recommend, at the beginning of the year, placing the most academically challenged student in the class in a group with the most gifted student. This situation could become frustrating for both at the start of learning to work in a *Learner-Active, Technology-Infused Classroom*. When designing the groups, seek to create a working mix of students in terms of achievement, gender, learning styles, personalities, and work habits. Spend a considerable amount of time on this: designing the lists, reviewing and modifying them, and perhaps returning to them the next day to ensure that the groups are well constructed.

The *home group* addresses the structures of taking responsibility for learning. Together, students discuss and plan out their time; they help one another find resources and make decisions about how to work; and they collaboratively assess progress. They also assist one another in mastering content, but the group's primary function is to provide each student with a sense of belonging to a group that collectively works together to tackle a *problem-based task*. The *home group* is the first tier for assistance, shifting the power, if you will, away from being primarily with the teacher. Working in a group for an extended period of time allows students to build important life and work skills in collaboration.

Switching groups for the next set of *ALUs* offers students the experience of engaging more closely with many members of the class. Working as part of a *home group* provides both comfort and challenges. Switching groups can minimize the amount of time a student must face any particular challenge when working with a group. For example, one group member might tend to take over the activities of the group. Although it's important for students to learn how to handle such peers, it's also pleasant to sometimes not have to deal with that particular challenge.

Some teachers like to allow students to create their own groups. This is possible after students learn how to work in a *home group* and understand how to best select group members. I would not recommend allowing students to establish their own groups until you are well-versed in running your *Learner-Active, Technology-Infused Classroom* and can create the structures to guide students through selecting a productive group.

Launching the *Authentic Learning Unit*

A well-crafted, authentic, open-ended, *problem-based task* should motivate students to learn—and learning is fun. Let me make a distinction here: being *taught* is not always fun, but realizing you've accomplished something you could never do before is. Launch your new *problem-based task* with an opening reflection that consists of a two- to three-minute period of thinking, drawing, or writing to focus students. For example, if you were going to launch a unit on the U.S. civil rights movement, posing the question of how far the country has or has not come in educational equity since *Brown v. Board of Education*, you might begin by asking them to write down thoughts, based on their personal experience, on the question, "what is opportunity?" or "what does equal mean when it comes to education?" Remember, the intent is to help students shift focus from whatever they were doing prior to this group *benchmark lesson* onto the subject at hand: civil rights. The opening reflection to an *ALU* is not intended to address any sort of learning objective, so keep it to a couple of minutes. This activity can be posted on the wall or classroom website as students enter the room at the beginning of a new *ALU*, so they can get started while everyone settles into the classroom. In the case of the virtual classroom, you'd ask students to complete this reflection before watching the opening video.

Then as you address the group through your opening *benchmark lesson*, you want to build their enthusiasm around the topic. This should be your "hook" that sends your students off looking for answers. Where possible, use world events, video, audio, and images to build a case for why you are presenting the question. In the case of "Justice for All" (Appendix G), you might show photos and build a timeline of schools before and after *Brown vs. Board of Education*; you might share newspaper headlines; and you might show photos of schools in various communities today to then pose the question, "Have we achieved educational equity?" Seek to captivate them around the topic. Strive for the "oooooh" reaction. The *ALU* launch and *problem-based task* introduction should only take about ten minutes.

Next, introduce students to the *analytic rubric* that will guide their work over the course of the *ALU*. After presenting the *problem-based task*, have students send a materials person to the *resource area* to retrieve copies of the *task statement* and *analytic rubric*. Ask students to read the *task statement* and then read down the *Practitioner* column of the *analytic rubric*, circling or underlining everything they are going to need to learn to accomplish the task. Note that I did not say "what they don't know." Focus on learning as a positive, productive experience rather than as a gap filler. You can also have them circle any vocabulary words they need to learn and see if others in the group know the meanings. After students read and discuss the *problem-based task* and *analytic rubric* with their group, return to a full group discussion to share what the class needs to learn, writing or projecting the list on the board. Then, let your students know you've designed a lot of *learning activities* that will help them accomplish their goals. This process allows students to see what lies ahead and consider what they need to learn, thus taking responsibility for their own learning. Depending on the age and ability level of the students, you might want to first have them review and discuss the *problem-based task* and then, afterwards, have them retrieve the *analytic rubric* for a similar reading and discussion.

You may choose to assign students articles or stories to read in advance of class to pique their interest in a topic. Then, the opening reflection might be relating their lives to the articles or generating questions from the articles or stories. When you introduce the *problem-based task* and *analytic rubric*, students should already be motivated to tackle it.

At this point, which could be the next class period, you're ready to hand out an *activity list* (more on that in a future section) and let them get started. Using these structures (the opening *benchmark lesson, problem-based task statement, analytic rubric,* and *activity list*) and strategies (having students reflect, presenting a case for the problem, having students read the *analytic rubric* on their own and consider what they need to learn), you will build greater *student responsibility for learning* and, thus, executive function skills related to empowerment.

Student Schedules

In the *Learner-Active, Technology-Infused Classroom*, students take responsibility for scheduling how they will use their time. You've developed a set of *learning activities* and *practice activities* for your *problem-based task*, outlined in your *scaffold for learning* (see Chapter 4). The next step is to create a structure that allows your students to schedule how they will use their time. In secondary grades, students typically move from class to class according to some time period. Rather than scheduling an entire day, as they have in elementary school *Learner-Active, Technology-Infused Classrooms*, students should schedule a week's worth of class periods, or a multi-day cycle if you run longer periods with an alternating schedule. For example, if you teach in eighty-minute blocks every other day, it takes two weeks to complete a cycle: two days one week, three days the next. You could choose to have them schedule weekly or for the entire two weeks. If students are fortunate enough to be engaged in *Learner-Active, Technology-Infused Classrooms* throughout the day, they will end up scheduling your class across the week or cycle and their full day, taking into account their other classes.

For virtual courses, students should schedule a manageable amount of time allocated to work on the course content. The amount of forward-looking activities students can manage will depend upon their grade level, the amount of time they have experienced your *Learner-Active, Technology-Infused Classroom*, and the amount of years they've studied in such classrooms in the school.

The goal across the grade levels is to have students self-assess using the *analytic rubric*, identify what they need to learn, then turn to the *activity list* to find the section with corresponding content, and decide from the available activities what they will do when. Note that it is the *analytic rubric*, not the *activity list*, that should drive student action. If students simply look at an *activity list* and start working through it, they are merely being compliant. Alternatively, if they have the overall *problem-based task* challenge in mind and they refer to the *analytic rubric* to determine what aspect they need to tackle next, they are building efficacy—the ability to produce an intended result.

> "Note that it is the *analytic rubric*, not the *activity list*, that should drive student action."

To schedule time, students need an *activity list* and a blank schedule. The *activity list* is developed from the *scaffold for learning*. (More on this in the next section.) The importance of having students indicate start and end times

> "The importance of having students indicate start and end times for their planned activities cannot be overemphasized; it is the foundation of time management, and it builds executive function."

for their planned activities cannot be overemphasized; it is the foundation of time management, and it builds executive function. If students merely determine the order in which they plan to complete activities and start working, an activity that should require twenty minutes of attention could end up taking forty minutes, and the student will be left believing that the teacher has assigned too much work. The *activity list* of learning options that you design should indicate an approximate range of completion times for each activity. As students begin to develop and/or contribute to *activity lists*, they will need to consider how long an activity should take. If the *activity list* indicates that gathering and graphing the data should take thirty minutes, students who find themselves still collecting data at twenty minutes will know to seek additional instructional supports. By scheduling start and end times, students can reflect on their ability to work productively and schedule realistically: two important twenty-first-century skills.

Some teachers use timers to cue students that a new time has started. The problem with timers is that the teacher is setting a time for all students and students soon simply work to the timer bell, which, again, sets up a compliance model. Plus, in a *Learner-Active, Technology-Infused Classroom*, students work to their own schedules, allowing them to allot different amounts of time to different activities, being mindful of the time to stay on schedule.

Early in the year, focus some of your *benchmark lessons* on how to schedule. Depending on students' prior familiarity with the *Learner-Active, Technology-Infused Classroom*, you may need to introduce them to scheduling by having them schedule just two days of activities, then three, to build to a week or two. You will use the *benchmark lesson* to introduce students to the scheduling process. Then, you can offer *small-group mini-lessons* for those who continue to need your help in building their skills in scheduling their time.

Use your *benchmark lesson* to teach students that there is a logical sequence to scheduling:

1. Identify the teachers' *benchmark lessons*, as those require your attendance, so you must put those on your schedule first.

2. Identify any *small-group mini-lessons* that you would like to attend and put those on your schedule next.

3. For the rest of your scheduling, be mindful of any due dates so that you prioritize activities related to those.

4. Do you have any group work to complete? If so, it is more difficult to find a common time among three or four people than to schedule individual activities. So connect with others and select a time when you can meet, and put that on your schedule next.

5. Do you have any pairs work in which to engage? Connect with your work partner and schedule that.

6. Are there any limited resources you plan to use for which you have to sign up? Find out what time slots are open, select one, and put it on your schedule.

7. Are there any conferences or other time-dependent activities in which you plan to engage? Put those on your schedule.

8. You should now be left with individual activities, which you can now fill in on your schedule.

When students simply order a set of required activities, they are mostly compliant, with some freedom to decide when to accomplish which activity. When students have to select which activities they want to complete from a larger list, taking into account how they prefer to learn, they have to additionally make choices regarding activities they like. This builds greater executive function. (Compliance requires only basic executive function skills.) When students have to orchestrate accessing *limited resources*, working with others, and meeting deadlines as they schedule, they build even greater executive function and skills that will serve them well in college, their future work lives, and life in general. When students have a voice in determining which activities to add to the *activity list*, they build further executive function toward empowerment and efficacy.

I met with some eighth graders in a school that had just begun the transformation to becoming a *Learner-Active, Technology-Infused School*. The students were complaining to me that they didn't like scheduling their time; they just wanted to get the work done. I realized that they'd been learning through a compliance model for years, and the goal of schooling for them had been to hand in assignment after assignment. So I carefully engaged in conversation hoping to have them see the importance of scheduling their time. Suddenly one student said, "Oh, but in Ms. D's classroom you just have to schedule time; you wouldn't survive if you didn't!" Those who also had Ms. D. as a French teacher agreed. They pointed out that in her activity list, you had to schedule time for a café conversation with a classmate, you had to sign up for a computer to complete the listening center, you had to meet with your group, and more. Essentially, Ms. D's activity list was so robust with opportunities to learn, that you could not simply pick one and start working without taking into account *limited resources* and scheduling time with others. The challenge was that in most of the other classrooms, the teachers had not yet created that level of complexity. Their activity list included many required activities and a few choices, without purposeful pairs and group work and without access to limited resources. The students were right! Scheduling in those other classes was not all that important. In Ms. D's class, they had a *felt need* to schedule their time. Your goal is to create a robust activity list with many and varied ways through which to engage in content.

The *Activity List*

The *activity list*, whether digital or on paper, should provide students with a reasonable number of activities to schedule over the course of the week.

Figure 5.1. Sample Activity List

Hydroelectric Power: The Basics			
Choose two of three (LA)	Explore water.usgs.gov to gain an understanding of how hydroelectric power works and take notes.	P	30 mins
	Watch the YouTube video "Energy 101: Hydroelectric Power" and take notes.	I	15 mins
	Read the article "Introduction to Hydroelectric Power" and take notes.	I	20 mins
Choose two of four (LA)	Read the two articles on the Three Gorges Dam of China and take notes using a double-entry journal.	I	40 mins
	Read the MoneyBox article on hydroelectric power and global warming and take notes using a double-entry journal.	I	20 mins
	Watch the YouTube video, the Mega project of the Niagara hydroelectric power plant and take notes. *May be chosen as homework.*	I	50 mins
	Explore the Inhabitat website on a 400-year-old abandoned open-pit mine's promise as a hydroelectric power source and take notes using a double-entry journal.	I	20 mins
Choose one of three (PA)	Run the Gold Sim online simulation of the Great Falls Hydropower Plant Project and log events and decisions.	I,, P or G	50 mins
	Run the MATLAB online simulation of hydroelectric power and log events and decisions.	I, P or G	50 mins
	Complete the hydroelectric power challenge using the Carolina Hydroelectric Power Kit and log your decisions and outcomes. *Sign up for limited resource.*	P or G	50 mins
Required (complete four LA and one PA)	Design and conduct an experiment to demonstrate the conversion of potential to kinetic energy with falling water at various heights.	P	60 mins
Optional	Read portions of the book *Microhydro: Clean Power From Water* to locate additional, relevant information. *May be chosen as homework.*	I	30–60 mins
Environmental Impacts of Hydroelectric Power Plants			
Required	Locate, read, and take notes on at least three online sources of information on the environmental impacts of hydroelectric power plants, take notes, and then schedule to meet with your group to discuss your findings.	I G	30 mins 20 mins
Optional	Read portions of the book *Recovering a Lost River* by Steven Hawley to learn more about the impact of hydroelectric power on an ecosystem. *May be chosen as homework.*	I	30–60 mins

Each entry on the *activity list* should offer a brief description of the activity, indicate any prerequisites to tackling this activity, provide an estimated timeframe for completion, and indicate if the activity should be completed individually (I), in pairs (P), or as a *home group* (G).

The *activity list* should be organized around the content presented in the *analytic rubric*. As students need to learn about a particular skill or concept, they can look to the *activity list* for opportunities to learn. Design your sections around the obvious content you feel will be needed by your students during the time period of the *activity list*. For example, for students tackling the *ALU* "Hydroelectric Power" (Appendix B), understanding how hydroelectric power works is important to achieving a variety of criteria on the rubric. The *activity list* would have a section for the basics of hydroelectric power with a variety of *learning activities* and *practice activities* from which to choose. (See Figure 5.1 for a sample activity list.)

Within each content section, you'll have up to three types of activities:

- *Choice activities*—Students must learn a required skill or concept. However, they have a choice as to how they will learn it. Choice activities should make up the bulk of your *activity list* to ensure an adequate amount of differentiation. For any given skill or concept, offer students a variety of ways to build mastery, including those that address different cognitive levels, learning styles and intelligences, and disabilities. For example, offer a podcast, text selection, *how-to sheet*, interactive website, and/or hands-on learning center. (You've already brainstormed the various participatory structures on your *scaffold for learning* in Chapter 4, though as you design your *activity list*, you will most likely add to the choices.) Group the choice activities for a specific skill or concept and indicate how many of the total you want students to complete. For example, you might indicate one or more from a choice of four, or two or more from a choice of five. Students decide how many and which activities to schedule to build personal mastery. *Small-group mini-lessons* are choice activities; however, I recommend posting them separately from the activity list, giving you maximum flexibility to schedule them as needed.

- *Required activities*—These are used when students must learn a required skill or concept through a specific activity, or demonstrate their understanding for you through an assignment. For example, if you have a video you want all students to view or a workbook page you want all to complete, you would put them as required activities. Given that they do not allow students choice, keep required activities to a minimum. *Benchmark lessons* are also required activities. As with the *small-group mini-lessons*,

I recommend posting those separately from the activity list, giving you the flexibility to make a last-minute change.

♦ *Optional activities*—Most *problem-based tasks* lend themselves to many extensions and digressions. Optional activities allow students to pursue related interests. This is particularly useful for students who are on or ahead of schedule to complete the main *problem-based task* and have the time to delve more deeply into areas of interest. For example, students who are developing a plan for constructing a waterfall to generate hydroelectric power may want to read a more in-depth book on the subject or read a book from the perspective of removing dams and hydroelectric power plants to reclaim the ecosystem of a river.

While there is no one right way to design your *activity list*, Figure 5.1 offers a sample page from an *activity list*. Note that students must learn about hydroelectric power, so they have several choices of *learning activities* from which to choose. The first set of *learning activities* addresses foundational concepts while the second focuses on hydroelectric power plants in specific geographic areas. Students then have a separate set of choices for *practice activities*. In this case they may engage in an online simulation or design a hydroelectric power simulation from a kit. You'll see a required activity of designing and conducting an experiment. It indicates that students must first complete the *learning activities* and the *practice activity*. The jagged black line indicates that there are more sections missing from your view of Figure 5.1. Note that the teacher has identified some activities that could be chosen for homework; the rest are to be completed only in class. The hydroelectric power kit is identified as a *limited resource* for which students will have to sign up. Where students have to create a "double-entry journal," if they don't know how, they will retrieve a *how-to sheet* from the *resource area*, and, if they still have trouble, seek out a *peer expert*.

This activity list would also include sections on other aspects of the *ALU*, such as understanding environmental impacts of hydroelectric power plants on the ecosystem, designing 3-D prototypes, and other content related to the *analytic rubric*.

Using an *activity list*, although you still have control over the activities to be completed, students have the freedom to make choices as to how they will use their time and the resources they will use to meet your academic expectations. Depending on your comfort level, allow students to suggest other activities to add to the list. An ambitious student may, for example, locate instructional websites that are unknown to you. A teacher was having students design scale drawings of a dream house in math class. One student found a 3-D modeling app that allowed him to feed in all of the dimensions and see a rotatable 3-D version of his house. He was excited to share this with the teacher who then set him up to run *small-group mini-lessons* on this *optional activity* as an extension to the plan design.

Special education students with expressive processing issues may know what they want to do but lack the language to explain it. The *activity list* provides them with that language. For *problem-based tasks* that involve writing, the *activity list* becomes a "word wall" of sorts for terms students might need in their writing.

Using the "Hydroelectric Power" *ALU* (Appendix B) again as an example, after learning about hydroelectric power plants, students will have to spend time developing a plan for addressing power needs in their local area. This is more of an application of knowledge than a *learning activity* or *practice activity*. Either your *activity list* should include required activity time for students to work on their solutions, or you can let students know that they should also include time in their schedule to work on their solutions.

Teaching Students to Schedule Their Time

Gradual Release

If you are teaching students that have previously attended classes in which teachers told them what to do and when to do it, scheduling their time will be an unfamiliar act. Sometimes, even the best activities, if unfamiliar, can cause students to be resistant. In this case, to ease students into scheduling. At first, provide them with a completed schedule, and let them know that you want them to be aware of the order in which you are going to offer and assign instructional activities. This schedule may, for example, indicate that you will start with them completing a journal entry, then offer a fifteen-minute lesson, have students complete a pairs activity for twenty minutes, and regroup for wrap-up for five minutes.

After a few class periods at this level, introduce some flexibility. Tell your students that the order in which they complete two activities doesn't matter, and allow them to fill in those blanks. Offer them choices as to three ways to accomplish the same learning and allow them to select the best fit for them.

Once your students are succeeding at this level, open up the schedule even further and provide them with a primarily blank schedule, allowing them to complete the rest, referencing the *activity list*. It is important to then approve students' schedules, applying your insights into the project and students' work habits. You may recognize that a student has not allotted enough time to complete an activity or has selected an activity that is too easy or too hard. In these cases, advise the students accordingly. Students will house their activity list in their folders, so you can review them and comment and/or approve.

Having Students Reflect on Their Progress

Upon completing and implementing a schedule, students should reflect on their success. Ask students who did not complete their scheduled activities to identify why. It may be that they did not schedule enough time; it may be that they were distracted. Secondary schooling is a time for discourse and debate, for tackling big concepts more than skill building. Discussing existentialism and its relevance today may not be easily contained in terms of time. One student shares that he read an article about the similarities between senioritis and existentialism, and the conversation takes an exciting turn. Before you know it, the class period is over, and while students were definitely engaged in something meaningful, it kept them from completing the rest of their activities. Upon reflection, students might decide that the conversation was so useful, it was worth the digression, and they will reschedule the missed activities, working more productively over the next few class periods. Alternatively, they might decide to stick to the schedule in the future and, in the case of a scintillating discussion, make some break-in-discussion notes and schedule another session in a future class period.

Student Work Folders

Each student should have a physical or digital *student work folder* that remains in class. I suggest that in the case of a physical folder, you use a two-pocket folder labeled "Work in Progress" on the left side and "Work Completed" on the right side. In the case of a digital folder, have students create those two subfolders into which they will place their work. When students arrive at class, they'll retrieve or open their *student work folders*, access their schedules, review any notes left by the teacher, and begin working. They'll move completed work that has been checked by the teacher out of the folder to take home. At the end of the class period, they'll ensure that their completed work is on the right, ready to be checked by the teacher. Managing papers or documents and categorizing work in progress from completed work will build executive function skills and serve students well in their lives.

Make sure your students keep the work folders organized and thin! The biggest challenge is the overstuffed folder with so many papers it takes additional time to find the work to be reviewed. Use a *benchmark lesson* to introduce this folder management concept, asking students to pull out the papers on the "completed" side, identify which are fully completed based on your comments, and remove those from the folder, placing the ones that may need more work, based on your comments, to the "in progress" side. Then create a "how-to" sheet for those who need more support.

The Student Work Folder–Assessment Connection

Given that running a *Learner-Active, Technology-Infused Classroom* requires a series of paradigm shifts, let's look at the dominant paradigm for checking and grading student work. Teachers tend to have students hand papers in, grouped according to activity. If the goal is to make it easier for the teacher to grade papers, it makes sense to have stacks of papers for each assignment. The teacher then takes a stack of papers, turns to the answer key, and grades them.

Although this approach may optimize the teacher's time, it does little to contribute to student achievement. Raising student achievement requires the teacher to know the abilities of the student as a whole and plan for that student accordingly. When you open up a *student work folder*, you are seeing the student holistically. At the secondary level, your *ALU* will be multifaceted, requiring students to demonstrate understanding of concepts and skills related to a variety of aspects of the *problem-based task*. In "Teachers, Schools, and Pop Culture" (Appendix F), students must read, analyze, design, write, and more. When you look at the folder, you may see that a student has difficulty in identifying sources and analyzing text but has creative ideas and is strong in design and in writing about her design ideas. The folder approach allows you to see and assess the student as a whole, providing you with insights into the student's overall ability and interests. In the case of this student, you might suggest she attend some targeted *small-group mini-lessons* and even provide one-on-one facilitation to help her strengthen her design work by building better research and text analysis skills.

During the course of the week, you may have met with a student to discuss overall progress and are therefore familiar with the contents of the folder. Generally, however, for departmentalized classrooms, you'll want to check *student work folders* weekly. (I recommend teachers in self-contained classrooms check them daily.) Even though you are facilitating and engaging with students as they work, your folder review will allow you to consider each student's schedule, completed work, and work in progress. You'll make notes to the student and suggest other activities. You'll use the data you glean from the class set of *student work folders* to schedule *benchmark lessons* and *small-group mini-lessons*.

It is important to instruct students to keep their *analytic rubrics* in their folders when they hand them in at the end of class. Additionally, they should indicate on the rubric what they have accomplished toward the *Practitioner* and *Expert* levels by checking off criteria. This way, you can see how students are progressing and make comments targeted to continued success.

Upon Entering the Classroom

Let's consider the moment when students enter the room. You want them to get started immediately, without any prompting from you. A common approach is to implement a "do now," but consider that a "do now" still has the teacher assigning the students an activity to complete, and the level of responsibility for the student does not extend beyond compliantly following the teacher's directions. In taking a problem-based approach to instruction, you can have students schedule how to use their own time. At the most basic level, that involves asking students at the end of the class period to identify what they should start working on the next time class meets and then having them reference that note at the start of the next session. This personal "do now" offers students empowerment and builds executive function. At higher levels of executive function, students map out how they are going to spend their time across the week or cycle. Students should enter the classroom and work on an activity that they scheduled previously. Even though it may be the day you are having students schedule their week, have them begin with an activity they decided on in an advance. Why? Scheduling requires a great deal of cognitive load (Sweller, 1988); that is, the amount of energy one's brain is using to manage information in working memory. Thinking through one's goals, choices of activities, choices of resources, timeframes, and so on requires a lot of information being manipulated in working memory, and, therefore, a lot of cognitive load. When students first walk in the room each day, their brains are already occupied by many thoughts. Retrieving their folders, reviewing teachers' notes, and getting started on an activity that is already written down will allow them to get started easily. After that first activity, then they can schedule the rest of the week, being better able to take on that level of cognitive load. Just to clarify, if you plan to have students schedule their week on Monday, make sure that in the prior week they established one activity to start the week. That may be the last item they accomplish on the prior Friday. If you have students schedule on Friday for the coming week, they will most likely be scheduling during the latter part of Friday's class period, so the start-of-class cognitive load challenge will not be an issue.

What administrative functions do you need to accomplish when students enter the room? Attendance? Collection of forms? Consider how you might accomplish these in ways that provide the students with the responsibility. If students retrieve a physical folder or log onto a class website upon entering class, you'll easily be able to determine who is absent without calling names off of a roster and consuming precious instructional time. Checklists posted on websites or physical classroom walls allow students to report in on issues such as field trip forms.

Analytic Rubrics

Analytic rubrics (see Chapter 3) allow students to self-assess and set goals. Key to using an *analytic rubric* to build *student responsibility for learning* is designing the rubric to drive instruction, rather than merely to evaluate the end product. *Analytic rubrics* designed to drive instruction offer students a clear path to success, introducing additional criteria in each column.

As you facilitate, expect your students to have their rubrics nearby with notes as to their progress. This might involve checking off a rubric box or highlighting criteria. As you sit with students, ask them to use the rubric to report on their progress and articulate their next steps.

Figure 5.2. Sample Rubric Row

	Novice	Apprentice	Practitioner	Expert
Bar Graph	includes properly drawn x and y axes with labels	includes three categories of data properly graphed, with axes and labels	includes a properly constructed stacked bar graph with two data sets for each of three categories of data with axes, labels, and legend	all of *Practitioner* plus overlays a line graph of related data

A well-written *analytic rubric* will free a student to pursue learning independent of the teacher's prompting. For example, an *analytic rubric* involving graphing data may ask students to create a stacked bar graph. The Novice column might require the student to set up properly labeled x and y axes for the graph; the Apprentice might require the student to graph three pieces of data; the Practitioner column might require the student to create a stacked bar graph using two data sets (see Figure 5.2). The student can easily begin to seek out resources for creating the graphs and check off those criteria that are satisfied. The student can then set a goal for mastering the next level of graph design and locate the necessary instructional resources. The *analytic rubric* empowers students to take responsibility for learning.

The *Resource Area*

As students are working on their *problem-based tasks*, they will need a variety of resources, including *how-to sheets*; instructional podcasts, screencasts, and videos; articles; the *analytic rubric*; activity direction sheets; and manipulatives. Typically, teachers hand out materials to students. If you hand out a direction sheet to your students and a student doesn't have one, whose responsibility is it? Yours. If you place the papers on a table and instruct students to retrieve them when they need them, and a student doesn't have the appropriate paper, whose responsibility is it? The student's. The *resource area* gives students responsibility for their own learning. One teacher pointed out that homework completion increased once she placed the assignments in the *resource area*.

Establish an area to place materials that students will need. If your students all have personal computing devices, you might create a digital filing cabinet for files and links to websites. If not, create a physical space. This could be, for example, a table, a filing cabinet, a crate of folders, pockets on a bulletin board that can hold papers, or shelf storage for tactile materials.

So as not to overwhelm students, it's a good idea to display the materials needed for the current set of activities in a prominent place in the *resource area* and avoid putting out materials to be used in the future. Materials used in the recent past that may need to remain for reference should be moved to a less prominent location in the *resource area*, such as the back of the table, or filed in a three-ring binder or file cabinet. Essentially, create an area where students can easily find what they need, are not distracted by materials they do not yet need, and can access formerly used materials if needed.

If you are teaching in a 1:1 technology environment, a digital *resource area* can offer links to video and websites as well as print materials. Begin to build digital resources, for example, by creating screencasts, and then encourage your students to design some of their own.

The *Peer Expert Board*

As described in Chapter 4, *peer experts* serve as powerful learning partners in the *Learner-Active, Technology-Infused Classroom*. As with other key learning engagement strategies, it's important to pair this with a structure to empower students to take advantage of *peer experts*.

Designate an area on the classroom wall or website as the *peer expert board*. As you cover key concepts and skills, post the names of students who can assist in learning them. Once other students become *peer experts*, add their names while removing those of the existing *peer experts*. This allows students to build mastery by teaching others without having them spend an inordinate amount of time on a skill or concept.

At secondary levels, students should be able to determine if they are peer experts, based on a description provided by the teacher. This might include taking a checkout quiz that includes, not only content, but methods through which the student will explain to others. It may be reviewing a checklist to ensure knowledge equal to the *peer expert* level.

The *Help Board*

As students begin working on the various activities toward the accomplishment of the *problem-based task*, you will facilitate instruction by moving around the room and sitting with a student or group for a few minutes. It would be extremely disruptive for students to be calling out for help. You want your facilitation to be proactive and not reactive.

Teach your students that their first line of help for academics is looking at the *activity list* and *resource area* to see if a related *how-to sheet* is available. Next, they should check the *peer expert* board. Then, they should turn to their *home group*. If they don't understand a direction, are not sure where to find a resource, or need help understanding a concept or skill, they should seek out a *home group* member. In either case, if students find they are in need of *your* help, they should write their names on the *help board*. This can be a space on a whiteboard, a paper on a bulletin board, or a digital comment on a Web-based help page.

Some teachers have students include the focus of their need for help, in addition to their names. The *help board* meets the needs of both the students and the teacher. While facilitating, teachers need to know who is in need of more immediate guidance. When the teacher is meeting with students, other students are not supposed to interrupt. They can, however, add their names to the *help board* to indicate their need. Often students write their names on the *help board* and then erase them, having found alternate ways to answer their questions.

As a teacher, your job is to keep an eye on the *help board* and provide assistance in a timely manner. When you finish facilitating with a group, check the *help board*. In the *Learner-Active, Technology-Infused Classroom*, you're not teaching lessons and then letting students work independently, in which case they would most likely require little of your attention. Rather, they are engaged in challenging *learning activities*, and you are teaching as you facilitate those experiences. Address those who need help in a reasonable period of time; however, teach your students to begin working on another activity if they find themselves in need of your help. No one should ever be simply waiting for the teacher; students should move on to another, less challenging, activity while waiting.

Monitor the amount of time you spend addressing the *help board*. Not all students will post their names on the board or feel they need your help. That does not mean, however, that they won't benefit from your facilitation. Students don't always know what they don't know. If you spend all of your time working down the *help board* list, you'll be more reactive than proactive. If you find this is the case, determine if your students have not yet become resourceful and are simply putting their names on the *help board* as a first step. Another problem might be that you do not have clear enough directions in your *learning activities*. If you find your time being driven by the *help board*, work to figure out why and correct that.

At the secondary level, if students have been learning in *Learner-Active, Technology-Infused Classroom* through their school experience, they will use the *help board* well. If this is their first experience in a *Learner-Active, Technology-Infused Classroom*, particularly at the high school level, students may not want to admit to the entire class that they need help. You might be able to overcome this mindset through some class discussions about the students as part of a learning community. You may need to create some alternate methods, which could be filling out a very short digital form that is fed to your phone or tablet.

The *Quality Work Board*

Teachers often use subjective words such as neat, descriptive, complete, and compelling when describing expectations. What does "neat" look like? It helps for students to see examples of high-quality work to gain a better understanding of expectations and to clarify any subjectivity. If you teach in your own classroom, you might use a bulletin-board area for this. If you move from classroom to classroom throughout the day, consider a three-ring binder. If every student in your classroom has a mobile computing device, consider a digital folder or website.

Include student work from previous years; include your own examples. If you want students, for example, to develop a plot line for a novel, you would develop one of your own, showing basic and advanced features, and including some innovative nuances. That way, you are showing an example of thinking through the plot of the novel and going beyond the ordinary. Post quality work without names, and refrain from posting work completed by students in the class. The point is not to create competition but to demonstrate what quality work looks like.

Obviously, quality work goes beyond those items that can be posted on a bulletin board. What do strong oratory skills sound like? What does a powerful song sound like? What does a well-crafted piece of pottery look like? Be creative! With today's technology, you can capture video and audio and post it to a digital folder. You can videotape yourself holding a piece of pottery and pointing out what makes it quality work.

A teacher whose students were studying the holocaust had students create a memory box of a key, historical figure. She shared an outstanding example of a memory box for Anne Frank, which she kept, with the student's permission, to share with future classes. Students will get a sense of what quality work looks like. It's not that they will copy it; they will be inspired by it, assuming your assignment is not constrained enough to make the outcome easily copied, that is.

A teacher who was introducing her students to myths decided to challenge students with selecting a product or sports team named after a mythological figure and write their own myth as to how this product or sports team got its name. In order to gain a better understanding of the *problem-based task* so she could construct the *analytic rubric*, she decided to write her own myth about how the Honda Odyssey got its name. She wrote a creative and humorous account of how Odysseus was called from his home in Ithaca to address a problem in New York City. He borrowed someone's Honda SUV to drive there. On the way, he encountered various challenges and picked up some traveling companions, such as Zeus, who had difficulty sitting up straight in the vehicle because of his size. Once Odysseus saved the day for New York City, he returned the car but wrote a letter to Honda offering some suggestions for improvements, such as more headroom (for Zeus). And that's how the Honda Odyssey got its name. She decided to have students read her myth as part of the *ALU* activities and found that, because of them reading a sample, high-quality myth, her students produced some of the best writing she'd seen from them. Quality work can produce even greater quality work!

The *Learning Dashboard*

The *learning dashboard* is a spreadsheet that each student uses to track individual progress. It has a tab for each content area and ones for executive function skills and, if applicable, Individualized Education Program (IEP) goals. Grade-appropriate content goals are listed down the first column. Students then place an x in the cell to the right depending on if they are just starting to learn the skill, practicing it, or have mastered it. Using conditional formatting in some spreadsheet programs, you can have the cell automatically fill in with colors (for example, orange, yellow, and green) for a more visual effect. Figure 5.3 shows an image from a high school math course.

You can download a learning dashboard template to use by heading to www.ideportal.com and the free content offering. Then search for dashboard to access information and a downloadable version with tabs.

Table Journals

One way to focus students on the effectiveness of their *home group* is with a *table journal*. At the end of a session during which students are working together, have them spend a couple of minutes reflecting on their effectiveness, using a set of questions or indicators. The reflection can be different from day to day, but the goal is the same: Have students assess how effective and productive they are and what they can do to become more effective and productive. The indicators will differ, depending on the age of the students, and will become more sophisticated over the course of the school year to build greater collaborative and executive function skills.

Figure 5.3. Learning Dashboard

	A	B	C	D	E
1	Student Name:				
2	Course:				
3					
4			Just Learning	Practicing	I Got This!
5		I can define vector quantities			x
6		I can represent vector quantities by directed line segments			x
7		I can find the components of a vector			x
8		I can add vectors end-to-end			x
9		I can add vectors component-wise		x	
10		I can add vectors using the parallelogram rule		x	
11		I can subtract vectors	x		
12		I can describe the magnitude of a sum of two vectors	x		x
13		Given two vectors in magnitude and direction form, I can determine the magnitude and direction of their sum	x		
14		I can solve problems involving velocity	x		
15		I can solve problems involving other quantities that can be represented by vectors			

Figure 5.4. Table Journal Example 1

Table Journal					
Each group member should rank the following statements on a scale of 1 to 5, with 1 being the lowest score and 5 being the highest. Rank independently. Then one person should record the results of the group by marking how many members rated each statement with a 1, 2, 3, 4, or 5. Be honest in your assessment!					
	1	2	3	4	5
The group arrived and got started immediately without any prompting from the teacher.					
The group involved everyone in all aspects of the work, but still divided responsibilities.					
Every member of the group participated throughout the work session.					
All members were encouraged to voice their opinions.					
The group worked through conflicts by discussing options and reaching consensus.					
Group members used their time well.					
Discuss how you might work even better as a group the next time and record ideas here:					

A *table journal* can be created as a digital or paper document. Figures 5.4 and 5.5 offer some examples of *table journal* pages.

Limited Resource Sign-Up Sheets

You will most likely have some limited resources (introduced in Chapter 4) in the *Learner-Active, Technology-Infused Classroom*, for example: math and STEM kits, microscopes, soundproof studio room, computers, listening center, aquarium, and/or *learning centers*. The key is that not all students can access the resource at the same time. *Limited resource sign-up sheets* coupled with *student scheduling* allow students to make use of limited resources easily. Many schools attempt to outfit classrooms with full sets of resources. An advantage of the *Learner-Active, Technology-Infused Classroom* is that you can save money on such resources because you don't have to

Figure 5.5. Table Journal Examples 2 and 3

Table Journal

As a group, discuss how you have worked differently as a group today as compared to prior days. What have you learned about working in a group?

Table Journal

This is your last chance to reflect on your work as a group! What was most effective about your group during this problem-based unit?

How might your group have been even more effective?

If you were to give other students advice on working well as a group, what would it be?

---

purchase an entire class set. You can provide students with more diverse offerings if you are willing to have students engaged in various activities at the same time; that is, giving up overt control in return for a structured environment in which students take charge of their learning.

As with all situations in the *Learner-Active, Technology-Infused Classroom*, you want to figure out how to build *student responsibility for learning* rather than overtly controlling the limited resources. Use a sign-up process. If you have a limited number of computers in the room, post a sign-up sheet with time slots, allowing a student to sign up, for example, at most, two slots across the week. If you want students to observe cells under a microscope, but not all at the same time, you can have them sign up for one slot per week. As students schedule the week, they determine when resources are available, sign up at the location of the resource or at the *resource area*, and indicate the time they will be using it on their schedule. This process builds tremendous executive function. See Figure 5.6 for two examples of a *limited resource sign-up sheet* (also can be used for a *learning center.*)

Limited resource sign-up is clearly a skill to demonstrate and walk students through during a *benchmark lesson* early in the year on using limited resources. Remember the seventh-grade science teacher from Chapter 1? He instructed his students to view a video and make a paper airplane by a

Figure 5.6. Limited Resource Sign-Up Sheet

Spectrometer (30-minute time slots)

Time	Name
Tue 9:00–9:30	
Tue 9:40–10:10	
Wed 9:00–9:30	
Wed 9:40–10:10	

3-D Virtual Reality Glasses Sign-Up (30-minute time slots)

Time	Group Members
Mon 1:10–1:40	
Tues 1:10–1:40	
Wed 1:10–1:40	
Thurs 1:10–1:40	

certain date. They then signed up for time slots to utilize the video station and he didn't need to be involved.

This structure applies to your time as well. Limit the amount of one-on-one conferences you have with students as they keep you from the rest of the class. However, if you are planning to meet with individual students or groups of students, create a sign-up sheet and have students select a time slot. Leave open time between conferences so that you can circulate the room to engage with students, and see whose names are on the *help board*.

Small-Group Mini-Lesson Sign-Up

As a differentiation structure, introduced in Chapter 4, the *small-group mini-lesson* allows you to provide a short, narrowly focused lesson to a small group of students who are ready to learn a particular skill at the same time. As a structure to build *student responsibility for learning*, the *small-group mini-lesson* requires students to self-assess whether or not they should attend the lesson and then, if attending, sign up for it. Here are some more tips for empowering students through structures related to *small-group mini-lessons*:

- Provide the tools for students to self-assess to determine if they should attend the lesson. These might include quizzes, checklists, pretests, and a set of questions.

- Announce *small-group mini-lessons* well enough in advance for students to consider them when scheduling their time. That might be the day before or the beginning of the week. From time to time you will find the need to add a lesson unexpectedly, based on your formative assessments, and students will have to adjust their schedules. This should be the exception to the norm, but, as previously stated, an important life skill is the ability to adjust to changing plans midstream.

- To announce the lessons, post them on a specific area on the board, bulletin board, classroom website, or other online venue. Include the start time and length of the lesson so that students can schedule accordingly.

Figure 5.7. Small-Group Mini-Lesson Sign-Up Sheet

Small-Group Mini-Lesson Sign-Up Sheet

Title: _____

Time: _____

Participants
1.
2.
3.
4.
5.

Overflow (I will schedule another session)

Given the *small-group mini-lesson* involves students signing up, use a structure that works for you. It might be a sign-up sheet in the *resource area*, a list on the wall, or a digital version. (See Figure 5.7 for an example of a sign-up sheet you could put in the *resource area*.)

Recognizing that you can't always ensure that the students who need it most will sign up, you can include a note in their folders or send them an email indicating you want them to attend.

The *small-group mini-lesson* is intended to address the targeted needs of and provide direct instruction to a small number of students; create a sign-up system with only five or six slots for the lesson. Create an overflow section so that others who may have wanted to sign up can let you know they also wanted to attend. That way you can schedule another *small-group mini-lesson* to handle the overflow. Obviously, you'll want to make adjustments as needed. If you have one student on the overflow list, you might allow them to attend or offer one-on-one facilitation to find out why they wanted to attend and address their challenges. If you encounter overflow situations regularly, make sure your students are aware of all of the options available for learning the skills and, as stated earlier, make sure your topic is narrowly focused. Sometimes students attend *small-group mini-lessons* because they fear they will not learn if they are not working in person with the teacher, which, as students acclimate, should not be the case in the *Learner-Active, Technology-Infused Classroom*.

It's a System!

The power of the structures of the *Learner-Active, Technology-Infused Classroom* lies in their interdependence. As you design your *Learner-Active, Technology-Infused Classroom*, consider how your structures are designed to support one another. Resources listed on the *activity list* should be in the *resource area*. Skills on the rubric should be reflected in *learning activities*, those listed as *peer experts*, and *small-group mini-lessons*. The expected solution presentation for *problem-based task* should be defined in the *analytic rubric*, and so forth. The stronger your system, the more effective your classroom.

RECAP

Engaging students in the learning process includes employing a variety of structures and strategies to create greater *student responsibility for learning*. As you design your *ALU* and learning environment, be sure to include the following:

♦ *Home-group* designations for students to have a sense of belonging and a first tier of support in their work;

- A compelling launch to the *ALU* that inspires and motivates students;
- Student scheduling of how they will use their time;
- *Activity lists* to guide student scheduling;
- A plan for teaching students how to schedule their time;
- *Student work folders* to encourage organization and teacher–student communication;
- *Analytic rubrics* to position students to self-assess and set learning goals;
- A *resource area* to empower students to gather necessary resources;
- A *peer expert board* to encourage student-to-student learning opportunities;
- A *help board* to allow students to manage their need for teacher assistance;
- A *quality work board* to promote higher levels of achievement;
- The *learning dashboard* to empower students to monitor their own progress;
- *Table journals* to encourage student reflection on process;
- *Resource sign-up sheets* to empower students to manage how they will utilize limited resources;
- *Small-group mini-lesson* sign-up sheets to empower students to avail themselves of teachers' lessons as needed;
- A systems approach to ensuring interdependence among the structures.

REFERENCES

Glasser, W. (1998). *Choice theory: A new psychology of personal freedom.* New York: HarperCollins.

Sweller, J. (1988). Cognitive load during problem solving: Effects on learning. *Cognitive Science 12*, 257–285.

6

Promoting Efficacy Through Facilitation of Learning

You walk into a classroom to find students actively engaged in diverse activities, clearly attending to the tasks at hand. The teacher is sitting and talking with a student. After a few minutes, the teacher moves to sit with a group of students. Again, after a few minutes, the teacher moves to sit with another student. At some point, you ask the teacher to tell you about a particular student. With ease, the teacher tells you what the student is working on, how he is progressing in his learning goals, where his challenges are, and what she plans to do to address them. How is the teacher able to do this with so much activity in the classroom? The answer lies in masterful facilitation of the learning environment, the subject of this chapter. I frequently use the following GPS metaphor to shed light on the teacher's role as facilitator of learning.

Teacher as GPS[1]

Global Positioning System (GPS) is a popular navigation partner, particularly in cars, for assisting the driver in meeting a destination. Did you ever stop to consider that a masterful teacher is a lot like GPS?

First, the GPS identifies the destination. A teacher identifies the destination as the curriculum standards that the students need to meet. Next, the GPS determines the best route for the driver to use to meet the destination.

---

1 Reprinted from the IDEportal (www.ideportal.com) with permission.

A teacher creates lesson plans and activities that are expected to help the student achieve the curricular goals.

During the trip, the GPS continually uses satellite communications to determine where the driver is. Based on that information and the destination, GPS ensures that the driver is "on track" to meet the destination. If the driver makes an incorrect turn, the GPS immediately recognizes that and develops a new plan for ensuring the driver arrives at the destination.

Masterful teachers use continuous formative assessment to determine students' progress and then modify lessons and activities to ensure student success. Quizzes, rubrics, verbal check-ins, gathering facilitation data, online assessments, and the like enable the teacher to track the progress of each student. If a student is having difficulty with a previously taught lesson, the teacher will meet one-on-one or in small groups, utilize a technology program, develop a *how-to sheet*, or use some other means to ensure that the student masters the skill or concept.

Of course, another wonderful aspect of GPS is that it never makes you feel like a failure. At each wrong turn, it merely recalculates the route. My GPS has never told me, "That's it! I'm not going to help you any more if you're not going to listen to my directions!" or "You just really don't have what it takes to get to your destination." On the contrary, my GPS always instills in me great confidence that I will arrive at my destination, as do masterful teachers.

CONSIDER

The goal of the *Learner-Active, Technology-Infused Classroom* is to move students beyond mere engagement in learning to empowerment and efficacy, with efficacy being the ability to identify a problem to solve or goal to achieve and put plans into action to reach a successful outcome. While the *problem-based task* and *analytic rubric* are designed to engage students in the learning process; and the various structures of the *Learner-Active, Technology-Infused Classroom* are designed to empower students; promoting efficacy stems from purposeful and deliberate facilitation by teachers in the classroom.

The Power and Purpose of Facilitation

Facilitating learning presumes that the teacher has already set up clear structures for the learning environment, as discussed in the previous chapters, and students are now engaged in the learning process. In a more conventional model of teaching, the teacher presents information to the entire class, typically from the front of the room, and then students engage in practicing what was presented. The teacher need only walk around the room to ask if students need help, as they are already armed with content from the lesson. In the *Learner-Active, Technology-Infused Classroom*, this is not the case. Students are learning in a differentiated environment in which content is presented in a variety of ways, rarely through the teacher in the front of the room. Therefore, the role of the teacher as facilitator during this time becomes critical. It is not enough to ask if students need help, as they may not know that they even need help. Facilitation must be deliberate and purposeful, aimed at the needs of individual students. Teacher facilitation is as important to the *Learner-Active, Technology-Infused Classroom* as are the *ALUs* for engaging students and the structures for putting them in charge of their own learning. There are three aspects to facilitation in the *Learner-Active, Technology-Infused Classroom*:

- ♦ Management: This is the most basic level of facilitation that occurs in most classrooms around the world. Teachers ensure that students are where they belong, address behavioral issues, and overtly coordinate the learning environment. As you shift your thinking regarding the role of the teacher in the classroom, you'll find that *Learner-Active, Technology-Infused Classroom* teachers need to spend little time on this. Instead they focus more of their time toward building student efficacy through the next two categories.

- ♦ Process: Given that the reality of students taking charge means that students must be able to manage themselves and their own learning process, building myriad executive function skills, you'll need to focus some of your facilitation on process. Ask logistical questions to guide students' efforts. Point them to their *analytic rubric* and ask them to share what they've accomplished so far and what goals they've set for the immediate future. Help them learn how to identify the proper resources to select. Work with them to think through how to design their schedule. Continually assess and track students' executive function skills and work to build them through the structures that involve the process of students taking charge: *problem-based task, analytic rubric, activity list, scheduling time, help board, home group*, and so forth. The time you spend facilitating students' learning process will pay off as they become better empowered to take charge of their own learning, using you as a resource in that quest.

- ♦ Content: Given that in the *Learner-Active, Technology-Infused Classroom*, you are not presenting skill instruction from the front of the room, you must provide students with a variety of differentiated *learning activities* through which to learn content. It is then imperative that you use your role as facilitator to ensure that all of your students are receiving the instruction they need and are achieving content mastery. The *Learner-Active, Technology-Infused Classroom* framework allows for the highest levels of differentiation, and the structures empower students to take charge of their own learning so they can work independent of a total reliance on the teacher. This allows the teacher to provide further, targeted differentiated instruction through facilitation. You'll proactively use formative assessment to track student progress and provide instruction, suggestions, and resources to ensure success. Your facilitation doesn't end with subject-area content mastery; you continue on to ask probing questions to stimulate higher-order thinking, inspiring students to higher and higher levels of content mastery. You also need to analyze the formative assessment data you collect during facilitation to drive your own instructional decisions, including what *benchmark lessons* and *small-group mini-lessons* to offer and what *learning activities* and *practice activities* to add to the *activity list*. The time you used to spend in the front of the room offering whole-class instruction now gives way to a more deliberate and purposeful engagement with individual and small groups of students.

Clearly, when you are offering *benchmark lessons* or *small-group mini-lessons*, you are "on stage" in front of the entire class or a small group of students. Beyond that time, you should be engaged as a facilitator. It's important to resist the temptation to think that students are well engaged and you can plan lessons, grade papers, or talk at length with a visitor to the classroom. Your deliberate (you decide when and how) and purposeful (you focus on what is important) facilitation time is a critical part of the teaching process.

Sit Among Your Students

As students are engaged in the learning process, you need to be moving around the room, pulling up a chair to sit with one or a group of students. "Never hover!" Again, if you only had to ask if students needed help, you could lean over their desks. If you are going to engage with them in the learning process in a meaningful way, you should be seated alongside them. When you walk into a well-run *Learner-Active, Technology-Infused Classroom*, it's hard to locate the teacher as he or she is usually sitting somewhere among the students.

James Coleman (1988) introduced the term *social capital* to mean that which is produced as a result of powerful relationships between adults and young people in a community. In a nutshell, consider a community in which the parents know the youngsters in the neighborhood by name, congratulate them for a sports win, offer a ride home from school, ask about an ill parent, and so forth. In such communities, students build confidence and are secure in the knowledge that there are adults who are interested in them. In such communities, students tend to fare well in school. Juxtapose that with a community in which the adults do not know the neighborhood youngsters and are not concerned about them. Students are left to fend for themselves with little formal or informal adult supervision. In such communities, students tend to fare poorly in school. Coleman's work in defining social capital has led large, urban schools to restructure into small learning communities (SLCs). In the *Learner-Active, Technology-Infused Classroom*, it reminds teachers that those critical, caring relationships between adults and students are best fostered during one-on-one and small-group facilitation, not from the front of the room.

The *Learner-Active, Technology-Infused Classroom* is a system of interdependent components. For example, facilitation works best when students are planning their entire week, scheduling activities across class periods, from different aspects of the *ALU*, tailored to their needs. As you facilitate, some students will be engaged in activities where they won't need much, if any, of your attention, for example, watching informational videos or researching a topic, whereas others will be involved in *learning activities* that are more cognitively demanding and could use your involvement. If you limit the choices or only offer students a small amount of time across the week to schedule their own time, you are more likely to run into a situation where everyone needs you or no one needs you. The power of your facilitation, therefore, begins with the strength of your *activity list*.

"The power of your facilitation, therefore, begins with the strength of your *activity list*."

Be Mindful of Balancing Your Energy in the Classroom

As you move around the classroom, you bring with you your energy. You take on the role of inspirer, cheerleader, coach, helper, guide, and so many others. As you move around the room to facilitate, be mindful of where you've been physically. If you are on one side of the room, move next to the other side. While it may seem to make sense to move, in order, around the room, that would cause your energy to be imbalanced, spending a lot of time one side of the room and then moving to the other. Instead, move back and forth across the room as you facilitate, unless the *help board* draws you to specific students. Students' positions on the *help board* take precedence. The key is to have few names on the *help board* as students learn to be more resourceful. Then your facilitation becomes more proactive.

Be mindful of your time as you move about the room, spending only a few minutes at each stop. Although at times you will be tempted to engage in a lengthy conversation with one or more students, consider that you would then be absent from the rest of the class. You might suggest that you and the student meet again to continue the discussion at a specified time. You might decide to schedule a related *small-group mini-lesson*.

Your facilitation experience will provide you with insights for further instructional design. If you find yourself feeling like you can't get to everyone, consider more group check-ins where three students meet with you to share their progress quickly and have you offer next steps. If you find you are not facilitating enough, you might be offering too many *small-group mini-lessons* or *benchmark lessons*, or you might be engaging in too many one-on-one conferences, which take you away from the class as a whole. If you are addressing the same challenges over and over again, you may need to offer more *learning activities* or a *small-group mini-lesson*. Use your facilitation data to inform your practice.

Every Student Will Benefit from Your Facilitation

Facilitation of learning is not about a reactive response to those who need help; it's about a proactive response to determining the best next step for each student. At first, some students may try to

> **"Facilitation of learning is not about a reactive response to those who need help; it's about a proactive response to determining the best next step for each student."**

push you away, claiming they don't need help. The reality is that they don't know what they don't know; it's your job to help them figure out what they do and don't know and then guide them in the right direction. Secondary schooling is a time of exercising your ability to learn, not just mastering academic content. It should be a time of thoughtful questioning, deep thinking, challenging the status quo, resourcefulness, debate, and idea generation. The skills one learns in elementary school in terms of how to learn should now become the cornerstone of one's secondary school experience.

Three Powerful Tools

Facilitation is an art and a science unto itself; it is a critical component of the *Learner-Active, Technology-Infused Classroom* that cannot be taken lightly. While the more tactile work of designing the *problem-based task, analytic rubric, learning activities*, and various structures may feel like the hard work of the *Learner-Active, Technology-Infused Classroom*, the real power of the teacher is evident through facilitation. It is that which can make or break your classroom. Students should not be teaching themselves; and they should not be discovering content on their own. The difference between an *ALU* in which students teach themselves and one in which teachers and students partner to ensure high levels of achievement is facilitation. This chapter will offer you three powerful tools: a *facilitation roadmap* to challenge your thinking as to how you can address individual students' learning needs; a *content facilitation grid* that you will use to capture formative assessment data and to make instructional decisions; and a guide for designing *facilitation questions* to probe students' thinking related to content. Mastering these three tools will help you focus on the new role of the teacher in the *Learner-Active, Technology-Infused Classroom*.

The Facilitation Roadmap

In order to make your facilitation more deliberate and purposeful, use the *facilitation roadmap* to guide your actions. This tool focuses on honing in on an individual student's state of mind and providing just the right support at the right time. An immediate win in running a *Learner-Active, Technology-Infused Classroom* is being able to look around and see all of your students seemingly engaged. I say seemingly because you don't really know how well they are understanding the content or how well they are managing their time until you sit with them and start asking questions. When you look out at that classroom full of engaged learners, can you identify how each student is feeling about their work at that point? Masterful *Learner-Active, Technology-Infused Classroom* teachers know their students and the work flow so well, due, in part, to the facilitation tools shared in this chapter, that they can tell you who is on target, who is bored, who is struggling, who is about to give up, and so on. Each of those students deserves a different response. The *facilitation roadmap* breaks that down. You would not necessarily carry it with you while facilitating, but it can give you some insights into ensuring your engagement with students is deliberate and purposeful. Facilitation is not about moving around the room seeing if everyone has mastered a skill or following some plan that you as the teacher have made; it's about ascertaining what, how, and when a student is learning, and then off ering guidance, information, and new challenges. You are a mentor; a coach.

"Facilitation is not about moving around the room seeing if everyone has mastered a skill or following some plan that you as the teacher have made; it's about ascertaining what, how, and when a student is learning, and then offering guidance, information, and new challenges. You are a mentor; a coach."

The *facilitation roadmap* begins with a challenge. Most likely you've given your students a challenge in terms of the overarching *problem-based task* of the *Authentic Learning Unit (ALU)*. The *analytic rubric* should also provide your students with learning challenges along the way. Sometimes in your

Figure 6.1. Facilitation Roadmap

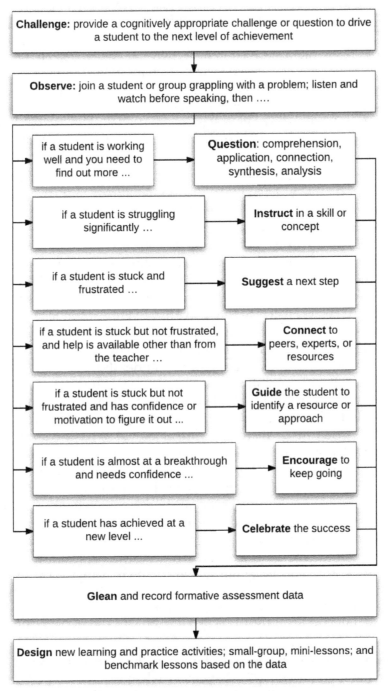

Challenge: provide a cognitively appropriate challenge or question to drive a student to the next level of achievement

Observe: join a student or group grappling with a problem; listen and watch before speaking, then ....

if a student is working well and you need to find out more ... → **Question:** comprehension, application, connection, synthesis, analysis

if a student is struggling significantly ... → **Instruct** in a skill or concept

if a student is stuck and frustrated ... → **Suggest** a next step

if a student is stuck but not frustrated, and help is available other than from the teacher ... → **Connect** to peers, experts, or resources

if a student is stuck but not frustrated and has confidence or motivation to figure it out ... → **Guide** the student to identify a resource or approach

if a student is almost at a breakthrough and needs confidence ... → **Encourage** to keep going

if a student has achieved at a new level ... → **Celebrate** the success

Glean and record formative assessment data

Design new learning and practice activities; small-group, mini-lessons; and benchmark lessons based on the data

Note: It's easiest to facilitate when students are grappling with a problem to solve or with a new skill or concept.

facilitation, you will offer up a new challenge for the next level of learning. People are engaged and in flow when a challenge is just above their ability level (Csikszentmihalyi, 2008). When students are given learning challenges that are slightly above their ability level, they thrive, demonstrating a powerful level of engagement with content. When the challenges are below their ability level, they get bored; when the challenges are too far beyond their ability level, they get frustrated and give up. The masterful *Learner-Active, Technology-Infused Classroom* facilitator seeks to identify the state of mind of the student and offer support, resources, and challenges to keep them in flow. Seek to ensure that students are engaged in learning challenges that are just above their individual ability levels. As they achieve one level of mastery, they should be given challenges at a slightly higher level. This "leveling up" (Prensky, 2006) increases the likelihood that students will be in flow and engaged in grappling with content.

As a *facilitator* of learning, focusing on the process and content aspects of facilitation, sit down next to a student or group of students and, at first, **observe** them. Your presence by their sides should not be unusual to them nor cause them to stop and attend to you. Over time, they will keep working until you ask them a question. Watch them work or, if students are engaged in collaborative work, listen to them. Within twenty seconds you will most likely get a sense of what is going on, but those twenty seconds will make what you do next that much more purposeful. Now, as you assess the situation, you decide how to engage with the student(s).

You'll see a list of possible options in Figure 6.1. If the student seems to be working well, **delve further** to determine how well they are understanding the content. Through a series of *facilitation questions* (discussed later in this chapter), you can see if students are at a level of basic comprehension, able to apply learning to new situations, or able to synthesize and invent new solutions or ideas from existing content. Based on your assessment, you'll ask questions at higher and higher levels to probe their thinking.

If a student is struggling significantly with the content, it's important to step in and simply **provide direct instruction**. You do not want to start asking probing questions, making suggestions, or offering resources when a student is about to give up due to excessive frustration; just teach! Show the student how you would go about tackling the challenge. Arm the student with enough knowledge to continue on, meeting with success. That being said, more often than not, you do not want to swoop in with the answer; instead, you want guide students toward succeeding at the challenge. Those situations are discussed next.

If a student is stuck or frustrated, but not to the point of giving up, **suggest a step**. "What if you tried …?" "Remember when we …? Let's try that!" The point is to offer an immediate step to take, not have the student attempting to find that step. Your facilitation stops just short of providing direct instruction in the skill or concept. Once the student has that aha moment and you have ensured that the learning momentum will continue, you can move on. If, however, it becomes obvious that, even with a next step, the student is becoming more frustrated, then you switch to providing direct instruction.

If a student is stuck but not really frustrated, rather than you being the critical resource that you would be in the prior two situations, **connect** the student to other resources to provide the content they need, including peer experts, outside experts that are available to them, or various learning resources that are available in the room or online. This is your opportunity to teach your students the powerful skill of resourcefulness. Suggest that the student connect with another student you know already has mastered a particular skill. Students learn well from one another, and those who have just completed a challenge are usually proud to share their breakthroughs with others.

If a student is stuck but has the confidence and motivation to figure it out, **guide** the student to finding the needed resource or approach to take. "Where might you find some help?" "Remember what you did the last time you were stuck?" "What are you thinking of trying next?" Note that this is subtly different from pointing the student to a resource or next step. This level of facilitation is more about asking the student to think through how they are going to locate a helpful resource. Often, students who have the confidence to push through are deflated when you give them the answer, as they wanted the thrill of figuring it out on their own. Your role is to simply ask them to share their thinking out loud with you. Often in talking about it, they arrive at the answer on their own.

If a student is doing well and nearing a breakthrough, **encourage** the student to keep going. "You almost have it!" "Keep going and let me know when you figure it out!" Those words of encouragement provide further motivation and let the student know that you are interested.

If a student has just successfully mastered a skill or concept, **celebrate the success**! Share some confirming words. Suggest the student posts something on the classroom blog, if you use one. Depending on the skill, see if the student is ready to be a *peer expert* or conduct a *small-group mini-lesson*. Once the student has basked in the success for a few moments, move on to present the next challenge. "Now what if you …?" "What's the next level on your rubric that you want to achieve?"

It is important to offer students the most purposeful facilitation to propel their academic achievement. Your words and actions will ensure that your students keep moving in a positive direction, making the best use of their time. It makes no sense for students to struggle futilely when you could help them; it makes no sense to let successful students work on their own, thinking they don't need you. Every student needs you to provide just the right facilitation in the moment.

While you're facilitating learning, you have the perfect opportunity to gather significant formative assessment data for your instructional decision-making. The key is to capture the data as it presents itself, not to attempt to move around the room assessing one particular skill or concept with all of your students. The tool for capturing formative assessment data is the *content facilitation grid*.

Content Facilitation Grid

Your *ALU* is designed around specific content that your students need to master. Given that students control when and how they learn, you need a way to capture formative assessment data throughout the day. In one short period of time, you might gather data on one student's math computational skills, another's ability to reason abstractly, and yet another's application skills. It may seem easier for you to gather assessment data when, in the more conventional approach, lessons are delivered to the entire class at the same time and all are working on the same content. As you shift responsibility for learning to your students, you give them significant choice and voice over their learning approach, but that comes with the challenge of ensuring you know everything that is going on in the classroom. The *content facilitation grid* allows you to capture data across students and subject areas across the day.

The *content facilitation grid* is a spreadsheet-type grid that includes students' names down the side and content skills and concepts across the top. As you observe and hear evidence of a student's progress toward mastering a skill or concept, you place a letter in the box, noting your assessment. Use the *content facilitation grid* as well to capture formative assessment data from quizzes; tests; and individual, in-class assignments. I do not recommend using it with any out-of-class assignments as it will be difficult to know the extent to which you are assessing the student's mastery given you won't know what kind of help was offered from others. The *content facilitation grid* will be described in more detail in the "Create" section that follows.

Facilitation Questions

As you sit with students, observe them in action, and then partner with them in the learning process, you will move between offering them instruction, guidance, and resources, and asking questions. Questions aimed at promoting content mastery, as opposed to those focusing on the learning process, should foster a culture of "leveling up" described earlier in the chapter.

When facilitating, most teachers tend to ask comprehension questions to ensure that students have a grasp on the basic content. Educational psychologist Benjamin Bloom worked with colleagues in the 1950s to develop a classification for intellectual activities inherent in the learning process. Bloom acknowledged that first someone must be able to *recall* information, then *comprehend* it, then *apply* it to various situations, then *analyze* it, which leads to the ability to *synthesize* and thus the create new information, and finally *evaluate* the creation of new information. Bloom's taxonomy remains a viable guide for teachers when considering *learning activities*. Also use it when considering the types of questions to ask students to probe their thinking. Note: a newer version flips the order of the last two categories, making synthesis a more higher-order skill than evaluation. I think you could argue both ways; the point is, however, give your students ample experience with both!

In the *Learner-Active, Technology-Infused Classroom*, teachers essentially ask five types of questions, somewhat mirroring Bloom's taxonomy, though not entirely:

♦ Comprehension—to determine basic mastery of the content

♦ Application—to determine the extent to which the student can apply the learning to another situation

♦ Connection—to determine the extent to which the student can connect and/or apply the learning to their own life

♦ Synthesis—to determine the extent to which the student can use the knowledge to generate new information, solutions, or ideas

♦ Metacognition—to determine the student's ability to reflect on the learning process

Your development of *facilitation questions* is intended to expand your thinking on the content and arm you with various levels of questions to ask. Unlike the *facilitation grid*, the *facilitation questions* are not necessarily intended to be carried around with you and are not intended to be used to ask every student these questions as you move around the room. They are meant to spark your own thinking. As you engage in conversations with students, your comments and questions should flow from that discussion. Thus, you may end up asking other questions similar to those you originally designed as a result of your conversations with students. The development of *facilitation questions* will be described in more detail in the Create section that follows. A well-run *Learner-Active, Technology-Infused Classroom* provides students with a differentiated, personalized learning environment. Students are engaged in solving real-world problems and empowered with the structures to support them in taking responsibility for their own learning. The road to efficacy is supported by the teacher's facilitation of learning, helping students identify problems to solve, set goals, decide on a path, locate resources, self-assess, consider further options, and so forth. As you design various tools to support your role as the facilitator of learning in the classroom, keep in mind that your ultimate goal is to propel students to academic success as efficacious learners.

> **"The road to efficacy is supported by the teacher's facilitation of learning, helping students identify problems to solve, set goals, decide on a path, locate resources, self-assess, consider further options, and so forth."**

CREATE

So far, you've developed a *problem-based task, analytic rubric, scaffold for learning,* and *activity list.* Once all this learning activity gets underway, you'll want to rely on your facilitation tools to gather formative assessment data to drive your instructional decisions. Avoid relying solely on your intuition, observations, or memory—gather the data!

Facilitating Process

The *Learner-Active, Technology-Infused Classroom* offers students many structures for managing the process of learning, including the *analytic rubric, activity list, schedule, help board, peer expert board, quality work board,* and more. Building greater *student responsibility for learning* involves expecting students to self-assess, make decisions about which activities to choose and when to complete them, select instructional resources, and make many other decisions. Part of the facilitation process is ensuring that students are carrying out these tasks successfully. When facilitating and sitting with students, ask them to show you where they are on their *analytic rubrics* for the *problem-based task.* Ask them what their next step is going to be and why. Ask how they decided upon the activities they've chosen. Ask how they will know when they've accomplished the next column in the rubric. Ask them if they are attending a particular *small-group mini-lesson,* and why or why not. Ask them how they decided upon the resources they selected.

These types of questions will help you feel confident in their decision making and will model for them the types of internal conversations they should be having surrounding their learning decisions. The more you teach your students how to take responsibility for decisions in the learning process, the more time you will have to spend on content mastery as opposed to process. You don't want to be the teacher reading off names to check whether or not students completed their homework. You don't want to be the teacher who asks students to put their homework on their desks and then walks around with a grade book recording the presence of homework. You don't want to be the teacher who is reprimanding individual students for not being on task or for not following directions. All of these actions take precious time away from what you do best: impart knowledge to your students and help them become lifelong learners. Have students self-report on homework. If they are inaccurately reporting, you'll know it from their performance and can talk with them about the importance of and your expectation for accurate reporting. The more you create structures that allow students to take responsibility for logistics, the more time you'll have to spend on content, which will have a direct, positive impact on achievement.

Advancing Content Mastery Through Facilitation Questions

A pair of students gathered data on the foods their colleagues ate over the course of a week. They used it to test their nutrition calculator to assess overall healthfulness of a student's eating habits. The teacher then asked what they might do with the aggregated data.

A group of seventh-grade students are designing a car that can drive on the surface of Mars. They've been focused on the rough terrain and possible icy surfaces and explained their decisions. The teacher asks what gravity is like on Mars vs. Earth, to ensure they also attend to that factor.

Students are developing recipes for printing food on a solar-powered, 3-D printer as part of their plan for providing food to third-world countries. The teacher asks if they can determine the optimal protein and nutrients intake of an adult and child who are suffering from malnutrition.

As part of an *ALU* based on the Indian caste system, students just finished reading the novel *Divergent*, in which survivors are divided into five factions based on personality characteristics. They share their thoughts on the story and compare and contrast them with the caste system. The teacher asks them if they were to write a similar book, how might they define the factions. They begin discussing, agreeing on some, disagreeing on others; the teacher moves on.

These types of questions probe students' thinking, sending their minds swirling with questions and ideas to pursue. Usually, one good question will send students off to pursue the next challenge and keep the learning momentum going. Before you can ask questions that probe higher-order thinking, however, you have to ensure that your students have a foundational understanding of the content they are studying. Using the *problem-based task* and *analytic rubric* you've designed for your *ALU*, select a content focus and develop a set of questions that you might use with students. Strive to write five to eight questions for each category:

1. *Comprehension Questions*—It is important to ask questions that ensure students understand the content and skills needed to solve the problem. Examples:

   a. What is the theme of a text?

   b. What are the seven elements of music?

   c. How is a ratio different from a fraction?

   d. What is feudalism?

   e. What are the pros and cons of hydroelectric power?

   f. In Spanish, what is a verb infinitive?

   g. What are five elements of writer's craft in narrative writing?

2. *Application Questions*—Ask questions that ensure the ability of students to apply the learning to new situations.

   a. What is the theme of the book?

   b. Describe the rhythm evident in the guitar track and drum track of Led Zeppelin's "Kashmir"?

   c. What is the length of the hypotenuse of a right triangle with sides of three and four units?

   d. How is the "cloud" similar to the concept of feudalism?

   e. How would you construct a time–distance graph of the marble moving on your roller coaster?

   f. What operational principles are at work in this video segment of the soccer game?

3. *Connection Questions*—Ask questions that ensure the ability of students to apply learning to their lives.

   a. How will you establish your theme in the story you are writing?

   b. How would you describe the rhythm of a favorite song of yours?

   c. How did Martin Luther King, Jr.'s work affect your life?

   c. Which artist's work here do you like the most and why?

   e. Where in your life could you apply ratios?

   f. Where in our community or your home do you see alternative fuel sources used?

4. *Synthesis Questions*—Ask questions that encourage students to create new information from existing data.

   a. What could the government of the country you are studying do to boost their economy?

   b. What techniques could you use to make the message in your poem even more powerful?

   c. What can you do to make your hydroelectric power plan produce even more power?

   d. How might the characters react differently if they lived in today's world?

   e. What claims and counterclaims can you use to build your case?

   f. What painting techniques might you use?

5. *Metacognition Questions*—Ask questions that prompt students to think about their own thinking processes.

   a. What was the hardest part of this task for you?

   b. How did you arrive at the solution?

   c. When do you realize your idea was not going to work?

   d. How might you go about solving this differently?

   e. How did you figure out how to change the color combinations in this graph?

   f. What did you like the most about this activity?

   g. What do you find most challenging about playing soccer?

When you finish writing up your questions, reread them and/or share them with a colleague and see if you can improve upon them. Again, once you've designed them, you typically don't need to carry them with you while facilitating. These are not meant to be a script nor answered by every student; they are meant to be used in the context of conversations. The process of crafting the questions focuses more on deepening your understanding of content and its application to the real world. While at first you may want to carry the list of questions as a reference, as you engage in content-rich conversations with students, you'll recall the relevant questions in the moment.

Using Formative Assessments to Drive Instruction

A GPS is constantly sending out satellite signals to determine the progress of the driver and modify the route if necessary. Masterful teachers use formative assessment constantly to determine how students are progressing. This is a key concept in the *Learner-Active, Technology-Infused Classroom*: teachers do not take comfort in the fact that they presented the content well; they only take comfort in the evidence that students learned the content well.

I heard a great analogy that states: formative assessment is to summative assessment as a physical is to an autopsy. Summative assessments are administered at the end of a unit of study or year in school to evaluate the level of success of the student. The understanding is that the teaching–learning process for this content is completed. The best information a summative assessment can offer the teacher relative to improving student achievement is in helping the teacher rethink the unit for the next group of students. Similarly, an autopsy will do nothing for the person being autopsied; however, the data can be used to advance the future of medicine. Alternatively, a physical is meant to assess the patient's condition and lead to prescribed actions aimed at improving patient health. Likewise, formative assessments are intended to provide data that will be used to prescribe learning activities that will lead to greater student success.

Formative assessments can be classified as follows: temperature gauges, breakpoints, student-directed assessments, and comprehensive assessments (Figure 6.2).

Consider these four categories and design assessments that you will use with your students.

1. *Temperature Gauges*—When you are presenting to the whole class, it's easy to take your cues from the handful of students who are smiling, nodding, and answering and asking questions. It's important not to be lulled into thinking this means your lesson is effective for the entire class. A quick check-in will provide you with important data. If you're talking about the periodic table, you can use a couple of temperature gauge questions, such as, "thumbs up if you know definitively where you would find an inert gas on the periodic table; thumbs down if not." I'm assuming I need not go into the danger of one-, two-, and three-"finger" check-ins with secondary students. This formative assessment tool must be carefully explained in advance; that is, which finger to raise if you're just raising one finger, and so on. If you're introducing a unit of study and have just handed out the *problem-based task, analytic rubric,* and *activity list;* you may want to see how students are feeling. Use the adjective check-in to have each student offer one word of how they are feeling. You'll hear words like interested, excited, confused, and overwhelmed. This allows you to get a read on the class. If you have a lot of students who are confused and overwhelmed, offer a *small-group mini-lesson* directly after the *benchmark lesson* for those who want to ask more clarifying questions and get more assistance before diving in. Keep in mind that students have to get used to these Temperature Gauge formative assessments. At first you might not get data as accurate as you want. Over time, students will realize this is critical feedback they are providing that is going to benefit them, and they will respond accordingly. The purpose of a Temperature Gauge is to provide you with the data to shift the focus of your lesson immediately. If you've just introduced the concept of foreshadowing, offer a three-finger check-in on whether or not a student could give an example of foreshadowing. If you find that few can provide one, you'll want to rethink your approach and offer perhaps some more examples.

2. *Breakpoints*—At the end of a day, class period, or whole- or small-group lesson, take the opportunity to gather assessment data. An exit card offers students a single, short question or request for information. The students write on an index card and hand it in

on their way out the door or upon leaving the lesson. If students are working on a variety of activities around governments, ask them to identify a form of government other than that of their country that appeals to them and why. Avoid closed-ended questions such as "list the major types of governments," as, given that exit cards are completed as students are packing up or transitioning, students might simply ask a peer for the answer. Quizzes are also Breakpoint assessments. At the end of the day or class period, you might offer a ten-question quiz to assess learning. The key to Breakpoint assessments is that they offer you valuable data to use to plan subsequent lessons, offering you more time to adjust than a Temperature Gauge assessment does.

3. *Student-Directed Assessments*—These are powerful because they not only provide you with information, but they force students to become aware of their own progress. Prior to handing in an assignment, have students complete a checklist to ensure they've included all of the learning objectives you expected. A reflective portfolio allows students to set goals, gather examples of progress, reflect on them, and share their insights with you. Sit with individual students and ask them to use the unit rubric to tell you where they are in their progress and how they are going to move to the next column. Student-Directed Assessments tend to take a little more time than the previous two categories, but they provide valuable data about the students' perceptions of their learning as well as data on their actual progress.

4. *Comprehensive Assessments*—Not to be confused with summative assessments, Comprehensive Assessments gather data across a variety of concepts and skills. Rubrics are one example as they contain indicators for all aspects of the unit performance. *Facilitation grids* gather data from across a set of concepts and skills. These allow you to get the big picture of how the unit itself is progressing so that you can provide clarifying information and new instructional activities as needed. In order to meet overall curriculum standards for the year, an *ALU* can only be allocated a specific amount of time. Even if students are thoroughly engaged in a particular unit, you cannot afford to let it simply continue, as you have other units to launch. If students are not progressing adequately, Comprehensive Assessments will make that obvious, allowing you to provide additional information on a classroom blog or website; offer some targeted *benchmark lessons* or *small-group mini-lessons*; or modify some activities or add new ones.

Figure 6.2. Four Types of Formative Assessment

Four Types of Formative Assessment

Temperature Gauges—Immediate, in-the-moment assessments that allow the teacher to get a sense of current student status. This often takes place while the teacher is presenting a lesson. Based on student response, the teacher can adjust the lesson content and pacing, and identify any urgent student needs. *Examples: Adjective Check-In, Three-Finger Check-In*
Breakpoints—Brief assessments given at a stopping point in instruction (such as the end of the class period or lesson), allowing the teacher to step back and revise the instructional plan. Based on student response, the teacher can plan instructional activities and whole-class lessons. *Examples: Exit Cards, One Sentence Summary, Do Now, Higher-Order Questioning, Quizzes*
Student Directed Assessments—Self-evaluative student reflection, giving the teacher insight into perceived needs. Based on student response, the teacher can direct the student to appropriate resources—small-group or one-on-one instruction, websites, learning activities, and how-to sheets. *Examples: Checklists, Self-Assessment on a Rubric, Peer Evaluation, Student Journals*
Comprehensive Assessments—Systematic data collection on individual skill & concept attainment. Based on student response, the teacher can offer targeted small-group instruction, re-teach core concepts, and provide additional resources. *Examples: Rubrics, Tests, Facilitation Grids, Individual Conferences/Oral Interviews, Student Folders, Notebook/Portfolio Check*

Formative Assessment Grids

The beauty and challenge of the *Learner-Active, Technology-Infused Classroom* is the level of activity going on in the classroom at any one time. A common fear of teachers is tracking classroom activity: how are you going to track everything that is going on? Two very effective tools are the *task management grid* (for facilitating classroom management) and the *content facilitation grid* (for facilitating content acquisition). These grids enable you to easily track and analyze assessment data. Both can be designed on a spreadsheet or with a table in a word processing document. Both can be invaluable when speaking with parents, colleagues, and students about academic progress.

Task Management Grid

The *task management grid* allows you to easily see which activities a single student or the class has completed. Across the top are the various activities presented to students; down the left side are the students' names. To design your *task management grid*, consider the various subtasks students will accomplish to complete the problem. What assignments will students hand in? These should be on the task management grid. You may choose to include all of the *learning activities* you've assigned to build to each of the subtasks; just remember that all students will not complete all *learning activities*, because of the many choices you'll provide, but they will have to complete all subtasks or assignments. Design the *task management grid* to help you best track student progress toward the final *ALU* project. For example, you may have students researching a topic of interest and writing an argumentative essay to be shared with someone who could make a difference. Figure 6.3 is a sample *task management grid* for writing a strong argument. Once students have researched the topic, they will hand in a list of their claims and list of their counterclaims. Then they will hand in a graphic organizer for you to grade. In this case, the *task management grid* includes all of the handed-in or graded assignments. For students who need more direction, you might include more of the activities listed on the grid, not all of which will necessarily be graded. Use whatever system works best for you in tracking each student's activities.

Reviewing students' folders will give you an idea of how well they are progressing in the curricular content, but it's not always easy to see which activities have been completed. The *task management grid* allows you to glance across a row to see how productive a student is. If you include all *learning activities* and *practice activities*, it will also allow you to identify very popular activities (those completed by many students) and unpopular activities (those that are not typically chosen). Some teachers hang a large

Figure 6.3. Task Management Grid

	List of Claims	List of Counter-claims	Graphic Organizer	Draft Essay	Peer Editing/ Two Students	Final Copy
Sancha B.						
Jesvin D.						
Frankie D.						
Isabella F.						
Manny F.						

✓ = Completed   S = Submitted   R = Return for Revisions poster board *task management grid* on the wall so that students can check off their progress; others use a digital file students update; and others record the data themselves based on students' *folders*. Although not assessing success in content mastery, it will provide you with data that you can use to guide students. Those who may have completed a lot of activities may not be spending enough time grappling with the content to receive the benefit of the activities. In this case, you'll want to slow them down and perhaps ask them to complete a reflection card or a learning journal on what they learned. Students who are not completing enough may need assistance in scheduling their time or on content mastery itself. You might want to encourage some of these students to sign up for a *small-group mini-lesson* with you to build scheduling skills.

Content Facilitation Grid

Perhaps the most important tool for using formative assessment to drive instruction is the *content facilitation grid*. When students are working and you are not offering a *benchmark lesson* or *small-group mini-lesson*, you should be facilitating learning. The *content facilitation grid* is similar in structure to the *task management grid* except that, instead of activities across the top, you enter concepts and skills (Figure 6.4). The highlighted columns are for prerequisite skills that you know were addressed in a prior grade or unit. As you pull up a chair next to a student or group of students, you'll be gathering valuable assessment data. Use the grid to make notations. For example, it you see evidence that a student has mastered a skill, write an "M" in that part of the grid. If a student has not only mastered the skill or concept but can explain it to another, use "PE" for peer expert. If a student seems to have an adequate knowledge base but you feel could use some practice, use "HW" to indicate that you should assign a specific homework assignment on that skill. "ML" indicates the student needs help and should attend a *small-group mini-lesson*.

Given that an *ALU* spans several weeks and involves a number of concepts and skills, it's best to design separate *content facilitation grids* for each week. You might want to carry them on a clipboard with the current one on top or use a handheld computing device with digital grids. Most of the data you'll be collecting will be from the current week's grid; however, sometimes you'll need to refer to past or future grids.

In addition to making notations while moving around the room, you can also use the *facilitation grid* to track assessment data when reviewing student work. As you review *student folders*, you can add notations under specific skills and concepts. I caution you against using homework to make notations regarding mastery as you cannot always determine how much help the student may have received at home. You could use a small check or slash to indicate the student completed homework on the concept or skill and still add an assessment notation later.

Figure 6.4. Content Facilitation Grid

Student	M mastered / PE peer expert / R needs reinforcement / HW needs homework / ML needs small-group mini-lesson	Identifies traits of an organism	Defines heredity	Defines DNA	Identifies location of DNA in genes	Explains how hereditary information is passed down from one generation to the next	Defines genotype	Defines phenotype	Compares and contrasts the probability of genotype and phenotype	Finds probabilities using Punnett Square	Finds probability using pedigrees	Defines meiosis	Defines mitosis	Finds probabilities using Punnett Square

As the *content facilitation grid* fills up, you can use it to assess students' progress and your own effectiveness. By looking horizontally, across a row, you can assess how an individual student is progressing on content mastery. This allows you to encourage a student to complete specific activities or attend specific *small-group mini-lessons*, assign homework, meet with the student to explain content, arrange for a *peer expert* session, and so forth.

By looking vertically, down a concept or skill column, you can assess your own success in designing the learning environment. If many students are having difficulty with a particular skill, you will want to rethink how you're delivering the instruction. You may need additional activities, a different explanation, an additional *small-group mini-lesson*, and so forth.

To get started, think through the concepts and skills students must master in this unit. Be sure that you are specific enough that you can assess a student effectively. For example, "solving various types of equations" could be an appropriate skill set for Calculus II, but for a Calculus I student, you would probably want to use one column for each type of equation, such as: linear, quadratic, polynomial, rational & radical, exponential & logarithmic, and trigonometric.

As demonstrated in Figure 6.4, you could highlight initial columns you consider to be prerequisite skills. That way, you know that most students should be able to easily demonstrate mastery of those skills, with the unit concepts and skills beginning in subsequent columns. See the *problem-based tasks* in the appendices for sample *content facilitation grids*. You could also group columns according to overarching topics such that the skills for each topic are easily found under a larger column heading.

It is important that you *use* formative assessment data daily. As a result of this data, you should make adjustments to the instructional activities you are offering. You'll want to allocate time to review each *student folder* and the *facilitation grids* in order to write a note to an individual student, providing direction for future activities.

Facilitating Executive Function

Your *problem-based ALU*, the structures you put in place to put students in charge of their own learning, and your facilitation work together to build greater student efficacy. In my book *Building Executive Function: The Missing Link to Student Achievement* (2018), I map specific executive function skills to key life skills, one of which is efficacy. Figure 6.5 offers a *facilitation grid* for those skills. While you are facilitating to build students' process skills in your classroom and their academic skills, you can also carry a grid to note their advancement in key executive function skills, like the ones included in Figure 6.5. While it's important that students know about history, literature, advanced mathematics, biology, wellness, world language, economics, fine

Figure 6.5. Executive Function Facilitation Grid

Conscious Control (CC)   Engagement (En)   Collaboration (C)   Empowerment (Em)   Efficacy (Ef)   Leadership (all)

Working Memory Storing and manipulating visual and verbal information (CC) Identifying same and different (En) Remembering details (CC) Following multiple steps (En) Holding on to information while considering other information (CC) Identifying cause-and-effect relationships (En) Categorizing information (En)	**Problem Solving** Defining a problem (Ef) Analyzing (Ef) Creating mental images (Ef) Generating possible solutions (Ef) Anticipating (Ef) Predicting outcomes (Ef) Evaluating (Ef)
Cognitive Flexibility Shifting focus from one event to another (CC) Changing perspective (En) Seeing multiple sides to a situation (C) Being open to others' points of view (C) Being creative (Ef) Catching and correcting errors (Em) Thinking about multiple concepts simultaneously (En)	**Inhibitory Control** Attending to a person or activity (CC) Focusing (CC) Concentrating (CC) Thinking before acting (CC) Initiating a task (En) Persisting in a task (En) Maintaining social appropriateness (C)
Planning Setting goals (Em) Managing time (Em) Working towards a goal (Ef) Organizing actions and thoughts (Ef) Considering future consequences in light of current action (Ef)	**Self Awareness** Self-assessing (Em) Overcoming temptation (C) Monitoring performance (Em) Reflecting on goals (Em) Managing conflicting thoughts (CC)
Reasoning Making hypotheses, deductions, and inferences (Ef) Applying former approaches to new situations (Ef)	

Adapted from Appendix A of *Building Executive Function: The Missing Link to Student Achievement* by Nancy Sulla, published by Routledge.

arts, and all of the other content taught at the secondary level, the ultimate goal of education should be to build efficacious learners.

RECAP

In the *Learner-Active, Technology-Infused Classroom*, teachers thoughtfully plan for the use of deliberate and purposeful structures and strategies to facilitate instruction. Together, with the *ALU* and structures you've put in place, teacher facilitation can and should promote student efficacy. Review the follow list to ensure that you have a plan for each in your *ALU*:

- ♦ Ask logistical questions about the student's goals, schedule, resource choices, activity completion, rubric progress, and so forth;

- ♦ Ask probing questions to push higher-order thinking, beginning with comprehension questions and then moving to application, connection, synthesis, and metacognition. Brainstorm questions in advance so they'll come to use easily during the facilitation process;

- ♦ Plan for a variety of daily, formative assessments, including temperature gauges, breakpoints, student directed, and comprehensive;

- ♦ Use a *task management grid* to track students' progress in completing activities;

- ♦ Use *content facilitation grids* to track students' progress in mastering concepts and skills;

- ♦ Use the data gleaned from the *content facilitation grids* to schedule *small-group mini-lessons* and modify the unit's *activity list*;

- ♦ Use a *facilitation grid* to track executive function skills toward student efficacy.

REFERENCES

Coleman, J. S. (1988). Social capital in the creation of human capital. *American Journal of Sociology*, Supplement 94, S95–S120.
Csikszentmihalyi, M. (2008). *Flow: The psychology of optimal experience*. New York: HarperPerennial.
Prensky, M. (2006). *Don't bother me, Mom: I'm learning!* St. Paul, MN: Paragon House.
Sulla, N. (2018). *Building executive function: The missing link to student achievement*. New York: Routledge.

7

Physical Classroom Design

The "Big Room" was a collaborative effort among three teachers who shared responsibility for teaching three homeroom groups of students. Based on their school's structure, the teachers taught their homeroom students language arts literacy, and then each of the three teachers taught all of the students either math, science, or social studies. Students moved from one class to the other throughout the day, sharing three teachers, as an introduction to greater departmentalization that was to come in subsequent years. My colleagues and I had been working in the school for three years, designing *Learner-Active, Technology-Infused Classrooms*, after which time these three teachers approached me indicating that they finally "got it" and wanted to run an amazing classroom by taking down the walls between the classrooms. I spoke with the superintendent, who had a knack for supporting teachers with great ideas, and he had the impeding wall taken down.

That summer, the teachers and I brainstormed, designed, and prepared for the fall, incorporating a lot of paradigm shifting. I questioned whether every student needed a seat facing the front of the room. If sometimes students are in their seats, sometimes conducting an experiment at a lab table, sometimes reading a book, why not design the room to be functional? The teachers agreed. In the end, the room had a discourse center with five couches (donated by parents), science lab tables, study carrels from the library for "quiet work," computers, collaborative work tables, a *small-group mini-lesson* area, and individual desks.

That was around twenty years ago. Today, everyone is talking about flexible seating, so it's not so hard to think that you could redesign your classroom to be more student-driven!

CONSIDER

In the *Learner-Active, Technology-Infused Classroom*, many of the decisions you make will be focused on the question "Why?" The physical layout of the classroom is no exception. The dominant paradigm for classroom layout is to provide each student with a seat and desk or tabletop space, and then provide additional areas such as lab tables, specialized computer stations, work tables, and so forth. The result is often a crowding of furniture in the room.

Instead, consider designing your class functionally so that when students enter the room, they go to the area that matches the function of the activity in which they will be engaged, based on the schedule they designed. In the *Learner-Active, Technology-Infused Classroom*, where students are scheduling their own time and learning activities are differentiated, using space functionally gives you the greatest number of options in the classroom. Of course, it begs the question: How do you offer a *benchmark lesson* to the entire class? As you design the space, think about what that particular learning situation might look like. If you have tables in the room, it may mean that more students sit at a table than usual in order to listen to your lesson. It may mean that students sit around the periphery of the room at lab tables or other specialized work tables. It may mean students are sitting on a couch and listening. You need to make it work for you. I'm not suggesting that you should only have one available spot in the classroom for each student; but I am suggesting that you do not have a seat at a desk for each student in addition to many other work areas in the room.

> "consider designing your class functionally so that when students enter the room, they go to the area that matches the function of the activity in which they will be engaged."

I've seen teachers focus so heavily on the concept of every student facing front to listen to a lesson, that they declined other furniture, such as round tables and couches, so as to preserve the desks facing the front of the room. My response to that is that you should design your classroom for what occurs in it 90 percent of the time, not ten percent. The amount of time you address the entire class should be minimal, so take the opportunity to design a rich and engaging physical environment for the more student-centered activities.

> "The amount of time you address the entire class should be minimal, so take the opportunity to design a rich and engaging physical environment for the more student-centered activities."

It may turn out that you have little control over your physical space. I have been in science labs where the tables were bolted to the floor. It may be that you share a classroom with other teachers and cannot make a lot of physical changes. If you are limited in the amount of control you have over physical space, read through this chapter to get a sense of the thinking behind the suggestions. You never know what change you may be able to effect over time. Remember that the three teachers in the "Big Room" managed to get their school district to take down a cinder block wall!

The challenge today is that furniture companies are heeding the call to develop more flexible seating for classrooms, and they are designing very attractive furniture. However, the dominant paradigm of teacher as lecturer still prevails in many of the choices. Small student tables on wheels roll together to form larger collaborative spaces. While new furniture is attractive and the idea of flexibility, ensuring a seat for everyone in the whole-class lesson, is appealing, it may actually not offer you the best solution in the end. As you read through this chapter, focus on the purpose of different types of furniture so you can make decisions that make the most sense for creating a culture of student engagement, empowerment, and efficacy.

CREATE

Create a functional and inviting space in which your students can work, offering them options that fit the activity. Students should be able to move around the room and work in a space that is most fitting for the activity: sitting comfortably to read, gathered together for a discussion, sharing a table for collaborative work, moving to an individual desk for individual work when quiet is needed. Try to wipe from your mind all of those images of classrooms in your past and envision students taking charge of their learning, using the space in a room so it makes the most sense in the moment.

A great way to start is to take a piece of paper and draw out your current classroom or, if you don't yet have a classroom, how you expect to set up your classroom. Include all of the various areas, furniture, and structures. Then, on a separate piece of paper, for each area of the room, write about *why* you chose to set it up that way. After you complete this reflective exercise, you'll be in a better position to rethink the physical layout of your classroom. Think through each of the following sections and consider how you could arrange your room. Be open to possibilities, but don't commit to anything until you've finished reading through all of them.

Some physical space could be used to serve the purpose of two or more areas. As you read through each, focus on the purpose and then find the physical space to address the need.

Collaborative Work Space

Engaging in learning in the *Learner-Active, Technology-Infused Classroom* is often a collaborative effort. Outside of school, students naturally learn from one another. Brainstorming and higher-order thinking are typically enhanced through collaboration. Students need a place with an unbroken tabletop surface to write, draw, and work with their peers. This tends to be the largest amount of physical space allocated in the *Learner-Active, Technology-Infused Classroom*. You will probably want to provide enough collaborative space to accommodate approximately fifty to sixty percent of your students at one time.

Moving student desks together does not provide the best collaborative environment as students still have their own desktop and clearly delineated personal space. Collaboration means working closely together, so the space between students needs to be minimized. Pushing desks together often results in students sitting forty-eight inches or more apart, which is too far for voices to carry without adding considerable noise to the classroom. Collaboration means sharing ideas and resources, and grappling with ideas to reach consensus. When students sit in arrangements where they still have their individual desks, they are not pushed to think as one unit as they are when they share an unbroken table top surface. Round tables that are forty-two inches in diameter are my choice, preferably with a writable surface to enhance the collaborative experience. Students share the table-top surface, no one has a specific, marked area, and the roundness and smallness foster a small-group environment. Although schools have a tendency to purchase forty-eight-inch round tables, that extra six inches adds tremendously to the overall noise in the classroom. Tables less than forty-two inches in diameter can be useful for conversations but not necessarily for having laptops, notebooks, and other materials in front of students. Consider a combination of forty-two-inch round tables and thirty-six-inch round tables. Rectangular and square tables tend to take up more space, and they do not engender a feeling of collaboration as well as a small, round table. Some teachers prefer the trapezoid tables that when paired create a hexagonal table. With these, however, the final table size tends to be very large and there's still a break down the middle, which I find does not foster collaboration as well as an unbroken, flat surface.

Clover tables are a more recent option. They are circular in overall appearance with an indentation where students sit. Students end up sitting forty-two inches apart from one another, for better discussion and collaboration, but the table juts out on the sides of the students to provide more space for materials. At this wider diameter, the table is forty-eight inches wide.

A French teacher wanting to ensure that her classroom was conducive to considerable conversation in the target language designed her classroom with small café tables so that students sat in pairs for discussions. On the first day of school she welcomed students to her café and served croissants.

Individual Work Space

Students need to work alone to build individual content mastery, particularly when it comes to skill building. They can certainly engage in individual work at a round table, but sometimes they will want to be separated from their peers to work on their own. Students can also work individually on soft seating, using a lapdesk, but sometimes it's just best to have a place to work at a desk away from everyone else. I advocate having two or three individual desks in the classroom for this purpose. This also allows students who has difficulty focusing or self-regulating to move to an area apart from the distraction of their peers.

Teachers ask me about students who are diagnosed with attention-deficit disorder (ADD) or attention-deficit hyperactivity disorder (ADHD) and may not be able to concentrate with the amount of stimulation that is typical of collaborative and student-centered classrooms. My answer is always that students need to learn to accommodate for their personal challenges, and what better place to learn this skill than in the classroom. The teachers in the "Big Room" borrowed a few study carrels from the media center. When students knew they needed to remove themselves to concentrate on their work, they moved to a study carrel.

The idea of "hoteling" has become popular in the corporate world. It speaks to the idea that not everyone is always in the building all of the time; so cubicles, desks, and offices should not remain vacant when they can be used by others. For example, if a company has 100 employees, but many of them are in sales or otherwise on the road such that no more than sixty are in the office at once, why should 40 percent of the physical space always remain vacant? Some of your students' parents may be working in such a situation; and your students may face this when they enter the work world. In the case of "hoteling," workers sign up to reserve a particular office, cubicle, or desk. This also can apply to certain areas in the classroom. I once saw a student move to a study carrel, pull out a picture of her family and a stuffed toy, set up her "office," and get to work. These items added a personal touch to the work environment. Note that a study carrel, or other furniture, may become in demand and require a *limited resource sign-up* sheet.

Discourse Centers

Oral communication skills are important yet not always supported in the conventional approach to classrooms. Verbal acuity is one of the outcomes of learning in a *Learner-Active, Technology-Infused Classroom*, both through collaborative work and meaningful discussions.

Suppose students need to sit and have a discussion about a *problem-based task* or a text they are reading. A couch area can provide a wonderful discourse center, making students feel like they're at home engaging in a conversation in the living room. When the area is not used for discussions, students may use it to work collaboratively or independently. I was in one classroom where I sat down next to a young man on the couch who was surrounded on the couch and floor by graphic organizers. I asked him about his work and he explained the writing project in progress. Then he looked up at me and said, "Aren't you the one who said to get couches in the classroom?" I responded, "I am," at which point he patted the couch surface next to him and said, "Nice touch." A couple of couches can give a nice, comfy feeling to a classroom. You can also create a discourse center using a carpeted area and/or beanbag chairs. Think about the best arrangement for you to provide your students with an area to have a discussion with you or among themselves.

Computer Areas

Nowadays, more schools are turning to laptops and one-to-one ratio of computing devices to students, so you may not need to allocate as much space to a computer area. In the "Big Room," each teacher originally had four computers in the classroom; so together, they had twelve. They designated eight of them as available for students to sign up for up to a forty-minute block. The remaining four were in a "Quick Lookup" area. Students could go to a computer to conduct a quick search for information, spending no more than five minutes at a computer. This way, there were always computers available to answer that spontaneous question or need for information.

Even if you are using laptop computers, you may want to have a desktop computer or two that offer special-purpose peripherals like a scanner, MIDI keyboard, or video camera. This could serve as a work area for multimedia production. You might have a STEM flight simulator computer; that would be in a specialized computer or STEM area.

Resource and Folder Area

In an effort to encourage students to take greater responsibility for their own learning, you'll need a *resource area* from which students can retrieve the printed materials, such as *how-to sheets*, and small resources they may need for their work. Additionally, you will need a place where students will deposit their two-pocket *student work folders* at the end of the day or class period and pick them up when they return to class.

Often, teachers utilize a rectangular table, located in some area of the room. Some teachers staple folders on a bulletin board so that students can retrieve papers from there. Others use storage boxes with file folders. Although it is more difficult to easily locate the desired material, storage boxes take up less room and can be stored away or moved if you share a classroom with other teachers. Storage boxes or crates also make a good receptacle for collecting student folders. In a 1:1 computing environment, the *resource area* becomes a Web-based or networked folder for most materials.

Small-Group Mini-Lesson Area

You will need a space that will accommodate approximately up to six students attending a *small-group mini-lesson* with you. Keep the space condensed enough that students can hear you without you having to speak so loudly that the rest of the class can hear you. You'll want the ability to display information for the group. Some teachers create this area near a whiteboard. Others use an easel pad on a tripod stand.

You want to be a part of the group, building *social capital*, so you would not want to sit behind your desk with students in front of you. Some teachers use kidney-shaped tables, others use round or rectangular tables, and still others use a set of individual chairs with an attached table surface. Given that students will be building skills, ensure that they will have a writing surface on which to work.

Limited Resource Area

I heard someone describing to me just recently how, in her school, students used math kits to explore certain math concepts, but then, when the lesson was done, the math kits moved on to another class. If some students hadn't quite yet grasped the concept, they would have to continue their work without the kits. I've seen science classrooms with class sets of microscopes stored on a shelf. This focus on "class sets" is not an uncommon occurrence in schools. The dominant paradigm for conventional teaching prescribes that all students have access to a particular resource at the same time. All students work with math kits; all students work on computers to construct a journal article; all students work with the STEM robotics kids; all students look at an onion skin under a microscope. This approach to resource utilization can prove to be costly and ineffective, and the underlying pedagogy does not lend itself to differentiation and student choice and voice all that well. Instead, consider having a smaller number of resources available in a classroom for a longer period of time. Five sets of math kits could remain in each classroom for the year, shared by students who sign up for particular time slots. One or two microscopes could be used by students through the year rather than by everyone for one particular lesson. In one school, we eliminated the idea of one, adopted, science textbook and instead had five sets of textbooks, with five books each. Students used them all as resources in their learning.

A limited resource may be set up in its own physical area, such as in the case of a microscope, fish tank, sculpting wheel, flight simulator, and so on. Other limited resources may be housed in containers and stored on a shelf, as in the case of math manipulatives, art supplies for a particular project, robotics kits, educational games, jump ropes, small percussion instruments, and so on. In both cases, however, students will sign up for an available time slot to make use of this limited resource. Decide what limited resources your students will need and where in your room you will allocate space for them.

Use the Walls

Consider how you will make deliberate and purposeful use of the classroom walls. Create a *quality work board* to offer inspiration for producing high-quality work. Designate a *help board* for students to sign up for your help when you are available. Provide areas for students to post their own work. Display various references around the room so that students gain valuable information at a glance. This might include a color wheel, regular polygons, the alphabet, a word wall, common words in a world language, parts of speech, the periodic chart, and more. If you share a room, consider a tri-fold presentation board with sample work that students can set up at the beginning of class and store away at the end of class.

Rather than thinking of your walls as something to decorate, consider how they can serve as a valuable resource for your students in the learning process. Creative use of the walls can add a lot of instructional space to the classroom.

How Big the Screen?

Shifting paradigms requires thoughtful reflection on the "why" of one's actions. The invention of the interactive whiteboard triggered a purchasing frenzy across schools. The interactive whiteboards were designated to be placed in the front of the classroom by the same administrators who were promoting a move from lecture-based instruction to student-centered instruction. This physical setup, however, perpetuates the dominant paradigm of whole-class instruction with everyone looking at the screen in the front of the room. This phenomenon demonstrates how difficult it is to shift paradigms. Alternatively, these devices could be installed in a corner of the room for student *collaboration* and *small-group mini-lessons*.

Some may point to the ability for students to share their presentations with the whole class. How often do you really want to spend class time having one student or group after another presenting to the class? Not often! Instead, designate an area of the room for collaboration and sharing with a large-screen television suited for the space. If you have the funds, install multiple screens around the room. A *Learner-Active, Technology-Infused Classroom* should not look like the perfect venue for movie night. When you walk in the room, the physical space should scream collaboration, movement, and functional work areas.

Any time you are inclined to set up an area of the classroom or purchase a resource that the entire class can use at the same time, stop and ask yourself why. You may find that as you apply the paradigm shifts of the *Learner-Active, Technology-Infused Classroom*, you arrive at a very different decision.

Media-Based Collaboration

Classroom media tables are one of the more recent additions to furniture catalogs. They look like a conference table cut in half across the width so that the flat end is against a wall with a large-screen display on it and the students sit around the curved edge. Students can then display their computer screen on the large-screen display to share their ideas and collaborate.

Most large-screen televisions and displays allow you to "cast" your computer onto them. They also allow for videoconferencing with others in remote locations. One or two of these added to a classroom can promote greater media-based collaboration.

Hospitals began using remote presence devices years ago to allow doctors to visit patients, and more recently to allow hospitalized students to attend school. I use the Beam by Suitable Technologies to visit one of the schools with which we partner. From my computer, I can drive the Beam around the school; I can see with 180-degree peripheral vision as if I were standing there in person. I think similar devices should be used to allow students in *Learner-Active, Technology-Infused Classrooms* to partner with one another across schools, states, and countries.

Comfortable, Fun, Dual-Purpose Furniture

Where do you like to work, read, and converse with others? Give your students some options. Consider some high-top tables, couches and armchairs, chairs with wheels, Adirondack chairs, and architect stations. Have you heard of the cardboard furniture (very compressed and heavy cardboard) that you can build or have students build? Innovative furniture abounds, particularly when you look at office and library furniture options. Seek out innovative seating for classrooms and you'll find some great inspiration for rethinking furniture in the classroom.

As I discuss in my book *Building Executive Function: The Missing Link to Student Achievement* (Sulla, 2018), recent research has shown that standing desks can improve executive functioning. Plus, as students are growing, sometimes standing instead of sitting eliminates fidgeting. You can provide stand-up workspace through high-top tables and stools or through individual standing desks. Exercise is another executive function builder, and you can purchase desks today that have bicycle pedals so students can be moving while reading or working. For students, this can help to focus them on their work while moving.

Search the Web and look for innovative furniture ideas.

The Teacher's Desk

Consider how much teacher space is designated in the classroom. In some classrooms, the teacher has a desk, side table, and a couple of file cabinets all positioned across the front of the room, away from the board, thereby designating about seven to ten feet of the front of the room for the teacher's use. In the *Learner-Active, Technology-Infused Classroom*, when students are in the room, teachers are never seated at their desks or working apart from students. Let me say that again: In the *Learner-Active, Technology-Infused Classroom*, when students are in the room, teachers are never seated at their desks or working apart from students. This is very important as teachers need to spend their time facilitating learning and instructing. So all of that "teacher space" goes unused.

I've had teachers decide to remove their desks from the classroom to provide for more space, indicating that when students aren't in the room, they can use any table or desk to accomplish their work. All they need are some file cabinets and/or bookcases for their belongings, and those can fit in a corner of a room or against a wall. I've had teachers ask for smaller desks and/or push their desks against a side wall to open up more space in the room.

In one co-teaching classroom, the teachers asked for two teachers' desks so that both teachers would be seen as being equally important. Within a short period of time, they both asked to have their desks removed, realizing they took up too much space.

Consider how much space is designated in your classroom for the teacher. Take time to rethink furniture choices and positions.

Put Students in Charge

As students become acclimated to the *Learner-Active, Technology-Infused Classroom*, particularly when they are in a school where they attend such classrooms in successive years, engage them in rethinking classroom furniture or in designating how existing furniture should be arranged. Student voice is powerful in designing their own classroom. (You can let them know what you need to make your work easier.)

A group of students were enjoying flexible seating, based on their teacher's resourcefulness. When students in other classrooms indicated a desire for flexible seating, the class wrote for an educational foundation grant and ended up securing the funds for other classrooms to have flexible seating as well. These students were quite proud of what they made happen (efficacy is powerful).

RECAP

The physical classroom space supports your philosophy of teaching and learning. As you design your *Learner-Active, Technology-Infused Classroom*, consider how you can rethink the use of physical space to create an environment that is aligned with your philosophy. This chapter outlined several areas for you to consider. Use these summary points as you reflect:

- ◆ Collaborative Work Space;
- ◆ Individual Work Space;
- ◆ Discourse Centers;
- ◆ Computer Areas;
- ◆ Resource and Folder Area;
- ◆ Small-Group Mini-Lesson Area;
- ◆ Meeting Area;
- ◆ Limited Resource Area;
- ◆ Use of the Walls as Instructional Resources;
- ◆ Media-Based Collaborative Spaces;
- ◆ Comfortable, Fun, Dual-Purpose Furniture;
- ◆ Teacher's Desk;
- ◆ Student Voice in Classroom Design.

REFERENCE

Sulla, N. (2018). *Building executive function: The missing link to student achievement.* New York: Routledge.

8

Principles and Paradigm Shifts

The *Learner-Active, Technology-Infused Classroom* embodies four major paradigm shifts and ten principles. Throughout this book, you've explored all of these. Review the *ALU* and classroom plan you're designing to see what structures and strategies you might want to add to foster the ten principles and what paradigm shifts you need to hold dear as you rethink your daily life as an educator focusing on increasing student engagement, empowerment, and efficacy.

Principle 1: Higher-Order, Open-Ended Thinking

Higher-order thinking relies on, and thus builds, executive function skills. Seeing multiple sides to a situation, changing perspective, thinking about multiple concepts simultaneously, making inferences and predictions, applying former approaches to new situations, and being creative are just some of the executive function skills that are activated when you offer students higher-order challenges to tackle. While it is true that one must master the lower levels of Bloom's taxonomy before achieving the higher, attempting to build higher-order skills creates a *felt need* for the lower order skills.

The focus of secondary schooling is typically promoting higher-order thinking and application of the many skills you've learned in your elementary years. It is important to challenge students with questions and tasks that promote higher-order, open-ended thinking. Problem-based learning provides the perfect venue for this as it begins with the big picture and causes students to then search for support among the lower-order skills they've learned.

Challenging students to launch a campaign to encourage people to vote sparks dozens of questions causing students to dive into facts, statistics, and topics in civics. Challenging students develop a solution to save the whales and other sea life from the devastation of ingesting plastics that are filling up the ocean involves myriad skills for reading, analyzing, experimentation, and writing. Attempting to design a waterfall that could be constructed to provide hydroelectric power locally causes students to draw on what they've learned about design process, scientific method, designing experiments, recording and analyzing data, reading, writing, calculating information, and more. Armed with a motivating challenge, students will work to accomplish the lower-order skills in order to be able to handle the higher-order skills.

I've been in many classrooms where teachers focus heavily on building basic skills absent of a greater context through lessons, demonstrations, guided practice, and independent practice. Students are, at worst, bored and tuned out, and, at best, compliant. Neither state promotes long-term retention of learning. Students, however, will work tirelessly to solve a motivating problem, opening the door for building the basic skills in the context of something larger. As a middle school math teacher, I noted that the opening chapters of the text covered the basic skills of addition, subtraction, multiplication, and division, which my basic skills students had probably been badgered with for years. I told them we were beginning with Chapter 7, ratio and proportion, and we began designing scale drawings of birdhouses to attract as many different species as we could to the area. They were engaged, engrossed, empowered; they realized the need for strong calculation skills, and they mastered them. The *Learner-Active, Technology-Infused Classroom* is a higher-order thinking arcade! Students are engaged in higher levels of understanding and application of content in order to address the *problem-based task*. They have a variety of ways of learning; and they utilize higher-order skills in their decision-making regarding when, how, and with whom they will learn.

What Higher-Order, Open-Ended Thinking Looks Like in the Classroom

- ◆ Rather than merely presenting back information that they learned, students seek out information while working to offer solutions to solve open-ended problems;

- ◆ Teachers construct problems in which the solutions reside in the "unknown," forcing students to grapple with content that drives them back to what is "known";

- ◆ Students are given carefully crafted higher-order problems to solve that drive them to learn lower-order skills;

- ◆ Teachers design instructional activities that provide students with a challenge level slightly higher than their ability level, continuing to build toward higher and higher levels of cognitive function;

- Teachers function as instructional facilitators, asking questions that cause students to think at the higher levels of Bloom's taxonomy;

- Students participate in a wide range of strategic learning activities that foster content attainment and reach for synthesis and evaluation;

- Students manage how they will spend their time, making numerous decisions involving increasingly higher-order thinking;

- Students themselves propose suggestions for enhancing the *problem-based task* or become problem-finders themselves, developing their own *problem-based tasks* to pursue.

Principle 2: High Academic Standards

Students can accomplish amazing things when faced with high expectations and instructional supports: the two go hand in hand. Conversely, raising academic rigor absent of instructional support will only result in more failure. Teachers must overcome the tendency to teach to the level of the lowest-performing students and resist the temptation to think students aren't ready or able to achieve at high levels. Instead, they must teach to a high level and help all students reach that level through appropriate resources, accessible tools, and differentiated opportunities to learn. That is the true meaning of educational equity.

"Students can accomplish amazing things when faced with high expectations and instructional supports: the two go hand-in-hand."

A high school decided to detrack its English 9 students, combining three different tracks of students into one classroom. Early in their training in designing *Learner-Active, Technology-Infused Classrooms*, one teacher remarked that she now realizes she needs three different *ALUs*: one for each level of student. The consultant replied that she actually only needs one, the highest level for all students; and her role was to provide students with the resources and supports they need to all achieve at that high level. In the end, the school found that its lower-level students showed tremendous gains. High academic standards, coupled with the supports to achieve, is powerful.

Teachers often design their *analytic rubrics* so that most students can meet the Practitioner column without too much effort and many can reach the Expert column. Here's a fun challenge for you. Take your *analytic rubric*, cut out the Novice column, shift the remaining columns to the left, and write a new Expert column. This will ensure that you are presenting academic challenges to all students.

Look at your wall hangings and make sure that you are posting materials to the bulletin boards that offer higher expectations rather than content your students should already know. Regardless of what subject you teach, model the proper use of the English language in everything you post. Post resources that students can glance at while working that support their success. This may sound obvious, but take a look at your classroom walls and ask yourself, "If students get stuck learning this skill or concept, what is posted on the wall that will help them?" I sat across from a student and, in French, said hello, to which she responded in French. I then, continuing in French, asked her how she was. She responded, in French, "so-so." I then asked her why and she told me, in English, that was as far as she could go on her own at this point; she then pointed to the wall behind me that had beginning conversation phrases. Empower students to find what they need in the moment!

When facilitating, ask probing questions to prompt higher-order thinking. Share information that raises expectations. Challenge students with suggestions. Ask "What if?" questions.

Finally, your own word choice in the classroom can be used to achieve *high academic standards*. Use terms that are related to your field. Most state standards now refer to these as academic vocabulary and domain-specific vocabulary. Choose your words carefully. Think about the number of times you use "do" during the course of a conversation and, instead, use "conduct," "complete," "accomplish," and the like.

Avoid teaching the vocabulary word and, instead, give students a *felt need* to know the word. Use a word in context that is new to your students, and then define it in the same sentence. For example, "I appreciate your tenacity … your willingness to persist until you succeed." The student just learned a new word. Cognitively, at the point you say "tenacity," the student will most likely wonder what the word means, creating a level of cognitive dissonance. By then hearing the definition, the student will most likely remember it.

What High Academic Standards Look Like in the Classroom

♦ The expert column of an *analytic rubric* pushes students to tackle extended content and greater higher-order thinking related to the content;

♦ The classroom walls are filled with resources to support students and push their thinking;

♦ The teacher introduces vocabulary words, defining them in the sentence, while speaking;

♦ The teacher uses sophisticated sentence structure and grammar as modeling for students;

◆ When facilitating, the teacher asks questions that probe thinking, offers new information, and presents challenges;

Principle 3: Learning From a Felt Need

Years ago, I was teaching a high school computer science class in programming. It was a time when text-based, computerized adventure games were popular—before computer graphics! On the first day of class, I had my students play these computer games and write about their experiences. At the end of the period, I told them that during the semester they were going to design original programs. First, they had to map out their ideas for their games; then they would begin to write the programs. When my students needed to display text on the screen, I taught them how by offering a *how-to sheet* or a *small-group mini-lesson*. When they needed to refer to the player by name, I likewise taught them how to store variables. When a few were ready to keep track of the items the player picked up during the game, I taught them to use arrays (multivariable structures.) I then established them as *peer experts* as an option for their classmates. I carefully constructed the *problem-based task* so that students would need to use all of the concepts and skills in the curriculum. They learned through a *felt need*.

It can be easier just to present content to students; however, it is unlikely that they will remember it past the test, if that far. When students experience a *felt need* to learn, and they are then provided with just-in-time instruction, they retain that learning.

What Learning From a Felt Need Looks Like in the Classroom

◆ Students develop or are presented with *problem-based tasks* at the start of a unit of study that drive the need to learn concepts and skills;

◆ Students develop or read the *analytic rubric* at the start of a unit, identifying what they will need to learn in order to address the problem. From there, the teachers design instructional opportunities;

◆ Teachers offer *small-group mini-lessons* based on students' articulated needs;

◆ Students can explain why they are doing whatever activity they are doing and connect it to a greater instructional goal;

◆ Students access learning resources as they need them from a *resource area* and online sources;

♦ Students seek out additional resources in order to explore their own interests further.

Principle 4: Global Citizenship

In his book *The World is Flat* Thomas Friedman (2006) presents ten major events that have led to the increasing globalization of our society. It was just the beginning of a rapidly advancing focus on preparing students to be global citizens, realizing we are all part of one world: one small interdependent world. Technology has played a significant role in leveling the playing field economically across the globe. In a flat world, someone using a product in South America may be helped by someone in India. The distance between people around the world is greatly reduced by the ability to videoconference, email, and send instant messages at a cost no different from talking to one's neighbor.

People are becoming increasingly aware of others around the world, helped, in part by social media and websites. Events in one part of the world affect the entire world economically, environmentally, and politically. We can no longer refer to ourselves as just citizens of our towns or countries: we are rapidly becoming world citizens.

The *Learner-Active, Technology-Infused Classroom* provides students with many opportunities for building their skills as *global citizens*. Make direct connections to other countries in your classroom activities. Students can engage in online activities with students in other parts of the world.

Build students' overall awareness of other countries. Students studying government structures can identify similar governments in countries around the world. Students can trace inventions to other countries; and they can look at today's manufacturing cycle in terms of other countries around the world.

Build students' cultural acceptance of others around the world. You can begin with your students' national heritage and explore cultural customs and beliefs that exist today in those countries. In their lifetimes, students may visit and/or work in other countries. Technology will allow them to work virtually with people from around the world.

Build students' higher-order skills of analyzing cause-and-effect relationships among countries. As your students work to solve problems, have them consider what impact, if any, their solutions will have on other parts of the world.

What Global Citizenship Looks Like in the Classroom

♦ Students gather information through the Internet on issues and events from around the world;

- Students engage in *authentic learning units* (*ALUs*) that require a knowledge of and consideration for countries around the world;

- Students follow news from around the world and relate it to their own studies;

- Students engage with outside experts and students around the world through technology, showing evidence of their understanding of cultural differences;

- Teachers provide learning opportunities for students to interact with members of the larger community in which they live;

- Students participate in service projects that have an impact on their schools, town, state, country, and the world;

Principle 5: Technology Infusion

The *Merriam-Webster* online dictionary definition of the word *integrate* is "to form, coordinate or blend into a functioning or unified whole"; the definition of the word *infuse* is "to cause to be permeated with something … that alters usually for the better." For far too long, the use of technology in the classroom has begun with the technology itself, assuming that if we take the goal of studying spreadsheets and the goal of studying population distribution patterns, we can blend the two into one project with two goals. This is integration.

When technology permeates the classroom setting, students who are studying population distribution patterns naturally turn to the Internet to search for information, use spreadsheets to generate graphs, use videoconferencing to interview others, use multimedia to present a position statement, and more. Technology is not the goal; immigration is. Technology is merely a ubiquitous partner in the learning process. This is the goal of technology infusion.

Computer technology should be seamlessly infused into the classroom curriculum, with perhaps key benchmarks at certain grade levels. Computing devices need to be as readily available as pencils; and with smaller and less-expensive computing devices, this is now a real possibility. While many popular uses of computers are automational, allowing students to accomplish that which they could without a computer, though with more difficulty, the power of technology lies in allowing us to accomplish that which without a computer is impossible or too complicated: transformational technology use. Gathering real-time data from around the world, engaging in simulations, programming robots, engaging in "what if?" analysis given a set of numeric data, collaborating with those in remote locations, and more are just some of the ways technology enhances the learning environment through transformational use.

Learning how to use technology should be a "just-in-time" experience. Teaching students the A to Z of using a particular application fails to honor brain research and the need to build sense and meaning to maximize retention. As students use various applications, *how-to sheets* and video resources can provide them with specific skill instruction to meet their needs. It is not important to learn how to center a title if you are not using titles in your paper. At the point you need to learn to center a title, it is important that you know where to look to find the information. These days, much of that information can be found on the Internet.

Technology should be seamlessly infused into the learning environment with students accessing hardware and software as needed to pursue the greater goals of completing their *problem-based tasks*. When used effectively, technology becomes a powerful partner in the learning process, and particularly, for differentiating instruction. A television ad for a tablet PC has the student using the device to communicate with friends, capture photos of interesting scenes around her, look up information, create, and more. An adult sees her lying on the lawn working on the device and says, "What are you doing on your computer?" Her response is, "What's a computer?" That's infusion!

What Technology Infusion Looks Like in the Classroom

- ◆ Students seek out technology when they need it, in the course of pursuing other learning goals;

- ◆ Technology is readily available all of the time in the classroom;

- ◆ Teachers use technology to deliver lessons and have students engage in *learning activities*;

- ◆ Teachers use technology to communicate and collaborate with students;

- ◆ Teachers use technology to gather and analyze student achievement data and communicate with parents;

- ◆ Technology is utilized to provide multiple means of representation (*Universal Design for Learning*) for students at various learning readiness levels.

Principle 6: Individual Learning Path

Clearly, there are not enough hours in a day to set up an *individual learning path* for every student and monitor each student's progress. This is why *individual learning path* and *student responsibility for learning* go hand-in-hand. If you provide students with tools for assessing their own learning style preferences, and you offer various learning options, they will learn to make appropriate choices, with you providing guidance on those choices.

A teacher had students begin the year by completing an online assessment of their learning styles, which provided a graph of their preferences. They then designed business cards to hand out to their teachers and *home group* members, so others would get to know them. More importantly, the students themselves became aware of how some preferred listening to someone offer directions while others preferred seeing a written set of directions and diagram.

Some teachers use the "Learning Styles and Readiness Grid" (see Appendix I, but consider different headings for student use) as a choice sheet from which students select *learning activities*, based on their preferences and abilities. It's not unusual for teachers to offers students content-related texts based on different levels of difficulty from which students choose.

Assessment should not be merely a tool of the teacher; students should self-assess to become aware of their cognitive strengths and weaknesses. They can use a *learning dashboard* (Chapter 5) to monitor their progress. As the teacher and student determine where the student needs to build greater skills, together they can lay out a plan for success. When students are treated as partners in their own instructional plan, they make many decisions independent of the teacher.

A seventh-grade math teacher and I developed structures to allow students to develop their own *individual learning paths*. She would give students a math pretest consisting of seven questions from each key skill in the unit. Students then self-scored the tests and analyzed their results. If they answered all seven questions on a skill correctly, they completed a challenge activity that presented them with a higher cognitive level problem using that skill. If they answered four to six questions correctly, they completed two to three activities that focused on practicing the skill. If they answered two or three questions on a skill correctly, they completed *learning activities* related to building the skill, including required computer activities, podcasts, *peer expert* sessions, or *small-group mini-lessons*. If they answered fewer than two questions correctly, they began with introductory skill-building activities. This may sound like a lot of work—and it is up front—but consider how this approach allows students to follow an *individual learning path*. Once the pretests and activities are in place, the teacher is free to facilitate, advise, and offer targeted, direct instruction. The following year, materials may need to be reviewed and modified, but with far less effort than the initial year. The initial outlay of effort on the part of the teacher to design structures to build an *individual learning path* pays off in higher student achievement, more meaningful interactions with students, and decreased effort in lesson design over the long-term.

What Individual Learning Paths Look Like in the Classroom

- ♦ Teachers and students utilize assessment data to craft individual student plans to address the standards, identifying specific activities or creating individualized expectations for students;

- ♦ Students follow personal *activity lists* that address their learning styles and cognitive levels;

- ♦ Students self-assess content mastery and skill level, sharing their analysis with the teacher to mutually agree upon a learning path;

- ♦ Teachers and students identify or create varied *learning activities* for building content and skill mastery such that students can engage in those that are most well-suited for them;

- ♦ Students make decisions about how they will learn a skill or build content mastery.

Principle 7: Student Responsibility for Learning

Consider three compelling reasons for building *student responsibility for learning*. First, it will make your work easier in that students will make informed decisions about how to master curricular goals. Second, students will not always have you around to guide them as they learn throughout their lives. Third, doing so builds executive function. Conventional wisdom places teachers in an authority role in which they tell students what to do, when to do it, and how to do it, with the belief that students would fail without that level of direction. In the *Learner-Active, Technology-Infused Classroom*, the emphasis is on building students' skills in self-assessment and decision making in the learning process such that they can truly become lifelong learners.

Children are inquisitive from birth. From the time they can talk, they start asking questions and they explore everything within their reach. The quest for learning is innate, and children learn a tremendous amount from their peers. A skateboarder sees an interesting move and begins to put a plan into place to learn that move. It may include watching others in person, on television, and on videos posted on the Internet. It may include creating a practice course and making it increasingly harder. It may include endless hours of practice. Your students know how to take charge of their learning, but schools teach them early on simply to listen to the teachers and do as they are told, thus squelching this natural pursuit of learning in favor of compliance.

If you asked me to teach you about figurative language, I could sit down and describe different examples, but that would merely be telling you and expecting you to memorize, not fostering a learning environment. Alternatively, I could design a set of activities that would allow you to engage with text and explore the power of figurative language in the context of a bigger writing challenge for you, thus building in you a *felt need* for and a knowledge of figurative language that would last a lifetime. The former is easier; the latter requires great forethought and planning. However, in the case of the former, I will be presenting that lesson over and over again with student after student, year after year. In the case of the latter, I will design it once and empower a great number of students to take responsibility for learning, with only minor revisions across the years. The upfront investment required for designing the *Learner-Active, Technology-Infused Classroom*, which depends heavily on the principle of *student responsibility for learning*, will pay off considerably in student achievement and a greater sense of efficacy for you, the teacher.

What Student Responsibility for Learning Looks Like in the Classroom

- ♦ Students schedule their own time in the classroom based on the teacher's articulated expectations, choices of a diverse range of learning activities, including those they propose, and availability of a variety of resources;

- ♦ Students use *analytic rubrics*, checklists, and other structures to self-assess and set goals, with the guidance of the teacher;

- ♦ Students access a *resource area, help boards, quality work boards,* and *peer expert boards* in their quest for learning;

- ♦ Students reflect on their progress and practices and make adjustments to become more effective and productive learners, both as members of *home groups*, and as individuals.

Principle 8: Connected Learning

Students are motivated by real-world events, fueled by accessibility via the Internet. Brain research demonstrates that it is important to connect learning to students' lives; the reality-based shift in society provides additional evidence of the importance of *connected learning*.

Problem-based tasks provide the real-world authenticity for learning; the next step is to make deliberate connections to students' lives. English teachers have students write stories about their personal experiences. A global issues unit begins with students reflecting on their personal access to water. Math teachers have students evaluate the social media network strength of a favorite personage or organization. Music teachers have students deconstruct a song of their choice. In designing *problem-based tasks*, consider the activities or requirements that could be used to connect the learning to students' lives.

Connected learning also means connecting learning across the disciplines. Given the departmentalized nature of school, students do not always see how one subject's skills and concepts relate to the next. Fractions are used in cooking; the Greeks invented geometry; informational text is present in every subject area; art is filled with the use of math skills; and so forth.

What Connected Learning Looks Like in the Classroom

- ♦ Students engage in *problem-based tasks* based on real-world scenarios;

- ♦ Students engage in activities that ask students to reflect on the content based on their own lives and experiences;

- ♦ Students articulate how content from other subject areas helped them in completing the *problem-based task*;

- ♦ Teachers present connections to other subject areas in their *benchmark lessons, small-group mini-lessons,* and other instructional materials;

- ♦ Teachers use the Expert column of *analytic rubrics* to encourage students to explore further related content of interest.

Principle 9: Collaboration

Cooperative learning describes a group working together and typically dividing up tasks to complete a particular assignment. The word *cooperate* intimates "putting up with one another" for the common good. For example, if the class wants to get dismissed on time, everyone should cooperate and pay attention to the teacher. *Collaborate*, on the other hand, intimates that some new knowledge is going to be developed based on the "two-heads-are-better-than-one" principle. *Collaboration* results in an end product that is enhanced by the input of more than one person; thus, collaborative activities are open-ended and focused on higher-order thinking.

"*Collaboration* results in an end product that is enhanced by the input of more than one person; thus, collaborative activities are open-ended and focused on higher-order thinking."

Problem-based tasks offer students rich opportunities to collaborate. Devising a platform for a new political party, creating a plan to reduce the carbon footprint of the community, deciding on how to dispose of nuclear waste, developing a proposing a plan and budget for a new business, writing an original song to promote school unity, and the like are all powerful venues for *collaboration*.

Consequently, it is important to carefully structure collaborative work. Students should work together to brainstorm, critique ideas, share relevant information, develop questions, and evaluate their work. They should work independently to research topics, build content mastery, and develop ideas to bring to the larger group. As you design your activity lists, be sure to build in a meaningful distinction between individual work and group work.

It can be useful to have students develop a set of "team norms" of expected rules of engagement, such as: one person speaks at a time, all members are encouraged to participate, and avoid monopolizing the conversation. Additionally, students need to be able to handle "roadblocks" that veer the discussion off topic. Construct a "roadblock management chart" by dividing a piece of paper into four quadrants. Label them:

- Off topic—save for a later discussion;

- We need more information that is not available right now—save until information is available;

- We do not have the authority to make this decision;

- We need other people to make this decision.

When students find themselves stuck in an unresolved conversation, they should stop and write down the current discussion points in one of the four quadrants. This allows them to capture the information and frees them to move on.

Students may also need collaborative brainstorming tools, such as Edward de Bono's ever popular "six hats" (1996) or "PMI" (1992). The six hats method has the students look at a problem or proposed solution from six perspectives. The yellow hat is optimistic, black hat is skeptical, red hat expresses emotion, green hat is creative, blue hat is into the organization of the process, and white hat focuses on objective facts. This method allows you to honor all perspectives, such as: "Put on your yellow hat for a minute and tell me what is great about this idea. Put on your black hat and tell me what could go wrong or why it won't work. Put on your green hat to see if you can come up with another idea."

PMI stands for Plus, Minus, and Interesting facts or questions. Students use a three-column sheet to analyze a possible solution or idea. In a short, designated amount of time, they write down two positive points, two negative points, and then two, related, interesting ideas or questions. Following personal reflection, each group member has an opportunity to share and be heard. Students in the group begin to see emerging trends and innovative ideas.

Both of these tools, and others, help students build their skills in critical thinking and problem-solving, which are important skills for collaboration. Consider introducing a new tool every couple of weeks to build your students' repertoire of collaborative work tools.

You'll want to establish a process for handling conflicts among team members as well. The first step should be to have the students sit down and talk about their differences to see if they can work it out. If that doesn't work, you might suggest the use of a peer mediator. Next, you might have the students sit down with you. Avoid allowing students to complain about one another to you without the other present. They are in a learning mode, so you do need to ensure that the collaborative relationships are productive and enhancing each student's individual progress. In your facilitation, you will get a sense if one student is not working to the effort of the rest of the team, if one student is being too bossy, and so forth. It is clearly better for you to assess the ability of the group members to work well collaboratively than it is for them to approach you and complain about one another. Ultimately, you want them to take responsibility for building collaborative relationships.

What Collaboration Looks Like in the Classroom

- Two to four students meet with a specific goal that is part of a greater problem-solving effort. For example, when deciding how to build a biodome to support life on Mars, an early group effort would be to brainstorm everything the students need to know to begin to make a decision;

- Students are challenged, in groups, to solve open-ended problems requiring them to apply curricular content, through which they build mastery in that content;

- Students use various structures, including protocols and norms, to ensure that all students have the opportunity to participate and that all group interactions are positive;

- Students take individual responsibility to contribute expertise and information to the group;

- Students take the responsibility for each member of the group being successful in both content mastery and group interactions;

- Students use Internet-based tools to work collaboratively both inside and outside the classroom;

- Students use Internet-based tools to work collaboratively with students in other classrooms and geographically distant locations.

Principle 10: High Social Capital

The term *social capital* dates as far back as 1916 (Hanifan) to an article on rural schooling pointing out that social networks bring a benefit to their members. A family is a social network as is a local community, work community, and, these days, online social communities. In more recent years, James Coleman (1988) popularized the term, suggesting that social networks, specifically local communities, had a direct correlation to the production of its members and the achievement of students in schools.

High social capital can be described as the relationships that are forged in a community between its adults and its young people. In communities that are characterized by *high social capital*, parents often know the names of other children in the neighborhood; they'll offer children they know a ride; they'll cheer for children at sporting events and congratulate individuals on their successes; they'll call one another to share what they saw, particularly if anything they see is suspicious. Children who grow up in communities with *high social capital* tend to do well in school. In communities that are characterized by low social capital, children move through the neighborhood seemingly unnoticed; often no one at home asks about them or their schooling; sometimes children are left home alone for long periods of time without anyone checking in on them; parents in the community do not necessarily know the other children nor engage with them. Children who grow up in communities with low social capital tend to struggle in school. Furthermore, children from communities with low social capital who attend private or parochial schools that foster *high social capital* tend to improve their academic performance.

Strong, caring relationships between adults and children contribute to improved student performance. These relationships are a characteristic of the *Learner-Active, Technology-Infused Classroom*. In conventional schooling, where teachers spent much of their time in the front of the room dispensing information, there are few opportunities to build relationships between adults and children. A student might enjoy a positive comment on a paper from a teacher, or the teacher might ask the student to linger after school to talk about accomplishments, and occasionally a teacher would be seen at a school event engaging in conversation with a student.

In the *Learner-Active, Technology-Infused Classroom*, teachers build strong relationships with students throughout the day. They increase social capital through the venue of the *small-group mini-lessons* where they are sitting with and talking to a small number of students, sharing information, asking questions, and encouraging students to succeed. Teachers have numerous one-on-one conversations with students throughout the course of the day. As teachers move throughout the classroom, the "never hover" rule causes teachers to pull up a chair and sit with students face to face, engaging in productive and motivating conversations about content.

In classrooms with more than one adult, such as the co-teaching classroom, and in classrooms that regularly involve parents and community members, students enjoy considerable interaction with adults who care about them. This builds *high social capital*, which yields results in increased student achievement.

What High Social Capital Looks Like in the Classroom

♦ Teachers spend class time largely sitting with students discussing their work, goals, and accomplishments;

♦ Multiple adults work in the classroom with students, thus providing greater adult–student interaction;

♦ Teachers and students design *problem-based tasks* and instructional activities that require students to engage with their parents, family members, and other adults in their lives;

♦ Parents and community members are regular participants in the learning process, either in person or through virtual connections;

♦ Teachers and students develop online or print newsletters for the community that celebrate the successes of the students.

Paradigm: Teaching From a Felt Need

As you move forward in implementing your *Learner-Active, Technology-Infused Classroom*, continuously ask yourself if you're responding to students' *felt need* to learn. At the unit level, that means either presenting students with a compelling problem that will motivate them, or, ultimately, having students identify problems they want to solve while you determine how their problems can build required curricular skills. Even at the skill level, however, how will you connect learning to meaningful purposes? Within your *ALU*, work to ensure that all learning stems from students feeling a need for the information. This includes encouraging them to decide how their solutions to problems could be even better, leading to new learning.

Paradigm: Teacher as Ferry Versus Teacher as Bridge Builder

As you design, reflect on, and redesign your *Learner-Active, Technology-Infused Classroom*, keep in the forefront of your mind the goal of becoming a bridge builder who empowers students. Compliance is no longer enough! Think through the smallest events in your classroom: what students do when they enter, how they hand in papers, how they get materials, how they get help, how they make suggestions, and so on. How can you build the structures to put them in charge of their own learning?

Paradigm: Don't Grade the Learning Process

While there is a tendency in schools to grade anything students hand in, remember that in the *Learner-Active, Technology-Infused Classroom*, you are using a *problem-based task* to build a felt need for learning and to launch a unit of study. Students should not be able to accomplish this without you at this point in their studies. Throughout the unit, you will be guiding them, offering feedback and suggestions, celebrating their successes. By the time their solution is ready to be presented, it should be in the *Practitioner* column of the *analytic rubric* because of your involvement; that's your job. Remember, to grade it would merely be grading yourself. Rather than grading the learning experience, offer a testing situation transfer task (Chapter 3) to grade individual content mastery.

Paradigm: Trigger Awareness

When you stand in front of your class, use all of your inspiration, talents, knowledge, expertise, experience, and tricks of the trade to trigger students' awareness of what they need to learn. Then, mic drop! Walk away! The true learning will take place when students engage in learning activities, not from you. If you feel the urge to teach the whole class because you want to ensure that they get it, forget it! Brain research will tell you that approach is futile, as not all of your students are ready to learn. Instead, identify a set of *learning activities*, including *small-group mini-lessons* for targeted audiences, to ensure that all students learn. Inspire, then lead students to learn through their own engagement with content.

RECAP

Consider your classroom, the unit you are designing, and the overall activities, structures, and strategies that take place in your classroom. Continually reflect on how you can foster these ten principles in your classroom:

- Higher-Order, Open-Ended Problem Solving;
- High Academic Standards;
- Learning from a Felt Need;
- Global Citizenship;
- Technology Infusion;
- Individual Learning Path;
- Student Responsibility for Learning;
- Connected Learning;
- Collaboration;
- High Social Capital;

Continually reflect on how you can reflect the four key paradigm shifts:

- Teaching from a Felt Need;
- Teacher as Ferry vs. Teacher as Bridge Builder;
- Don't Grade the Learning;
- Trigger Awareness.

REFERENCES

Coleman, J. S. (1988). Social capital in the creation of human capital. *American Journal of Sociology*, Supplement 94, S95–S120.
de Bono, E. (1992). *Serious creativity*. New York: Harper Business.
de Bono, E. (1996). *Six thinking hats* (2nd ed.). Boston: Back Bay Books.
Friedman T. (2006). *The world is flat*. London: Penguin.
Hanifan, L. J. (1916). The rural school community center. *Annals of the American Academy of Political and Social Science*, 67, 130–138.

9

Special Considerations

The *Learner-Active, Technology-Infused Classroom* is a framework for putting students in charge of their own learning. It holds much promise for increasing student engagement, empowerment, and efficacy leading to stronger student achievement. Given that it is a framework for instruction, it is flexible enough to accommodate most of the instructional approaches that schools are pursuing, such as co-teaching classrooms, STEM and STEAM, career academies, Advanced Placement courses, Universal Design for Learning (UDL), Response to Intervention (RTI), and more. It allows you to address the needs of all students in one, fully differentiated classroom environment, including students with disabilities, English-language learners, gifted learners, and those who struggle with learning content. This chapter will address a number of the various ways that the *Learner-Active, Technology-Infused Classroom* can meet the needs of your classroom, school, or district. It focuses on understanding and higher-order application of content. It's important to remember that the *Learner-Active, Technology-Infused Classroom* is not a strategy that you use some of the time; it's an umbrella, of sorts, that pulls together all of the programs, resources, and approaches you wish to incorporate into your classroom.

> "the *Learner-Active, Technology-Infused Classroom* is not a strategy that you use some of the times; it's an umbrella, of sorts, that pulls together all of the programs, resources, and approaches you wish to incorporate into your classroom."

No matter what your instructional need, you can emphasize different aspects of the *Learner-Active, Technology-Infused Classroom* to address it. You can incorporate customized language to promote a specific approach. For example, if you are implementing Accountable Talk (University of Pittsburgh), your discussion protocols would include language related to the types of questions and statements they will make, such as affirm, agree, disagree, clarify, and so forth.

No matter what your overarching goal, given that your *Learner-Active, Technology-Infused Classroom* is a departure from conventional classrooms, take care to introduce students to the various structures and strategies so that they meet with success from day one. This is accomplished through a *priming plan*. Beyond that, customize your classroom structures and language to meet your needs: just stay true to the paradigm shifts and the "why" behind each structure as you do.

The Priming Plan

In many cases, students in a *Learner-Active, Technology-Infused Classroom* will experience a variety of new structures and have different responsibilities from the classrooms from which they came. In order to avoid having students begin the year or course with confusion and frustration, it's important to begin with a *priming plan*. This is a one-week unit (if you meet with your students daily) or two-week unit (if you meet with them every other day) that engages students in a variety of activities aimed at three overarching goals:

- ◆ Introducing students to all of the structures of the *Learner-Active, Technology-Infused Classroom;*

- ◆ Priming students for academic success through hope, confidence, and optimism;

- ◆ Gathering assessment data related to academics and social interaction to make decisions for the first *Authentic Learning Unit (ALU)*.

You will design a variety of activities such that, throughout the *priming plan*, students will be engaged individually, in small groups, and in pairs both with and without your direct involvement. Given that you want to observe student interactions with others, change *home groups* daily and have every activity focusing on different ways in which to learn with and without others. That means, you will not use a typical *ALU*, since an *ALU* is meant to be collaborative in nature and span a period of several weeks. You will introduce students to the structures of *problem-based tasks* and *analytic rubric*, but one that can be addressed in a few days.

Your role in the *Learner-Active, Technology-Infused Classroom* is to act as a bridge builder to empower your students, not as a ferry moving them along. However, in the beginning, you need to start out somewhat like a ferry to offer enough overt direction and gradually release the control to your students over the course of the *priming plan*. After the *priming plan*, you'll launch your first *ALU*.

Walking Through the Door

As you envision your students walking into your classroom space for the first time, how will you immediately engage and empower them? One approach is to engage them in a scavenger hunt of sorts to locate structures and learn the meaning of different places in the classroom.

Imagine students walking into the room and having you hand them a piece of a picture. Their job is to find the other two or three people that make up the full image, which then has directions on it. Students engage in various activities related to the subject area that cause them to need to:

♦ Retrieve items from the *resource table;*

♦ Set up their physical or digital *folder;*

♦ Add their name to the *peer expert board;*

♦ Learn about special areas or structures specific to your content area;

♦ Use a *rubric* to self-assess;

♦ Engage in curricular activities you would consider to be a starting point for the course.

You could offer math or science students problems to solve where they must arrive at an answer and find a group based on common answers. You could offer world language students a sentence in the target language that leads them to their group. You could offer English students quotes from well-known literature. It's fun to watch students try to figure out who is in their group. Be careful to structure it so that they must find their group members before finding their location. Otherwise, students will just go to a location and wait for others to arrive; that's mere compliance. Get them engaged in problem-solving from the start: who else has an excerpt from the same author? How will I find the students who arrive at the same answer upon solving the problem on their cards? Who else has synonyms for the word I was given? Who else has a matching puzzle piece?

Secondary teachers often designate areas of the room and have students move to all of them over the course of the week. In each area, students find a description of the use of the area and complete some related activity. For example, you might have a soft seating area or conference table at which students engage in discussion, and have them use a discussion protocol to engage in a practice session. You might designate lab tables for experiments and have students review safety rules. You might have study carrels for students who wish to work on independent work and offer an assignment that will give you insights into their current knowledge level.

The key is to put students in a position of being in charge of their own actions as soon as they walk through the door. That means coming up with a way to have them find a group, a set of activities or locations, and clear directions they can follow on their own.

Priming Plan Task

Unlike in an *ALU*, the *priming plan* task should be short, lasting for just a week or two. Here are some ideas to start the year:

◆ What's your problem? Have students consider the overall content for the year, perhaps reading some articles, and identify several problems they might want to solve related to the content. This is especially good for students who have been learning in *Learner-Active, Technology-Infused Classrooms* for years.

◆ Let's make this year a success! As you learn more about the course goals, your job is to create a guide for you and for me to ensure you have a successful experience in this course. Students will write about their goals for the course, assess themselves on a *Great Student Rubric*, take a learning styles inventory, and more.

◆ Learning is social! Have students develop a plan for how they can successfully engage in the course, learning from peers while still taking personal responsibility for content mastery. This is a good way to get to know your students and have them reflect on their strengths and weaknesses as a student.

◆ The Game of Classroom! This is especially good for students who have learned in *Learner-Active, Technology-Infused Classrooms* in the past and have some level of knowledge of the structures. Students get to know the classroom, subject-area content focus, and you as a teacher and develop a board game, digital game, or app that others can play. Given the complexity of this, you might have students develop the games in pairs and allocate time for them to work on it throughout the *priming plan* while using other time to have them engaging with others. The games should require students to have to know the ins and outs of this *Learner-Active, Technology-Infused Classroom*.

Try to identify a *problem-based task* that may involve some learning but focuses more on knowledge students already have. The *problem-based task* in an *ALU* is meant to be used to launch a unit through which students are learning new content; that's why they span four to five weeks. However, if your students already knew all of the content, that same *ALU* would probably take a day or two; that's the intent here. You're seeking to find out what skills and content they possess, who they are as a learner, and how they interact with others, while teaching them to utilize the structures of your *Learner-Active, Technology-Infused Classroom*.

Priming Plan Activities

Unlike the activities that are part of an *ALU*, which are meant to promote learning new content, during the *priming plan*, the activities will focus more on strengthening foundational skills and learning how to use the classroom structures. Offer short assessments of their content knowledge. You might use a facilitation grid of some key prerequisite skills you expect them to have. You might offer some pre-assessments to see if some students have already mastered some of the content of the next unit.

Offer *benchmark lessons* on content needed for the *problem-based task*, how to succeed in the classroom, and to set the stage for the *ALU* that will start soon. At the start of the year, particularly if students are used to teachers presenting content, conduct one short *benchmark lesson* each class period. As you move into your first *ALU*, transition students to fewer across the week, ensuring they understand that the *benchmark lesson* will offer them an idea of what they need to learn to succeed in finding a solution for their *problem-based task*. During the *priming plan*, offer benchmark lessons on the purpose and use of the *two-pocket folder, analytic rubric, activity list, schedule,* and more.

The *learning activities* and other resources should include *how-to sheets, direction sheets,* and *protocols*. Have students engage in small-group discussions following a *protocol*. Have them follow *direction sheets* as a group to engage in an activity. Have them retrieve skill-based *how-to sheets* from the resource table. The sooner students learn to independently follow printed instructions, the better the classroom will run.

Create activities that will ensure students understand all of the structures of your *Learner-Active, Technology-Infused Classroom*. Take time to offer assessments and to gather facilitation data so you have a strong sense of what each student will need to succeed on your first *ALU*.

Some teachers write their students a letter for each to open and read, sharing their interest and experience in their subject area, then asking that students write a letter about their previous experiences and interest in the subject area in return. This can serve as a writing assessment.

Great Student Rubric

Introduce students to rubrics in the *priming plan* by using a *Great Student Rubric* in which you offer clearly articulated expectations for student behavior and work habits. See Appendix J for sample *Great Student Rubrics*. Develop one that works for you and your students. Have students assess themselves, set goals, and reflect on their progress. Strong work habits and behavior lay a strong foundation for academic achievement. Your *Great Student Rubric* can address key executive function skills as well. Depending on the level of familiarity your students have with the *Learner-Active,*

Technology-Infused Classroom, you can have them offer suggestions for designing the *Great Student Rubric.*

Sociograms

Observe how students work with one another. Who are the natural leaders? Who are inclined to take over? Who are inclined to depend too heavily on others? Which students seem to work well together? Which do not? You can create a sociogram by asking students to write down three other students in the class with whom they like to work, explaining that you may not always be able to have them working together, but you will try for at least some of the time. Then put a set of circles on a page with one student's name per circle. Draw arrows from each student to the ones they said they would like as work partners. Once all the lines are drawn, analyze your sociogram. Some students will have a lot of arrows pointing at them, designating them as stars. You can use your stars wisely to teach them to model productive behaviors and proper use of structures. Some students will have few to no arrows pointing at them, designating them as isolates. You'll want to keep an eye on these students to ensure they are well placed in groups in which they can thrive. Two students who choose one another are said to have made a mutual choice. Three or more students who all mutually choose one another are known as a clique. The insights you glean from a sociogram can be useful as you start creating *home groups* for the first *ALU.*

Response to Intervention (RTI) and Multi-Tiered System of Supports (MTSS)

While RTI was originally introduced at the elementary school level, it is gaining more popularity at the middle and high school levels. The RTI framework is a powerful approach to instruction that avoids labeling students by ability or disability, and instead speaks to the need for different types of instructional interventions. Educators begin with "Tier I" instruction for all students, using high-quality, differentiated strategies, and formative assessment to gauge student progress. If some students begin to fall behind in content mastery, educators are asked to apply "Tier II" intervention methods, involving small-group instruction. The goal is to position students to succeed through Tier I instruction. If students receiving Tier II interventions are still failing to master content, educators are asked to provide them with "Tier III" interventions, involving one-on-one instruction, often with a specialized teacher. The *Learner-Active, Technology-Infused Classroom* provides the perfect venue for offering Tiers I, II, and III instruction, potentially, all in the same physical classroom. With students managing their own time in a fully differentiated instructional environment, it's easy for teachers to provide Tier II *small-group mini-lessons* and provide students who are struggling with specific content more targeted, ability-based *learning activities*. A coteacher can join the classroom working with small groups or individual students, maximizing productivity in this classroom that is characterized by minimal whole-group instruction. The *Learner-Active, Technology-Infused Classroom* is a model RTI classroom.

A multi-tiered system of supports (MTSS) includes RTI but expands beyond its academic focus to include social and emotional supports. It involves continual progress monitoring through formative assessments. *Home groups, Great Student Rubrics,* and *peer experts* are just a few structures of the *Learner-Active, Technology-Infused Classroom* that can provide social supports. Given the differentiated learning environment and heavy reliance on teacher facilitation, the *Learner-Active, Technology-Infused Classroom* provides the perfect venue for supporting students in social and emotional learning as well as academic achievement. Varied formative assessments and *content facilitation grids* provide for continual progress monitoring.

If you are attempting to embrace an MTSS or RTI approach to instruction, this book will help you design an effective classroom aligned with a multi-tiered system of supports.

The Co-Teaching, Inclusive Classroom

An inclusive classroom is one in which students with and without disabilities learn together. The differentiated nature of the *Learner-Active, Technology-Infused Classroom* makes it the perfect venue for an inclusive setting. Students will be working on different activities, often oblivious to what anyone else is working on. Teachers can offer all students the support they need to excel.

To address the needs of a diverse class of learners, some of which are identified as having learning disabilities, typically two certified teachers, at least one with special education certification, join together to co-teach the group of students. In a conventional classroom setting that focuses on the teacher first presenting content, followed by students practicing toward mastery, having two teachers in a classroom can present some challenges. Often the sharing of teaching falls into one of three categories: one teacher presents content while the other quietly kneels or sits next to a student offering cues, such as pointing to the place on a paper; the teachers split the group and both teach to a subset group; or one teacher teaches and the other grades papers or prepares for a future lesson. None of these is optimal, however, as the structure of a teacher-centered environment does not easily lend itself to co-teaching.

The *Learner-Active, Technology-Infused Classroom* is a student-driven learning environment that offers teachers new possibilities for joining together to promote student achievement. It is the optimal framework for co-teaching.

There are four distinctly different ways in which co-teachers engage in the *Learner-Active, Technology-Infused Classroom*:

- **Group and Guide**: While one teacher is offering a *small-group mini-lesson*, the other is facilitating the rest of the class, guiding them academically and in their processes. Both teachers take turns offering *small-group mini-lessons* so that one is not always the instructor in this setting.

- **Dual-Focus Facilitation**: When students are working on various activities they've scheduled, both teachers move around the classroom facilitating learning. While both teachers will assist students as needed, they each have a specific focus for their facilitation and utilize a *facilitation grid* tailored to that focus. For example, one may be looking to glean data related to student mastery of the unit content while the other may be focusing on executive function skills. The teachers would carry both *facilitation grids*, to capture formative assessment data as it emerges; however, their questions would be geared to their facilitation focus.

- **Balanced Benchmark Lesson**: During a benchmark lesson, rather than having one teacher present while the other watches, both teachers play a role. This requires some level of planning and coordination, but strategically, the teachers can play off one another. One might ask questions while the other responds. One might offer a statement or explanation followed by the other then contributing, which causes students to have to attend and shift focus from one to the other, thus building executive function. The two teachers might act out a skit.

- **Individualized Inspiration**: One teacher holds individual conferences with students while the other facilitates learning. In a *Learner-Active, Technology-Infused Classroom* with one teacher, it is difficult to offer one-on-one conferences as it takes the teacher away from the rest of the class. With two teachers, one can hone in on individual students to review their progress and inspire them to tackle new challenges. Teachers can share this responsibility, with one meeting with part of the class and the other meeting with the rest. These conferences can also be offered to a subset of students who are at a point where the conference makes sense.

It is important to create a culture of equal adults in the co-teaching classroom. Both names should be on any materials related to the course.

Students should see themselves as having two teachers, not a regular education teacher and a special education teacher. I am not a fan of the big teacher desk in a classroom as it takes up a lot of precious space. While teachers may need space for their belongings and materials, during class they are with students and, when students are out of the room, they can use any table space in the classroom to accomplish their work. So two desks would definitely not be my preference; however, equality is important in creating a co-teaching culture. Both teachers should have space for materials in the classroom. If there is going to be a desk, it should be shared or the teachers should each have a small desk.

STEM/STEAM

Computer automation has shifted the job market away from the rote, factory jobs of the last three centuries to a focus on design. At this point, people are needed to solve problems and design product solutions; computer-automated factories build those products. Consider the rise of the 3-D printer that allows students to create models that they otherwise would have had to build by hand. Are we developing a future workforce of design-oriented people? Add to that the need for more workers in the areas of science, technology, engineering, and math. Job positions lie vacant for months waiting for qualified individuals.

STEM (science, technology, engineering, and math) and STEAM (arts added) education has emerged as a priority in schools. Additional letters have entered into the name as well. For the purpose of this section, I will use the term STEM, acknowledging that the additional foci are addressed here as well. As with most innovations, schools are challenged by the idea of infusing the concept into the current instructional plan. Instead, they add a course, specialized teacher, or program. You will often hear of STEM days, the STEM lab, the STEM teacher, and so forth. The problem, still, is that students can learn to program objects, build prototypes, and land flight simulator jets without making connections to or tapping into their passion for STEM careers. Until we view STEM as a part of a rich, bold tapestry of every student's daily experience, we will fall short of preparing students for STEM careers for the following reason.

What is most obvious about STEM in schools is what I will refer to as the "stuff": 3-D printers, robot kits, programmable objects, computer simulations, 3-D goggles. These are all very exciting and, for students, a wonderful departure from their typical daily instructional resources. STEM resources can be expensive, and in a conventional setting in which every student needs a pair of 3-D goggles or a robot kit, budget constraints can limit access to a wide variety of materials. Given the *Learner-Active, Technology-Infused Classroom* is a place where not all students are working on the same activity at the same time, you can purchase fewer of each STEM item and, thus, a wider variety of items. Students will then sign up for *limited resources* so that the class can get the most out of the resources available.

It is incumbent upon educators to attach the STEM "stuff" to a greater purpose, which, in the *Learner-Active, Technology-Infused Classroom* is a *problem-based task*. In the case of STEM, that would be a real-world problem to solve that requires the STEM "stuff" to solve. Students can design solutions to the challenges faced by disabled persons in everyday life. Given the heightened concern about the reduction in the population of our natural pollinators, bees and bats, they can seek to design an automated pollinator drone. University students, organizations, and even K–12 students are engaging in designing and printing prosthetic hands for those in need. One organization of volunteers, enablingthefuture.org, as of the writing of this book, allows you to obtain a hand, build a hand, or volunteer to help in building hands for others. Might students design an app for a tablet or phone to improve people's daily lives that doesn't yet exist? Given a real-world problem to solve, students engage even more deeply in learning how to use the "stuff" of STEM. However, even that's not enough to prepare students for STEM careers.

The *Learner-Active, Technology-Infused Classroom* is a perfect venue for STEM. Students engage in a *problem-based task* and they can sign up for the use of limited resources. What makes someone passionate about STEM and pursuing a related career? It's the way a person's mind works, the way they think about the world around them, the way they see connections among the disciplines and possibilities for solutions. They possess what I call the mindsets of STEM. I believe if we are truly to prepare students to pursue a STEM career, it is our moral imperative to ensure they possess the mindsets of the scientist, technologist, engineer, and mathematician (see

Figure 9.1. The Moral Imperative of STEM

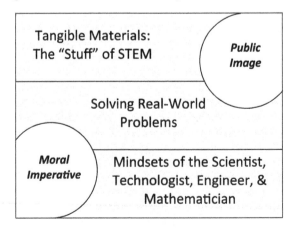

Figure 9.1). Otherwise, all we've given them are great experiences with fun STEM "stuff." In order to transfer their learning to the world around them, seeing the world through a STEM lens requires that students possess the mindsets of STEM. While watching students look through 3-D goggles and print on 3-D printers is exciting, hearing them make connections and speak in ways that demonstrate their true understanding of STEM is even more exciting!

Accomplishing this simply requires tapping into some powerful ideas that are already available to you. The Next Generation Science Standards (www.nextgenscience.org) offer a set of crosscutting concepts that transcend the disciplines: patterns; cause and effect; scale, proportion, and quantity; systems and systems models; energy and matter (flows, cycles, and conservation); structure and function; stability and change. Several of those are concepts that are easily identifiable in other content. Making those concepts visible to students across the subjects builds in them the mindset of a scientist. The Common Core offers math practice standards which, similarly, cross all subject areas. A technologist considers all the ways in which technology can help in solving problems, including: information retrieval, communication, collaboration, simulation, modeling, design, and presentation. An engineer uses a design process, which can be applied across all subject areas. See Appendix K for a chart illustrating these mindsets.

In the problem-based learning environment of the *Learner-Active, Technology-Infused Classroom,* students can engage in real-world problem-solving using an engineering design process and STEM technologies while building the mindsets of a scientist, technologist, engineer, and mathematician.

Design Process

Throughout school, students learn the scientific method: a series of six steps for uncovering a scientific truth. Scientific method seeks to explain what exists. A well-conducted experiment will prove that certain plants

Figure 9.2. Design Process

(c) 2016, IDE Corp. - reprinted with permission

thrive in sunlight, gravity pulls objects to the Earth, oil and water do not mix, and so forth.

When solving an open-ended, authentic problem, there is no one, right answer or known truth. The solution to the global water crisis does not yet exist. Inventions and innovations are, by nature, that which does not yet exist. While various experiments and the use of the scientific method are necessary in solving open-ended problems, the overarching approach should be guided by a design process. A design process seeks to create that which does not exist. IDE Corp.'s (www.idecorp.com) design process is depicted in Figure 9.2 and explained in what follows.

♦ Formulate—Think through the problem and ensure that you understand it fully. Ask yourself:

   – What is the reality?

   – How does this situation affect others?

   – What is the ideal situation?

   – What must it be like for those affected by this problem?

   – What would happen if the problem was not solved?

♦ Explore—Delving into the problem more deeply, search for existing information, conduct experiments, and gather as much knowledge as you can about the various aspects of the problem. This is where subject-area, content learning takes place. Ask yourself:

   – What do you know?

   – What do you need to know?

   – How will you learn that?

   – What are some reliable sources you can use to gather your information?

   – Who would be affected by solving or ignoring the problem?

♦ Ideate—Generate as many possible solutions as you can, being careful not to judge any. Just let your creativity flow. Ask yourself:

   – What are some solutions to the problem?

   – Do you need to explore further before you can create a solution?

♦ Sift—Consider all the ideas generated to see which, if any, would work. Ask yourself:

- Which ideas could work?

- Which ideas are feasible?

- What are the possible unintended consequences of each idea?

- What else could go wrong?

- Do you need to explore and/or ideate further? Do you need more ideas?

♦ Simulate—Once you have an idea you think will work, give it wings! Create a prototype, mock-up, sample, model, or anything else that will allow you to test it to build your confidence that it is a viable solution. Ask yourself:

- How might you create a prototype or mock up that you can test out?

- How can you test your solution?

- What did you learn from this prototype that will help you with the next one?

- Were you able to test your solution?

- Should you return to sift or ideate further solutions?

♦ Advocate—No idea will change the world if it isn't implemented or shared. The final step of the design process is to promote your idea: share it with an appropriate audience. Ask yourself:

- Who needs to know this; who is your audience?

- Who can help you put your ideas into action?

- How will you share your ideas (a video, website, model, etc.)?

- Where will/can your ideas end up?

While the design process is linear in that you must move through the steps in order, at any point, you can return to a prior step. Once you simulate your chosen idea, you may find it doesn't work. At that point you would return to either sift through other ideas, ideate some more, or explore the topic further.

Given that in the *Learner-Active, Technology-Infused Classroom*, students are always working to solve real-world problems, offer them a design process to guide their work. Whether they're developing a prototype for a space vehicle for Mars, a poem, or a plan for engaging in civil war, students can use a design process to guide their process. The discipline of the process and the individual, purposeful steps will help build executive function and increase likelihood of success.

Equity-Focused Instruction

Not all students come to school with the same background, skills, learning styles, or prerequisite knowledge. Educational equity involves providing students with the supports that they individually need to succeed. Instructional lessons delivered to the entire class do not necessarily take into account the differences among students, and if they do, the presenter is hard-pressed to meet the needs of all students from the front of the room.

A classroom provides students with **resources** (such as audio recordings, texts, primary sources, and videos), **tools for learning** (such as calculators, computers, manipulatives, and rulers), and **opportunities for instruction** (such as *learning activities*, *peer expert* assistance, teachers' facilitation, and teachers' lessons). Equality means offering all students the same resources, tools, and opportunities; equity means offering each student the resources, tools, and opportunities that student needs to succeed. While one student might need an auditory explanation of a concept, another might need a visual to accompany any description. While one student might easily follow a *how-to sheet* to learn a skill, another student who lacks strong executive function might need additional visuals and chunking of content. While one student may access a *learning activity* on a skill listed on the *analytic rubric*, another might be missing a prerequisite skill and first need instruction in that skill. While one student might learn a skill after one instructional lesson, another might need two or three. While one student might engage immediately with a *learning activity*, another might need support in feeling emotionally safe to engage.

The level of differentiation and individual activity inherent in the *Learner-Active, Technology-Infused Classroom* allows each student to engage in the *learning activities* needed and progress at a pace that will maximize success. With teacher facilitation being the predominant mode of student–teacher interaction, individual students are more able to receive the instructional guidance and support they need. Given students learn to schedule their own time—determining what, how, and when they will learn—they are empowered to select the resources, tools, and opportunities to learn that would most benefit them. For those who lack the experience or executive function to make such choices, a teacher's *small-group mini-lesson* guides them through the process to design their schedules.

Regardless of students' abilities or background, all students deserve the right to learn through compelling problems, seeking solutions that require higher-order thinking. All too often, students who lack executive function or grade-level skills are relegated to endless practice of lower-order skills, which can be boring and demoralizing. Beginning the study of a unit with a problem to solve allows all students to set their sights on finding a solution; equity means providing all students with the supports they need to achieve at high levels. The "bar" is the same, whether inside the classroom or outside the classroom; equity means providing each student with the differentiated supports needed to achieve. Using problem-based learning, students can also engage in solving problems relate to equity issues in their community and the world at large.

The *Learner-Active, Technology-Infused Classroom*, with its emphasis on problem-based learning and student voice and choice, facilitated by a masterful teacher, is the quintessential educational equity environment.

Universal Design for Learning (UDL)

UDL was developed by David Rose, a Harvard School of Education Lecturer and the Chief Education Officer at the Center for Applied Special Technology (cast.org). It is "a framework to improve and optimize teaching and learning for all people based on scientific insights into how humans learn" (cast.org). At the core is a philosophical commitment to access for all. A great metaphor I've heard for understanding that is the difference between a retrofitted building and the Guggenheim Museum. Years ago, buildings were constructed with the assumption that all people were ambulatory, thus many included stairs. The Americans With Disabilities Act of 1990 ushered in a time when buildings were then retrofitted with ramps, as an afterthought, in order to provide those with disabilities access. Frank Lloyd Wright's design of the Guggenheim Museum, whether intentional or not, provided access for all in its design. One navigates the museum via a spiral ramp, which has a grade of three degrees. Thus, the Guggenheim, built in 1959, was constructed with access for all in mind. Classroom curriculum, throughout history, has been designed with the academically able in mind. When students are deemed to have academic disabilities, teachers make modifications and accommodations (instructional retrofitting). What would it look like if classroom curriculum were designed with access for all in mind?

If you are thinking the *Learner-Active, Technology-Infused Classroom*, you're right! The intent of its instructional design is to provide all students with the instructional resources, tools, and instructional opportunities they need to succeed. As you design your *activity list*, you take into account learners of all learning styles and cognitive levels and offer appropriate *learning activities*.

The UDL framework addresses affective networks (the why of learning, or engagement), recognition networks (the what of learning, or representation), and strategic networks (the how of learning, or action and expression.) The UDL guidelines for addressing these three networks include, as just a sampling, providing options for recruiting interest (choice and autonomy; relevance, value, and authenticity; and minimized threats and distractions); providing options for perception (customizing the display of information, alternatives for auditory information, alternatives for visual information); and providing options for executive functions (goal setting, planning and strategy development, and progress monitoring). As you review the full list of guidelines at cast.org, you will see that the *Learner-Active, Technology-Infused Classroom* is the ultimate UDL learning environment.

English-Language Learners

Students who do not speak the native language of the classroom environment need additional supports to maximize their achievement. They benefit from visual cues; scaffolding allowing them to transition, at times using their native language, such as in journal writing; supports for understanding culturally unique expressions, which might include videos or pictures explaining terms such as "drive up the wall" or "piece of cake"; and engaging in small-group work where they are continually hearing the language and may be willing to speak in a more risk-free environment. Three obvious advantages of the *Learner-Active, Technology-Infused Classroom* for ELLs is that the level of individualized learning and differentiation allows students to receive the instructional supports each needs; the classroom is a social environment that exposes students to a significant amount of spoken language, including that of peers; and the framework lends itself to a teacher trained to support ELLs engaging with students in the classroom through one-on-one facilitation and *small-group mini-lessons* as well as partnering with the teacher to design customized *analytic rubrics, activity lists, learning activities*, and so on. Learning is social, and students learn well from one another. There is not a learning environment more socially oriented than the *Learner-Active, Technology-Infused Classroom*. ELLs will thrive in a well-run *Learner-Active, Technology-Infused Classroom*.

The Flipped Classroom

Some equate the *Learner-Active, Technology-Infused Classroom* with the flipped classroom; but they are, in fact, different approaches. The flipped classroom seeks to reverse the actions of the conventional classroom in which teachers deliver content through classroom lectures and students engage further and practice at home. In the flipped classroom, students watch video lectures, collaborate with others through digital venues, and research information at home; they then engage in discussions and other activities to deepen their understanding of content in the classroom.

In the *Learner-Active, Technology-Infused Classroom*, all *learning activities* take place in the classroom, where assistance from the teacher is readily available. However, aligned with a key goal of the flipped classroom, students do not sit and listen to teachers' lectures, and content is not presented primarily by the teacher. Rather, the teacher develops a comprehensive, differentiated collection of *learning activities* that offer alternative ways for students to grapple with content, with teacher-directed lessons being one of the options.

Both models utilize technology, though the *Learner-Active, Technology-Infused Classroom* relies more on the use of technology in the classroom than outside of the classroom. Both models give students more responsibility for their own learning, with the flipped classroom focusing on student responsibility at home to complete key activities and the *Learner-Active, Technology-Infused Classroom* focusing on students managing all of their activities, in class and at home. The key paradigm shifts involving "felt need" (beginning a unit with an authentic problem-based task) and "Teacher as Bridge Builder" (allowing students to manage their individual learning path) are also unique to the *Learner-Active, Technology-Infused Classroom*.

The Virtual *Learner-Active, Technology-Infused Classroom*

The *Learner-Active, Technology-Infused Classroom* can easily be implemented as a virtual classroom. *Benchmark lessons* would be offered through either live video conference sessions or pre-recorded videos. *Small-group mini-lessons* would be offered through live video conference sessions. In more conventional virtual learning environments, students digitally submit assignments and await teacher feedback. In the *Learner-Active, Technology-Infused Classroom*, teachers actively facilitate learning as students are engaged in *learning activities*, meaning they would review work in progress and, in a cloud-based environment, offer comments directly in student documents. It is important, therefore, to select an online environment that allows for that level of virtual teacher facilitation.

Gifted Learners

While many students in school may be intelligent and high achievers, few are truly gifted. The former are easily served in the *Learner-Active, Technology-Infused Classroom*; truly gifted people (approximately 1 percent of the population) can be well served in the *Learner-Active, Technology-Infused Classroom* if teachers recognize the attributes and needs of gifted learners. While gifted learners possess many unique attributes, such as a love of problem-solving, strong vocabulary, and abstract thinking, most of their attributes are addressed in the overall structures and strategies inherent in the *Learner-Active, Technology-Infused Classroom*. Here we will consider those that require a specific understanding on the part of the teacher:

- A propensity to daydream—One of the attributes of gifted people is creativity, which is not always nurtured in school but fits well with the problem-based nature of the *Learner-Active, Technology-Infused Classroom*. One of the habits of highly creative people is daydreaming (Kaufman & Gregoire, 2015), which does not tend to align well with teachers' expectations for learners. It is important to allow gifted students the time to wander in their thoughts.

- An interest in doing things differently—Your gifted learners will be the ones to recommend alternative *ALUs*, *learning activities*, classroom structures, and the like. As long as you are comfortable and their ideas are in line with the underlying paradigms and principles of the *Learner-Active, Technology-Infused Classroom*, let them! If you are not able or willing to allow them to pursue an idea, be honest as to why not.

- High levels of frustration—Your gifted learners may exhibit frustration and a temper when having difficulty meeting performance standards. While the *facilitation roadmap* would indicate that in cases of extreme frustration, you should provide direct instruction, this may not be the case with gifted learners. Noticing when the gifted learner is reaching a level of frustration and intervening is an important first step. Talk the student through the situation, offering them perspective in the situation and helping them develop a plan for working through the difficult situation.

- Wide interests—Gifted learners can appear to be distracted by ideas and unfocused in their work at times. That is because their minds are taking in everything, making connections, and exploring, most likely, far beyond the content you've set before them. In most cases, the gifted learner will be able to meet your expectations and keep running with multiple ideas and interests. However, in the case that the giftedness prevents the student from focusing on the basic content-related requirements, use a graphic organizer that has those requirements in one area, with other areas for the student to capture ideas and questions to which to return after addressing the requirements.

These are just a few attributes to consider. If you have gifted learners in your classroom, seek out a more complete list of attributes and consider how they will be addressed in the *Learner-Active, Technology-Infused Classroom*.

Executive Function

The *Learner-Active, Technology-Infused Classroom* is a veritable executive function playground. As outlined in *Building Executive Function: The Missing Link to Student Achievement* (Sulla, 2018), executive function skills are necessary for key life skills: conscious control, engagement, collaboration, empowerment, efficacy, and leadership. These key life skills are aligned with the intended outcomes of the *Learner-Active, Technology-Infused Classroom*.

Students build significant executive function through the structures of the *Learner-Active, Technology-Infused Classroom*. Consider that when students manage a *two-pocket folder*, they must store and manipulate visual information, identify same and different, follow multiple steps, hold on to information while considering other information, categorize information, shift focus from one event to another, catch and correct errors, think about multiple concepts simultaneously, set goals, manage time, work towards a goal, organize actions and thoughts, consider future consequences in light of current action, attend to an activity, focus, concentrate, think before acting, initiate a task, persist in a task, monitor performance, and reflect on goals. That's twenty-one executive function skills exercised in just one of the structures of the *Learner-Active, Technology-Infused Classroom*. Similar lists could be generated for all of the structures. Putting students in charge of their own learning builds tremendous executive function.

While one might argue that students need executive function in order to function successfully in a *Learner-Active, Technology-Infused Classroom*, in fact, this classroom model builds executive function every day. Returning to the structure of the *two-pocket folder*, if students are weak in executive function, they would attend a *small-group mini-lesson* in which the teacher would walk them through daily folder management. The teacher would provide checklists or *how-to sheets* that they could learn to use to gradually take responsibility for their *two-pocket folders* on their own, as they build the necessary executive function skills.

The problem-based nature of the *Learner-Active, Technology-Infused Classroom* builds the executive function skills of defining a problem, analyzing, creating mental images, generating possible solutions, anticipating, predicting outcomes, evaluating, being creative, applying former approaches to new situations, changing perspective, seeing multiple sides to a situation, being open to others' points of view, and more.

A masterful teacher with a strong working knowledge of executive function can support students in building executive function through the various structures and strategies of the *Learner-Active, Technology-Infused Classroom*.

Mapping Other Instructional Approaches to the *Learner-Active, Technology-Infused Classroom*

The *Learner-Active, Technology-Infused Classroom* is a framework for putting students in charge of their own learning, focusing on engagement, empowerment, and efficacy. Most instructional approaches aimed at specific content mastery fit within this framework. If you are looking to stay true to the *Learner-Active, Technology-Infused Classroom*, before adopting curricular programs and approaches, consider the extent to which they align to two of the key paradigm shifts:

♦ Felt Need—The *Learner-Active, Technology-Infused Classroom* uses a problem-based task to launch a unit of study, focusing on the application aspect of content mastery at the start of the unit. Does the curricular program or approach in question allow for the development of a problem-based task to serve as the core of the unit?

♦ Teacher as Bridge Builder—The *Learner-Active, Technology-Infused Classroom* allows students significant choice and voice, with the teacher creating the venue through which that should happen. It is students who decide how they will learn, with the teacher's guidance. It is students who decide when they will tackle various *learning activities*, *practice activities*, and application of content in designing the final product or performance. Any program or instructional approach, for example, that requires all students to study the content at a particular time of the day would significantly conflict with student voice and choice in the classroom. While some programs may presume all students will be engaged in studying the subject area at the same time (since the *Learner-Active, Technology-Infused Classroom* is unique in the concept of allowing students to study different subject areas at times that make sense to them), that does not necessarily mean that you could not apply the principles and strategies of a particular program or approach within the framework of the *Learner-Active, Technology-Infused Classroom*.

The *Learner-Active, Technology-Infused School*

Once all of the teachers in a school are running *Learner-Active, Technology-Infused Classrooms*, you have a *Learner-Active, Technology-Infused School*! It's important to realize that as students are progressing through the grade levels, entirely immersed in this framework, they need to have the structures becoming more complex as they go. Just as standards increase in complexity from year to year, so should the structures of the *Learner-Active, Technology-Infused Classroom*.

For example, ultimately the *analytic rubric* should drive students' action. If in "More Friends Good, Fewer Friends Bad?" (Appendix A), the rubric for their analysis of a local company's social network indicates they must apply Metcalfe's law, students will have a "felt need" to learn about Metcalfe's law. As they see, for example, that their solution to the worldwide water shortage should include a biomimicry component, they will have a "felt need" to learn about biomimicry and will pursue that learning. When first introduced to the *Learner-Active, Technology-Infused Classroom*, the *activity list* offers students choice, required, and optional activities for learning idioms. At some point, once students understand the path to learning, and assuming adequate technology is available, the *activity list* can be eliminated and replaced by a hyperlinked rubric. On the *analytic rubric* for addressing the worldwide water shortage, the term "biomimicry" would be hyperlinked to a page that contains choice, required, and optional activities. Students would recognize from the *analytic rubric*, the need to learn about biomimicry, rather than being prompted by the *activity list*, and pursue that learning.

If students are learning in a *Learner-Active, Technology-Infused Classroom* from earlier grades, you can move to reduce the dependency on the *activity list*. Also, at the secondary level, students can also be given fewer, predetermined *learning activities*, and instead build their resourcefulness to pursue learning absent of a clear structure. Much of the skills they need for learning will be developed in their elementary years of the *Learner-Active, Technology-Infused Classroom*, so at the secondary level you can expand students' thinking by having them depend on those skills.

As students progress through the grades, problems, too, should become less defined so that students have more voice in specifically what they would like to pursue related to the problem. Eventually, students can become problem-finders most of the time. After students have spent years addressing problems presented by the teacher, even though some may be open to student ideas, they will understand the nature of open-ended, authentic problems and be able to identify them on their own. By middle school, you should be able to allow students to explore a content area to identify current problems they would like to solve. As students are more able to work effectively in the *Learner-Active, Technology-Infused Classroom*, you may feel comfortable having different groups of students pursuing different problems.

Rubrics, too, will become more open to student voice. You might offer several rows and have students design additional rows based on their interests. For example, in *Digital Serfs?* (Appendix E), some students might decide that they want to look at feudalism through lenses other than those listed. Assuming the ideas are in line with content, as opposed to being peripheral and thus taking time away from the subject-area focus, let students have increased voice in their rubrics.

Students can play a greater role in self-assessment and reflection as the years progress. If students become familiar with the use of the *learning dashboard* in the early grades, they can build toward simply taking curricular standards and designing their own *learning dashboards*, thinking more deeply about what they need to accomplish. They will be better able to assess their progress and report to you on that, along with their future learning plans. They will be better able to answer more metacognitive questions about their learning process. As the years progress, students should be challenged to think at much higher levels in the *Learner-Active, Technology-Infused Classroom*, given they've mastered the structures through which they learn.

In terms of the physical classroom, as the years progress, where possible, students should be given much more voice in the classroom setup; after all, it is their learning environment. Where students are involved in interdisciplinary *ALUs* across multiple classrooms, you could designate certain rooms for specific activities, allowing students to move freely among the classrooms and teachers to serve as a resource team. You can also have students take greater responsibility for the school outside of their classrooms, adding their voice to how the media center and cafeteria are used, hallways are decorated, and outside areas are landscaped and used.

Figure 9.3. LATIC Rubric Rows

		Emerging	Practitioner	Reflective Practitioner
Engaging the Learner	**How-To Sheets and Videos**	the teacher(s): ❑ designs how-to sheets, podcasts, and screencasts on concepts and skills students will need in order to address the problem-based task (learning activities) ❑ provides directions that are detailed, easy to follow, and designed to ensure success ❑ includes graphics and screenshots to enhance learning	the students: ❑ seek out and use how-to resources to learn skills and concepts as needed ❑ identify and locate additional how-to resources as needed both in and out of the classroom ❑ design how-to sheets and videos once they've mastered a skill	meets all of the criteria in the *practitioner* column plus: ❑ students demonstrate a deeper understanding of what makes a quality how-to podcast, screencast and vodcast by incorporating wait time/pauses and voice inflection to capture the listener's attention ❑ teachers and students contribute to a collection of how-to resources that ensure all students can learn prerequisite, requisite, and advanced content through a variety of modalities
	Small-Group Mini-Lessons	the teacher(s): ❑ designs narrowly targeted skill acquisition small-group mini-lessons that last 5–15 minutes ❑ establishes a sign-up procedure with a maximum of six students and overflow slots ❑ makes students aware of small-group mini-lessons in advance so that they can sign up and/or be "invited" to them ❑ allows for small-group mini-lessons to be offered by various adults who work in the classroom	the students: ❑ identify their need to attend a small-group mini-lesson(s) ❑ use a "checkout" quiz or other assessment in order to attend an advanced-content (challenge) small-group mini-lesson ❑ seek out opportunities for skill practice following a small-group mini-lesson	meets all of the criteria in the *practitioner* column plus ❑ generate requests for small-group mini-lessons ❑ serve as appropriately vetted peer experts who offer some small-group mini-lessons ❑ teacher and student develop guidelines for outside experts to offer small-group mini-lessons

portion of LATIC Rubric from www.ideportal.com, copyright 2017, IDE Corp. — www.idecorp.com

"Whereas choice is a matter of working from a set of possibilities created by the teacher, voice is a matter of designing those possibilities."

Overall, you want to move toward greater student voice and less dependence on teacher-defined structures. Whereas choice is a matter of working from a set of possibilities created by the teacher, voice is a matter of designing those possibilities. As the years progress, teachers can put more of their effort into being critical resources and thought partners for students.

The *Learner-Active, Technology-Infused Classroom* Rubric

As you design your *Learner-Active, Technology-Infused Classroom*, you'll be happy to know there's a rubric to guide you. The journey to rethinking your classroom to break the mold and pave a new road for your students to change the world can be both exhilarating and daunting. Reading the book is a great first step. As for implementation, just start! It's a journey of one *ALU* at a time; one structure after another building to create a new special place called your classroom.

If you are not working directly with IDE Corp. consultants, you still have several ongoing resources to guide you, including my blog, YouTube channel, Twitter feed, Twitter chat, and other books—you can find links to each at nancysulla.com. You can also reference some *ALU* ideas and instructional planning tools, including the *LATIC Rubric* as part of the free content available at www.ideportal.com.

In your first year of implementing a *Learner-Active, Technology-Infused Classroom*, do not even attempt to assess yourself with a rubric. Use this as a horizon line. In your second year, you can begin to self-assess and set goals from it. Figure 9.3 offers two rows from the area "Engaging the Learner" that address *how-to sheets* and *how-to videos*, and *small-group mini-lessons*. Note that this rubric is different from the ones you'll be using with your students. It has three columns:

- ♦ Emerging is the place you'll flourish in for approximately three years, so be good with that! You could have an entire rubric around that one column; however, for our purposes, it's giving you the end goal. This is the column that explains everything you, as the teacher, will design, put in place, and execute. This column represents what you will do to create your *Learner-Active,*

Technology-Infused Classroom. However, the goal of all that you do is to empower students to take charge of their own learning and move toward efficacy.

♦ Column two describes what students will do as a result of all of your effort in column one. If you've designed an effective *Learner-Active, Technology-Infused Classroom*, the students will visibly take charge of their own learning. So essentially, your students earn you the second column score. They can only succeed; however, if you've put in place all the structures and strategies in the first column. In your third year of implementation, take a good look at this second column to see where your students are taking charge of their own learning. Where they may not be, return to the first column to see how you might modify your implementation. Ultimately, the goal is to build efficacious students who can partner with you to co-create the learning environment.

♦ Column three describes how students and teachers will create classroom structures and strategies together. This is your year-five target, so you can begin looking at this column in year four. The reason you don't want to attempt to accomplish this in year one is that you and your students have to gain complete familiarity with and internalize the paradigm shifts of the *Learner-Active, Technology-Infused Classroom* first, in order for third-column implementation to be accurate and successful.

Brain surgeons have, as their goal, performing successful brain surgery; however they do not attempt this in their first year of residency. They may, in fact, engage in five years of residency toward becoming masterful at brain surgery. So consider this rubric your five-year residency program for designing your own amazing, world-changing, *Learner-Active, Technology-Infused Classroom*. Read, design, implement, read again, reflect, redesign, and enjoy every minute of it. The destination is rewarding; but the journey is life changing.

RECAP

Get your students off to a good start with a *priming plan*. Develop a series of activities for the first week or two of school, including those that:

- Introduce students to the structures of your classroom;

- Prime students for success, building hope, confidence, and optimism;

- Gather assessment data.

The *Learner-Active, Technology-Infused Classroom* is a framework that can serve as the backdrop for most other programs, including:

- RTI/MTSS;

- The Co-Teaching/Inclusive Classroom;

- STEM/STEAM;

- Design Process;

- Equity-Focused Instruction;

- Universal Design for Learning (UDL);

- English-Language Learners;

- The Flipped Classroom;

- The Virtual *Learner-Active, Technology-Infused Classroom;*

- Gifted Learners;

- Executive Function;

- Other instructional approaches that can be mapped to the key paradigm shifts.

Once enough teachers are implementing the *Learner-Active, Technology-Infused Classroom*, you can begin to address the unique nature of a *Learner-Active, Technology-Infused School*. This means developmentally modifying structures across the years to match the growing understanding of the model by your students.

Over the course of the next five years, keep reflecting and revising, using the "LATIC Rubric" available at www.ideportal.com. Keep in mind that the columns indicate:

- What you will do;

- What your students will do when they are empowered;

- What you and your students will co-create as they build efficacy.

REFERENCES

Kaufman, S. B. & Gregoire, C. (2015). *Wired to create: Unraveling the mysteries of the creative mind.* New York: Penguin.

Sulla, N. (2018). *Building executive function: The missing link to student achievement.* New York: Routledge.

Appendix A
More Friends Good, Fewer Friends Bad?

Social networking sites, like *Facebook*, *Twitter*, or *Instagram*, provide a way to connect with "Friends"—people you have added to your profile. Some people have many more "Friends" than others—does this make their network better?

There are offline social networks as well. A sports team, a tribe of hunter-gatherers in the Amazon rainforest, or even your math class: anywhere that groups of people form and interact is a kind of social network.

The engineer Robert Metcalfe suggested a mathematical law that essentially states: the more friends you have, the better the network. In fact, his law says that the value of the network is equal to the square of the number of friends. This means that two smaller networks with a combined total number of friends more than another single network could actually have less total value for their owners than the one large network for one owner. Does having a huge network of friends on a social networking site always mean that the network is going to have a much better value? In fact, more than two thousand years ago, Pythagoras created a theorem that allows you to compare just that!

But can a 2500-year-old idea really help us understand the value of modern social networks? Pick an organization or company of interest and determine the number of followers on their social media networks, including the breakdown if they have multiple sites on the same social media platform. Using Metcalfe's law and the Pythagorean theorem, evaluate the strength of their network. Share your findings with them and offer suggestions for improving their network.

More Friends Good, Fewer Friends Bad? *Rubric*

Evaluator's Log		Novice	Apprentice	Practitioner	Expert
Pythagorean Theorem: Proof		construction and explanation of a right triangle on graph paper or with objects, focusing on its angles and sides	includes a logical proof of the theorem with graphical representation and written descriptions	• two different logical proofs of the theorem with graphical representation and written descriptions • includes constructed right triangles for at least three Pythagorean triples • logical proof of the converse of the theorem with graphical representation and written descriptions	all of *Practitioner* plus identifies at least 4 examples of the Pythagorean Triples and explains their significance
Pythagorean Theorem: Two and Three Dimensions		• includes at least two measurable qualities of social networks • combined measure of at least two qualities	• includes at least three measurable qualities of social networks • combined measure of at least three qualities	• justification of at least three measurable social network qualities • shows application of Pythagorean theorem to create combined measure of at least three qualities of a social network	all of *Practitioner* plus weighting of different qualities using coefficients / scaling factors to differentiate importance of factors
Organization or Individual		description of an individual or organization with a social media network	• description of individual or organization and at least two of its social media sites	• description of individual or organization and at least two of its social media sites, with network sizes • list of the individual's or organization's use of multiple sites on the same social media platform, with network size for each • list of at least two competitors' sites and relative size	all of *Practitioner* plus tracking of the growth of the social media sites over a three-week period

(Appendix A continues on next page.)

	Novice	Apprentice	Practitioner	Expert
Evaluation Using Pythagorean Theorem and Metcalfe's Law	use of triangle side lengths to represent the size of social networks, on a coordinate grid	◆ interpretation of social network size on a coordinate grid with right triangles ◆ application of theorem to determine the distance between two points on a coordinate grid ◆ calculations of value for two smaller social networks	◆ interpretation of size of social networks, on a coordinate grid with right triangles ◆ application of the Pythagorean theorem to determine the distance between two points on a coordinate grid ◆ calculations of Metcalfe's law value for two smaller social networks ◆ comparison of the value of one social network with two others	all of *Practitioner* plus evaluation of the effectiveness of Metcalfe's law based on data and own assessment of the value of surveyed networks
Recommendation	◆ aimed at a local, national, or international group that encourages social networks among its members ◆ recommendations are focused on the size of the social network	◆ aimed at a local, national or international group that encourages social networks among its members ◆ recommendations are focused on the size of the social network, and at least one other quality	◆ aimed at a local, national, or international group that encourages social networks among its members ◆ recommendations are focused on the size of the social network, and at least two other qualities ◆ includes mathematical evidence for recommendations-	all of *Practitioner* plus evaluation report is presented to the group to implement suggestions with an offer to discuss further and help in its implementation

Appendix B
Hydroelectric Power Source

Did you know that Niagara Falls is so powerful that it generates some of the least expensive electricity anywhere in the world? For generations, the Niagara River has fascinated camera-ready tourists and admiring visitors with its overwhelming power and strength. It's really no wonder why Niagara Falls is widely known as one of the great, natural wonders of the world.

Since the early 1900s, a hydroelectric power facility has captured that potential energy, becoming the largest electric producer in New York State. This natural, nonpolluting, publicly owned power source has existed in harmony with the beauty of Niagara for nearly a century. According to the New York Power Authority website (www.nypa.gov/), this power plant generates 2.4 million kilowatts—enough power to light 24 million 100-watt bulbs at once! This low-cost electricity saves the state's residents and businesses hundreds of millions of dollars a year. In 2007, they predicted that the Niagara Power Plant will continue to produce steady supplies of clean, carbon-free hydroelectricity for another fifty years.

Are waterfalls an untapped natural resource in other places? Where could this massive energy potential be harnessed and used to create electricity? What about places that don't have a natural waterfall?

Marmore's Falls in Italy is the world's tallest *man-made* waterfall. Marmore's Falls is an incredible 165 meters high, compared to the world-renowned Niagara Falls, which is only 53.6 meters high. But even more amazing is that it was constructed by man during Roman times, dating back to 271 EF. So, there's no reason that we can't be constructing waterfalls today!

How could you strategically create man-made waterfalls in your area to supply local residents with clean, affordable hydroelectricity? Where and how could this be done? Develop a proposal to either construct a hydroelectric power facility on an existing waterfall or a new, man-made waterfall. Tap into the awe and majesty of waterfalls to advance renewable clean energy technology!

While developing your proposal, use the IDE Design Process to create a novel solution and explore the economic, social, environmental, and geopolitical costs, benefits, and risks. To ensure that you have the most feasible and optimal solution, consider a wide range of constraints to your proposal. Let's help to responsibly manage our natural resources!

Hydroelectric Power Source: *Rubric*

	Novice	Apprentice	Practitioner	Expert
Solution Design	◆ includes a solution to a problem ◆ demonstrates some use of the design process	◆ includes a solution to a real-world problem, based on scientific knowledge ◆ demonstrates use of the design process and scientific method	◆ includes a solution to a complex real-world problem, based on a wide variety of scientific knowledge related to hydroelectric power ◆ demonstrates effective use of the design process and scientific method ◆ includes a wide variety of student-generated sources of evidence, including competing ideas and evidence ◆ includes prioritization of criteria and tradeoff considerations	all of *Practitioner*, plus the solution offers alternative options to increase the persuasive value of the proposal
Explanation	◆ outline of the key points of the proposal ◆ some textual evidence to support the need for either a waterfall or a hydroelectric power source	◆ detailed proposal ◆ some cited textual evidence to support the need for a waterfall and a hydroelectric power source ◆ includes proposal evaluation that considers some possible constraints, such as cost	◆ detailed proposal with maps, images, data tables, and/or other illustrative examples ◆ ample, relevant, cited textual evidence to support the need for both the waterfall and the hydroelectric power source ◆ includes proposal evaluation that considers a range of constraints, including cost, safety, reliability, and aesthetics, and to consider social, cultural, and environmental impacts	all of *Practitioner*, plus includes evaluation of competing design solutions (such as dams) based on scientific ideas and principles, empirical evidence, and logical arguments regarding relevant factors (e.g., economic, societal, environmental, ethical considerations)

(Appendix B continues on next page.)

	Novice	Apprentice	Practitioner	Expert
STEM Connections	includes use of science, technology, engineering, and math in solution design	• includes scientific knowledge to support both the need and the solution • includes some use of technology in the solution-finding process • includes a plan for an engineered 3-D prototype of solution • includes mathematical computations in the decision-making process	• includes scientific knowledge through sources and experiments to support both the need and the solution • includes use of technology for modeling and exploring "what-if?" scenarios • includes engineered 3-D prototype of solution • includes a mathematical analysis of costs and benefits as a critical aspect of decision-making	all of *Practitioner*, plus explains how STEM thinking helped in the development of the solution
Human Impacts on Earth Systems **Human Impacts on Earth Systems**	offers some of the benefits of less pollution and waste with the use of hydroelectric power	• explains the responsible management of natural resources • highlights the possibility of less pollution and waste with the use of hydroelectric power	• details the sustainability of human societies and the biodiversity that supports them through the responsible management of natural resources • highlights the contribution the proposal makes to society by producing less pollution and waste and precluding ecosystem degradation	all of *Practitioner*, plus describes various predictions based on scientific evidence or empirical data for the long-term impact on the primary community that would profit from the proposal, as well as any secondary or tertiary community impacts
Audience and Format	• writes to inform – • by including basic scientific procedures and some evidence or technical processes • includes visuals to support solution	• writes to inform and explain by including scientific procedures, evidence, and/or technical processes • uses domain-specific vocabulary to manage the complexity of the topic • presents arguments to support solution with some evidence • includes visuals and graphical data to support solution	• writes to inform, explain, and persuade by including scientific procedures, evidence, and/or technical processes • uses precise language and domain-specific vocabulary to manage the complexity of the topic • presents arguments to support claims in an analysis of substantive topics, using valid reasoning, as well as relevant and sufficient evidence • anticipates the audience's knowledge level and concerns • uses technology to enhance presentation, including visuals and graphs	all of *Practitioner*, plus presents claims and counterclaims fairly, supplying evidence for each while pointing out the strengths and limitations of both

Appendix C
A Place for Robots

Have you ever watched a movie or a cartoon where robots can complete tasks in the place of humans? In the animated movie *WALL-E* robots help humans after the Earth is considered no longer habitable. Some robots go and take care of the humans on a floating space station, while others stay on Earth and clean up the leftover debris. Another group travels back and forth between Earth and the Space Station looking for signs of life, which would mean that the humans can go back to Earth.

In the real world, NASA (National Aeronautics and Space Administration) has done a great deal of work with robotics. Robotics is the branch of technology that deals with the design, construction, operation, and application of robots. One of NASA's biggest use of robots is in space exploration. NASA uses robots to travel to and explore places that aren't safe for humans, such as Saturn and Mars.

NASA is preparing for another space exploration mission to Europa, Saturn's icy moon. It is a high priority to explore due to a salty underground ocean found under the moon's crust. This excursion is planned to take place in the 2020s; it will take NASA several years to develop and create the equipment. Once NASA has access to data from Europa, it needs to determine if the moon can sustain life. What makes a planet sustainable?

NASA is still designing the robotic tools necessary for this particular mission. Every mission uses different robots for different purposes. How will robots help us determine if Europa is a habitable moon? Why do companies use robots instead of humans for similar missions? What would it take to design a robot that can collect, preserve, and return evidence of one of the three necessities to sustain life? What would the process of this design and creation look like?

Your challenge will be to create a working model for this mission that can be shared with the education department at NASA, including an argument for why your design is essential to the mission.

A Place for Robots *Rubric*

	Novice	Apprentice	Practitioner	Expert
Design Process Journal: Initial Research (Explore)	includes the purpose of robots and examples of their use in space exploration	includes: • summary of the various use and purpose of robots • key ideas and details from research • citations for multiple sources	includes: • evidence from informational texts to analyze, reflect, and research space exploration and robotics • relevant information from experiences, print and digital sources • summary of information in notes • multiple, valid, cited sources to build knowledge about investigation of space exploration and the use of robotics in space	all of *Practitioner* plus, includes an interview with an expert in the field of space exploration or robotics
Design Process Journal: Use of Design Process	documents some of the steps in the Design Process to attempt to create a robotic model	• documents all of the steps in the Design Process to create a robotic model • includes both process and reflection notes • states one way to improve design from initial idea	• documents, in detail, of all steps of the Design Process • provides evidence of reflection and rounding back to earlier stages in the Design Process to improve model • includes relevant information from experiences to provide organized, detailed description of the Design Process in action	all of *Practitioner* plus, provides analysis of errors, and addresses any constraints to the Design Process
Robotic Working Model	reflects design as specified in the Design Journal	• functions as specified in the Design Journal • moves based on remote control or programming	• functions as specified in the Design Journal • moves based on programming • responds appropriately to obstacles • navigates rough terrain • collects a sample of evidence and preserves the sample for return to Earth	all of *Practitioner* plus: can collect and preserve multiple samples of evidence for sustaining life

(Appendix c continues on next page.)

	Novice	Apprentice	Practitioner	Expert
Final Proposal	◆ introduction of concepts of robotics used in space exploration ◆ some facts and detail ◆ a list of resources used at the end of the proposal	◆ introduction of concepts of robotics used in space exploration as hook ◆ findings presented using the Design Process system view framework ◆ research embedded throughout proposal ◆ sources cited at the end of proposal ◆ opinion is supported with fact and detail to strengthen the argument for the design	◆ introduction with claim supported by research and a logical sequence ◆ integrates information from several texts on robotics or space exploration ◆ cites sources throughout the proposal ◆ includes evidence and direct quotes from multiple credible, timely sources ◆ references using Design Process, showing journey through several attempts at model design ◆ includes words, phrases, and clauses to create cohesion and clarify relationships between claim and evidence ◆ includes concluding statement that supports argument and addresses their audience	all of *Practitioner* plus: includes an online tool e.g., website to advocate solution beyond the classroom

Appendix D
Deadly Encounters

African Dust and Coral Reefs

Waiting for rains that never fall, West African farmers watch soil turn to gray dust, too powdery to grip plant roots. On the other side of the Atlantic Ocean, scientists are pondering why coral reefs in the Caribbean are dying. Could the two environmental disasters – 4,800 km (3,000 mi) apart – be related?

The world's coral reefs are dying. Approximately 10 percent of the world's coral reefs may already be beyond saving. Scientists studying the Caribbean coral reefs are linking part of the problem to dust from the Sahara Desert. They are also investigating the effect that warming ocean waters are having on coral. Should we be worried? What other environmental issues may be related? How might this affect our local environment? What impact might this have on our lives?

What can you do to help? What recommendations would you make as to future actions on the part of your state or national government or some other organization? Pick your audience, design your solution, and pitch your idea.

Deadly Encounters Causal Map Rubric

	Novice	Apprentice	Practitioner	Expert
Number of Events	fewer than five different events/ situations	five to seven different events/ situations	eight to ten different events/situations	more than ten different events/ situations
Content	events beginning with the Sahara desert leading to the damage to coral reefs	♦ comprehensive chain of events detailing cause-and-effect chain from dust in the Sahara to damage to the coral reefs ♦ includes events with multiple effects	♦ comprehensive chain of events detailing cause-and-effect relationships ♦ includes events with multiple effects, with chains continuing from each ♦ includes predictions as to the effects of the death on the coral reefs to the environment and people	all of *Practitioner* plus includes other contributing factors at various points in the chain
Arrows	arrows point from cause to effect	♦ arrows point from cause to effect ♦ comments on arrows to describe relationships	♦ arrows point from cause to effect ♦ comments on arrows to describe relationships ♦ arrows are differentiated by color according to strength of relationship, e.g., major cause vs. contributing cause (includes key)	all of *Practitioner* plus arrows showing introduction of other contributing factors
Story-Telling	diagram tells a partial story of the events surrounding the problem	diagram tells a story of the events surrounding the problem, from dust in the Sahara to compromised coral reefs in the Caribbean	diagram: ♦ is easy to read and follow ♦ tells a clear story of the events leading to the problem	all of *Practitioner* plus images used to enhance the message

Deadly Encounters Solution Statement: Rubric

	Novice	Apprentice	Practitioner	Expert
Problem Development	includes opinion statement as to the coral reef–Saharan dust connection	includes: • clear claim stated in opening and closing paragraphs case for the coral reef – Saharan dust connection • includes supporting evidence from at least three different sources	• builds a case for the coral reef–Saharan dust connection and/or other environmental threats to coral reefs • includes relevant, supporting evidence from at least three different credible sources • includes timelines to show progression • explains how coral anatomy and life functions are being affected • projects effects over the next ten years	all of *Practitioner* plus • projects effects over the next fifty years • references several of the ocean literacy principles related to the claim
Content Focus	includes effects on the Earth's atmosphere, biosphere, geosphere, and/or hydrosphere	includes current and future effects on the Earth's atmosphere, biosphere, geosphere, and/ or hydrosphere with plans for rectifying any damage	details current and future effects on the Earth's atmosphere, biosphere, geosphere, and hydrosphere with plans for rectifying any damage to each	all of *Practitioner* plus offers a systems perspective of how threats to the coral reef affect the four spheres
Opposing Claims	includes one counterclaim	• includes one counterclaim and evidence to refute it	includes: • at least two counterclaims • evidence to refute all counterclaims introduced • use of multiple valid sources to refute counterclaims	all of *Practitioner* plus offers reasoning behind counterclaims
Solution	one actions that will positively affect the situation	two different actions that are: • feasible • will positively affect the situation	three or more different actions that are: • feasible • financially possible • will positively affect the situation • broken down into actionable steps	all of *Practitioner* plus all actions will positively affect the situation both short-term and long-term
Writing Structure and Style	• logical sequencing of ideas • transitions between supporting information	• use of domain specific vocabulary • logically organized reasons and evidence • cited, credible sources	• formal writing style • use of academic and domain specific vocabulary • logically organized reasons and evidence • properly cited sources • words, phrases, and clauses used to create cohesion	all of *Practitioner* plus deliberate use of figurative language and transitions to make the message more powerful

Deadly Encounters The Pitch: Rubric

	Novice	Apprentice	Practitioner	Expert
Components	fewer than five of the seven items listed in *Practitioner*	five to six of the seven items listed in *Practitioner*	• causal map • position statement • supporting information • action plan • data graphs • maps • images	all of *Practitioner* plus additional components such as relevant sound or video clips
Screens	at least five screens used	• each screen focuses on a message • at least seven screens used	• each screen focuses on a specific message • at least nine screens used	all of *Practitioner* plus • all components on each screen enhance the message
References	includes facts, graphed data, and images	• cited facts • cited anecdotal stories • cited graphed data	• cited facts • cited anecdotal stories • cited graphed data • cited images, sound clips, and/or video clips • includes referenced items for claims and counterclaims	all of *Practitioner* plus personally gathered data
Theme	consistent use of colors and fonts	consistent use of colors, fonts, and/or graphics to create a theme	consistent use of colors, fonts, and graphics to create a theme that supports the position statement	all of *Practitioner* plus • a theme statement repeated throughout • different colors used for different sections
Style and Mechanics	◆ no errors in spelling, capitalization, punctuation, or grammar	• concise writing or script • no errors in spelling, capitalization, punctuation, or grammar	• concise yet comprehensive writing or script • no errors in spelling, capitalization, punctuation, or grammar • use of various features to strengthen presentation	all of *Practitioner*, plus employs compositional risks

Appendix E
Digital Serfs?

As technology continues to rapidly change the world in which we live, what impact will it have on our economic system? Author Gary Marx suggested "social and intellectual capital will become economic drivers."

Back in the Middle Ages, feudalism was a land-based economic and political system in which the upper nobility class maintained control over all the land, providing the lower classes with no other choice but to work for the local king or lord. Is it possible that in the new era of technology land has become the Internet? Are we back to a new form of feudalism?

Can you imagine buying a new phone and having to enter all of your contacts manually? Luckily, with Internet cloud storage, all of our information, including contacts, photos, email, and so on, are backed up and can be synchronized among devices. Consumers trust companies like Amazon, Apple, Google, and Microsoft to maintain all of their data for convenience and security. But in exchange for all of that trust, we give up a great deal of control and freedom. Does that make us digital serfs in the land of the Internet?

Some may find it disconcerting that everything connected to the Internet can be tracked and monitored. However, the Internet has also revolutionized human society. According to the World Economic Forum, in one year alone, Facebook apps created over 182,000 jobs. As technology continues to rapidly change the world in which we live, what impact will it have on our economic system and human autonomy? Do these technological advances have the potential to take us back to a feudal system similar to that of the Middle Ages?

Based on economic, political, and social structures, consider the possibility of the rise of "digital feudalism" in the twenty-first century. What are the potential short-term and long-term impacts to our emerging global society? Will the next generation of technologists have no choice but to live as "digital serfs" inside the fiefdoms of today?

Spread the warning or support the cause. Make your opinion heard. Develop a multimedia presentation that could be submitted to *Open Source Bridge* to share at their annual conference, a news channel, or any other organization that will provide their citizens with a voice.

Digital Serfs? *Rubric*

	Novice	Apprentice	Practitioner	Expert
Research	• gathers facts on all of the following: feudal system overview, social pyramid—roles at each level	• gathers accurate facts on all of the following: feudal system overview, social pyramid—roles at each level, benefits and costs of the system to individuals • gathers accurate facts on one to two of the following: 　religion □ health 　homes □ clothing 　arts □ education	• gathers reliable and detailed facts on all of the following: feudal system overview, social pyramid—roles at each level, benefits and costs of the system to individuals • develops an original visual of feudalism's social pyramid • gathers accurate and detailed facts on three or more of the following: 　religion □ health 　homes □ clothing 　arts □ education	all of *Practitioner* plus: • researches history of the feudal system including its precursor economic system and its decline
Evaluation of Proprietary Knowledge System	• outlines one to two ways in which the current situation is similar to feudalism • determines opinion of the current system • identifies sources	• outlines three ways in which the current situation is similar to feudalism • identifies three short-term or long-term effects of the current system • develops one cause-and-effect diagram for a positive or negative effect of feudalism • develops opinion of the current system • supports claim with reasoning • cites all sources	• describes three ways in which the current situation is similar to feudalism • describes one to two ways in which it is different • develops cause-and-effect chains for three positive or negative effects of feudalism • identifies three short-term and one long-term effect of the current system • develops opinion of the current system • supports claim with logical reasoning and relevant, accurate data • offers a feasible alternate solution • properly cites all sources	all of *Practitioner* plus: • develops cause-and-effect chains that map feudalism to current situation
Multimedia Presentation-Content	• focuses on the current method of knowledge management, referencing feudalism	• focuses on the current method of knowledge management through the lens of the feudal system • includes information from the *Evaluation* row • incorporates facts from the *Research* row	• focuses on the current method of knowledge management through the lens of the feudal system row • includes all information from the *Evaluation* row • incorporates facts seamlessly from each component of the *Research* row	all of *Practitioner* plus: • uses questions for viewers to ponder to drive home the message
Presentation Format	• video • narration is clear	• three to six minute video • images, design, and sound support the content of the presentation • narration is clear	• four to five minute narrated multimedia presentation • images, design, and sound support the content of the presentation • narration is clear and concise • no errors in any text or word pronunciation	all of *Practitioner* plus: • has overarching theme/slogan to punctuate the message

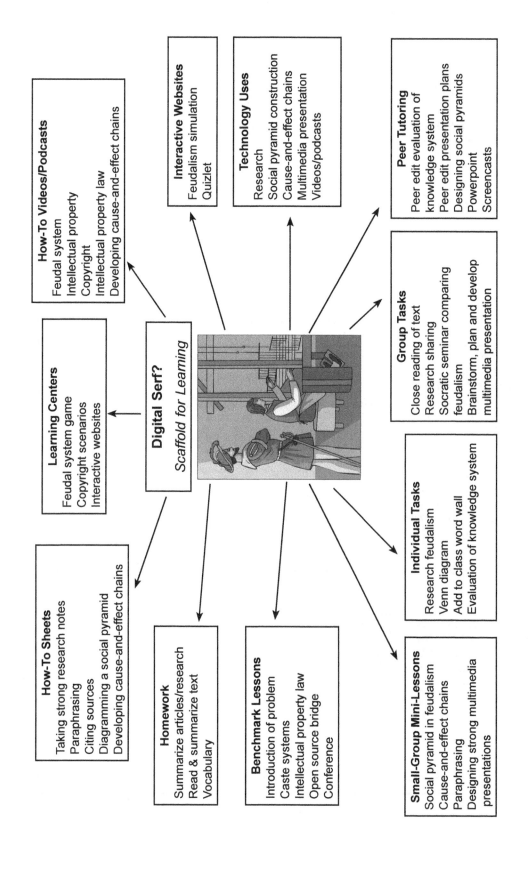

How-To Videos/Podcasts
Feudal system
Intellectual property
Copyright
Intellectual property law
Developing cause-and-effect chains

Interactive Websites
Feudalism simulation
Quizlet

Technology Uses
Research
Social pyramid construction
Cause-and-effect chains
Multimedia presentation
Videos/podcasts

Peer Tutoring
Peer edit evaluation of knowledge system
Peer edit presentation plans
Designing social pyramids
Powerpoint
Screencasts

Learning Centers
Feudal system game
Copyright scenarios
Interactive websites

Digital Serf?
Scaffold for Learning

Group Tasks
Close reading of text
Research sharing
Socratic seminar comparing feudalism
Brainstorm, plan and develop multimedia presentation

How-To Sheets
Taking strong research notes
Paraphrasing
Citing sources
Diagramming a social pyramid
Developing cause-and-effect chains

Homework
Summarize articles/research
Read & summarize text
Vocabulary

Benchmark Lessons
Introduction of problem
Caste systems
Intellectual property law
Open source bridge
Conference

Individual Tasks
Research feudalism
Venn diagram
Add to class word wall
Evaluation of knowledge system

Small-Group Mini-Lessons
Social pyramid in feudalism
Cause-and-effect chains
Paraphrasing
Designing strong multimedia presentations

Digital Serfs? *Content Facilitation Questions*

COMPREHENSION: *Ask questions that ensure students understand content and skills needed to solve the problem.*	What is the feudal system? What is the Internet cloud? What is copyright?
APPLICATION: *Ask questions that ensure the ability of students to apply learning to new situations.*	What was the importance of the relationships within the feudal system? How does feudalism compare to the Internet? The cloud? How does feudalism provide protection? Who would be considered the lords in today's digital era?
CONNECTION: *Ask questions that ensure the ability of students to apply learning to their lives.*	How are you dependent upon technology, particularly the Internet? Do you visualize yourself as a digital serf? What would be your role within the digital feudal system?
SYNTHESIS: *Ask questions that encourage students to create new information from existing data.*	How can we stop digital feudalism? How might school represent a form of feudalism? What do you think is the future of our economic system? If digital real estate is status, what would today's social pyramid look like?
METACOGNITION: *Ask questions which prompt students to think about their own thinking process.*	What was the hardest part of this task? Why? How did you go about contrasting the two different times in history? How did you divide responsibilities and keep all group members on task? How did you know when you found a truly compelling visual for your presentation?

Digital Serfs? *Task Management Grid*

Students	Research	Social pyramid	Venn diagram comparing feudalism and the Internet	Evaluation of systems draft	Evaluation of systems peer edit	Evaluation of systems final	Multimedia presentation brainstorm	Multimedia presentation draft	Multimedia presentation final

✓ = Completed   S = Submitted   R = Return for Revisions

Digital Serfs? *Sample Content Facilitation Grid*

Students	Describes how and why feudalism emerged	Describes the different tiers of the feudal pyramid and the responsibilities of each level	States the pros and cons of the system	Compares and contrasts the feudal system of the Middle Ages to digital feudalism	Describes and explains digital feudalism	Describes how the ancient culture transformed due to feudalism	Offers an opinion on the current economy and digital feudalism	Supports claim with evidence from various print and digital sources	Quotes or paraphrase the data and conclusions of others while avoiding plagiarism and following a standard form of situation

M = mastery   *P = peer tutor level*   *HW = needs homework for reinforcement*

W = working on it   *ML = needs a mini-lesson*

Appendix F
Teachers, Schools, and Pop Culture

Everyone is a consumer of pop culture. All around us are advertisements, television shows, movies, radio talk shows, pictures, books, magazines, social media posts, and so on. Whether we realize it or not, the pop culture media in which we are immersed has a strong influence and impact on us, not only personally, but societally as well.

According to a study published by the *Journal of Social and Political Psychology*,[1] "The media play a central role in informing the public about what happens in the world, particularly in those areas in which audiences do not possess direct knowledge or experience." In this way, the role of the media can be positive, because it informs us about issues about which we would not normally know. At the same time, however, the study also found that the media can "severely limit the information with which audiences understand these issues" and that it can "limit understanding of possibilities of social change."

---

1 http://jspp.psychopen.eu/article/view/96/37#d2e356

One example of this might be in the world of education. Teachers, students, and schools are often depicted in pop culture. Just think about it! How many movies, TV shows, advertisements, or books have you encountered where the main setting was a school building or college? How many of your favorite protagonists are teens? But, upon taking a closer look, how accurate are all of these depictions? In this case, is pop culture serving as a positive influence, informing people who are on the "outside" about the real issues and situations that occur? Or do you think that, in this case, pop culture is actually limiting the wider public's understanding of what really goes on in schools?

Conduct a study in which you closely analyze the way that teachers and schools are depicted in pop culture (e.g., books, movies, television shows, advertisements). How are they being represented? What (both consciously and unconsciously) is being messaged to the wider public about them? To what extent do the depictions of teachers and schools actually match reality?

Teachers and those who serve in education deserve recognition for the work they do. Now let us work to ensure that they are properly and accurately represented! After conducting your research, choose at least one current media outlet with whom you can communicate. Perhaps this is an author of a book, a TV network station, an advertiser, a radio show, or a producer. Create a product to convince them to depict teachers and schools more accurately. The form of the product will be up to you, and can include mediums such as an essay, a presentation, a podcast, or a letter.

Teachers, Schools, and Pop Culture: *Rubric*

	Novice	Apprentice	Practitioner	Expert
Planning Notes: Choice of Sources	◆ one source from pop culture that depicts teachers/schools ◆ created within the last 30 years	◆ two sources from pop culture that depict teachers/schools, one of which is a literary text ◆ sources created within the last 30 years ◆ at least one source from a suggested list provided by the teacher	◆ at least three sources from pop culture that depict teachers/schools, of which: — at least one is a literary text — at least one is a TV show or movie ◆ sources created within the last 30 years ◆ includes your own sources outside the teacher's suggested list	◆ all of *Practitioner* plus collection of sources represents a wide range of cultures and experiences
Planning Notes: Analysis of Sources	for **each** pop culture source: ◆ determines specific adjectives/archetypes that describe the characters (i.e., teacher, principal, etc.)	for **each** pop culture source: ◆ determines specific adjectives/ archetypes that describe the characters (i.e., teacher, principal, etc.), supported with at least three pieces of evidence ◆ identifies the author's point of view on teachers/schools	for **each** pop culture source: ◆ determines specific adjectives/ archetypes that describe the characters (i.e., teacher, principal, etc.), supported with at least three pieces of evidence ◆ identifies the author's point of view on teachers/schools ◆ explains how the author developed his/her point of view (e.g., use of word choice, mood, tone, characterization, camera angle, music, lighting)	◆ all of *Practitioner* plus explains why the author may have depicted the teacher/school in that manner
Planning Notes: Development of Claim	◆ compares or contrasts the extent to which the depictions are accurate, based on personal experience	◆ compares and contrasts the extent to which the depictions are accurate, based on personal and/or peers' experience	◆ includes surveys/interviews of peers from other schools/states/countries to seek their opinions as to the accuracy of the depiction of the teachers/school in the chosen source ◆ compares and contrasts the extent to which the depictions are accurate, based on your experience, your peers' experience, and the results from your survey/interviews	◆ all of *Practitioner* plus compares and contrasts the extent to which the depiction is accurate, based on information gleaned from nonfiction informational articles on the topic and/or different cultural perspectives

	Novice	Apprentice	Practitioner	Expert
Product Content	the product should: ♦ name the title of the source that you are critiquing ♦ contain your findings ♦ formulate a claim as to whether the depiction of teachers/school is accurate ♦ outline at least two reasons to support your claim ♦ outline at least one piece of evidence to support each reason	the product should: ♦ be addressed to a specific audience (e.g., individual or company) ♦ name the title of the source that you are critiquing ♦ present your findings supported by specific examples ♦ contain a clear claim as to whether the depiction of teachers/school is accurate ♦ support the claim by including reasons and relevant evidence in the form of personal anecdotes and facts/statistics ♦ Offer at least 1 realistic suggestion for how to better represent teachers/ schools in the media	the product should: ♦ be addressed to a specific audience (e.g., individual or company) ♦ name the title of the source that you are critiquing ♦ present your findings, supported by specific examples ♦ contain a clear claim as to whether the depiction of teachers/school is accurate ♦ support the claim by including reasons and relevant evidence in the form of personal anecdotes, facts/statistics, and opinions from experts in the field ♦ offer two to three realistic suggestions for how to better represent teachers/ schools in the media	all of *Practitioner* plus includes predictions for the next twenty years if changes are not made
Grammar / Mechanics	♦ complete sentences (i.e., no sentence fragments and run-on sentences)	♦ complete sentences (i.e., no sentence fragments and run-on sentences) ♦ transitional words and phrases to: – add to ideas (e.g., also, in addition, as well, furthermore) – indicate a shift in ideas (e.g., however, despite, though, yet, but) – give examples (e.g., for example, for instance)	♦ complete sentences (i.e., no sentence fragments and run-on sentences) ♦ transitional words and phrases to: – add to ideas (e.g., also, in addition, as well, furthermore) – indicate a shift in ideas (e.g., however, despite, though, yet, but) – give examples (e.g., for example, for instance) ♦ formal style, avoiding slang terminology and vague language (e.g., some people, things, stuff)	all of *Practitioner* plus utilizes parallel structure to emphasize ideas

Teachers, Schools, and Pop Culture
Scaffold for Learning

How-To Sheets
- How to determine author-s point of view
- How to storyboard
- How to create a podcast
- How to maintain formal language and style

Homework
- Analyzing commercials and TV shows you watch (conscious/unconscious message, author's POV, archetypes, craft)
- Interviewing/surveying others

Group Tasks
- Sharing sources that depict teachers/schools
- Sharing of students' findings
- Survey/interview others
- Peer revising of products

Benchmark Lessons
- Pop culture & its impact on societal beliefs
- Author's craft: What is it and what's the point?

Interactive Web Sites
- Camera Techniques in Filmmaking
- Film Techniques
- Author's Craft Techniques
- Archetypes Definitions & Examples
- Archetypes

Small-Group Mini-Lessons
- Determining author's point of view
- Making inferences/drawing valid conclusions
- Identifying author's craft techniques
- Maintaining formal language

Individual Tasks
- Researching, reading, and choosing sources to analyze
- Analyzing each source
- Journaling/reflecting
- Creating the choice product

Learning Centers
- Exploration of pop culture sources that depict teachers/schools
- What are archetypes?
- Reasons v. Evidence
- Camera Techniques
- Author's Craft Techniques
- Transition words

Peer Tutoring
- Determining author's point of view
- Making inferences/drawing valid conclusions
- Identifying author's craft techniques

Podcasts/Screencasts
- Determining author's point of view
- Author's craft techniques
- Cinematography techniques
- Archetypes in Literature

Technology Uses
- Using devices to watch movies/videos
- Using devices to create the product (e.g., videos, podcasts, presentations)
- Using Internet to connect to students in other cities, states, countries

Teachers, Schools, and Pop Culture: *Facilitation Questions*

COMPREHENSION *Ask questions that ensure students understand content and skills needed to solve the problem.*	◆ What is an archetype? What are some common archetypes that exist? ◆ What is an author's point of view? ◆ Name some craft techniques that authors use. ◆ Name some craft techniques that filmmakers use. ◆ How do you make an inference?
APPLICATION *Ask questions that ensure the ability of students to apply learning to new situations.*	◆ Do you think that this character represents an archetype? Which one(s)? ◆ What is this author's point of view on teachers/schools? ◆ How does this author develop his/her point of view in this text? ◆ What craft techniques that you use in the creation of your own product?
CONNECTION *Ask questions that ensure the ability of students to apply learning to their lives.*	◆ What is your opinion about how this author depicts teachers and schools? ◆ Do you think that you or anyone that you know represents an archetype? ◆ Do you think that these depictions and representations of teachers/schools are correct? ◆ Do you think that these depictions have influenced the way that you think about school in any way?
SYNTHESIS *Ask questions that encourage students to create new information from existing data.*	◆ What impact do you think pop culture and media has on public opinion and policy? ◆ How do you think this representation of teachers/schools affects the opinions of society? ◆ In looking across the different sources, do you notice any patterns? (For example, do authors who have the same target audience have similar representations of teachers/schools? Has the depiction of teachers/schools changed over time?) ◆ What advice might you give this author to make the representation more accurate?
METACOGNITION *Ask questions which prompt students to think about their own thinking process.*	◆ Why did you decide to pick this particular source/author to whom to send your product? ◆ What revisions do you make between your first draft and your final? Why did you make them and how does it make your piece better? ◆ What was a challenge you came across and how did you overcome it?

Teachers, Schools, and Pop Culture: *Facilitation Grid*

Students	Makes accurate inferences	Supports inferences with relevant evidence	Defines archetype and give common examples	Identifies archetypes on demand	Accurately identifies author's point of view	Explains how an author developed his/her POV	Identifies various craft techniques in literature	Identifies various craft techniques in film/TV	Formulates a claim with reasons	Understands difference between reasons and evidence

M = mastery   *P = peer tutor level*   *HW = needs homework for reinforcement*

W = working on it   *ML = needs a mini-lesson*

* The sample facilitation grid should be clearly designated as a sample and may only cover a single week.

Teachers, Schools, and Pop Culture: *Transfer Task*

Now that you have studied the depiction of teachers in popular culture, choose another sub-group to analyze. For example, how are girls represented in the popular culture? What about boys? What about parents or police officers? LGBTQs?

Choose a sub-group of your choice to analyze and find two recent sources that depict this particular group. Analyze these sources, and then write an essay in which you present your findings and analyze the extent to which those representations are true.

In your essay, be sure to:

♦ Include at least one source that is literature (text).

♦ Refer to specific adjectives and archetypes that describe the characters in the sub-group, supported by specific evidence.

♦ Identify the author's point of view about the chosen sub-group.

♦ Explain how the author developed his/her point of view about the chosen sub-group.

♦ Clearly state your claim as to the extent to which these representations are true.

♦ Support your claim with specific facts and evidence.

♦ Utilize transition words to create cohesion between thoughts.

♦ Maintain a formal style.

♦ Use proper grammar and mechanics.

Appendix G
Justice for All

"Injustice anywhere is a threat to justice everywhere."

(Dr. Martin Luther King Jr., Letter from the Birmingham Jail)

In 1954, the U.S. Supreme Court declared racial segregation in public schools unconstitutional, in turn bringing an end to the legal doctrine "separate but equal." The landmark case that brought forth this monumental decision is known as *Brown v. Board of Education*.

Despite the Supreme Court ruling, there are those that still argue the effectiveness of this decision. Have the goals of *Brown v. Board of Education* been fulfilled? Are American schools still segregated? What other obstacles have arisen since 1954 that keep students from having a quality education, and how has this affected your education? What can you do to ensure that every child receives an equitable educational experience?

Explore both past and current forms of segregation and desegregation in education across the U.S. Choose one area of education where segregation is most prevalent today or an area that is of the most interest to you. Develop a plan of action to share with the State Department of Education, Congress, a Senator, and so on. Educate others regarding the importance of achieving equity. How can you persuade others in power to take action? What supportive evidence will be necessary to help others view your claim as credible? Fannie Lou Hamer, a civil rights activist, once said, "When I liberate others, I liberate myself." Does treating people equally mean treating them the same? As the future of this country, it is your job to continue to embrace diversity and ensure justice for all.

Justice for All: *Rubric*

	Novice	Apprentice	Practitioner	Expert
Exploration of Past Events	• defines civil rights • includes one example of past segregation • includes one example of past desegregation efforts	• defines civil rights and the purpose behind them • includes three examples of segregation and desegregation in the past • provides detail of the events and their implications on society	• defines civil rights, the purpose behind them, and their evolution over the years • includes at least five examples of segregation and desegregation in the past, including in education • provides detail of the events and their implications on society • correlates how segregation and desegregation efforts relate to the U.S. Constitution and civil rights	all of *Practitioner* plus: reflection on the importance of diversity, and equity and one's duty as a U.S. citizen
Current Examples	includes • one recent example of how/where segregation is still an issue • one recent example of a desegregation effort	includes • more than one recent example of how/where segregation is still an issue in education • the implications of these examples on society • recent examples of efforts to desegregate education	includes • multiple, recent examples of how/where segregation is still an issue in education • the short-term and long-term implications of these examples on society • recent examples of efforts to desegregate education, both through laws and by choice • varied and credible digital and print sources	all of *Practitioner* plus: examples of segregation and desegregation in education in at least one first, second, and third world country
Commendation or "Call to Action"	includes • opinion regarding a segregation issue in education • support of opinion with several pieces of evidence	includes • solution to a segregation issue in education • support of opinion with several cited, pieces of evidence • recommendations for "next steps"	includes • solution to a segregation issue in education, supported by evidence, including data and statistics • list of reasons for putting this proposal into action that relate to civil rights • multiple perspectives and sources • detailed "next steps" to ensure justice for all • implications for the short-term and long-term, based on plan for action • counterclaims to the solution • ramifications of dismissing the call to action	all of *Practitioner* plus: shares solution and action plan with person(s) of power and ability to make a difference

	Novice	Apprentice	Practitioner	Expert
Writing Style	includes ♦ claim ♦ supporting evidence for claim ♦ concluding section that follows from the argument	includes ♦ precise claim ♦ claims, counterclaims, reasons, and evidence ♦ supporting evidence for claims and counterclaims ♦ precise words and phrases, telling details to convey the significance of ideas ♦ clear and cohesive ideas using varied sentence structure ♦ concluding section that follows from and supports the argument presented	♦ includes precise claim, distinguished from alternate or opposing claims ♦ includes clear relationships among claims, counterclaims, reasons, and evidence ♦ includes supporting evidence for claim and counterclaims ♦ includes strengths and limitations of claim and counterclaims ♦ demonstrates anticipation of audience's knowledge level and concerns ♦ demonstrates cohesion among major sections ♦ includes precise words and phrases, telling details to convey the significance of ideas ♦ creates clear and cohesive ideas using varied sentence structures ♦ includes concluding section that follows from and supports the argument presented	all of *Practitioner* plus: demonstrates anticipation of and addresses challenges that may be faced in pursing this call to action

Justice for All

Scaffold for Learning

How-To Sheets
- How to use Google Slides (or any other presenting platform)
- How to leave a comment on a GoogleDoc
- How to find an audience

Homework
- Summarizing research/data
- Locating current examples of segregation
- Finding an audience

Group Tasks
- Exploring the past
- Creating a solution
- Creating a plan of action

Benchmark Lessons
- Human rights or civil rights?
- Separate but equal?
- Equality vs. equity
- Claims and counterclaims

Small-Group Mini-Lessons
- Sentence structure
- Citing a source
- Supporting a claim
- Using precise vocabulary
- Reliable sources
- Supporting evidence
- Is my plan of action realistic?

Interactive Web Sites
- Primary Source Documents
- Segregation map
- Parable of Polygons—A parody of the shape of society
- The Rise and Fall of Jim Crow
- EdPuzzle

Individual Tasks
- Defining our civil rights
- Evolution of our civil rights
- Describing events to highlight segregation and desegregation efforts
- Developing a timeline
- Developing an argument organizer

Learning Centers
- Cause and Effect
- Pros and Cons to Diversity
- Separate but Equal
- Diversity in America
- Bias—Difference of Opinions

Peer Tutoring
- Peer editing
- Credible sources
- Citing a source
- Supporting a claim

Podcasts/Screencasts
- Citing a source
- Supporting a claim
- Data and statistics

Technology Uses
- Researching current issues
- Typing plan of action -
- Peer review others' plans
- Determining an audience

Justice for All: *Facilitation Questions*

COMPREHENSION *Ask questions that ensure students understand content and skills needed to solve the problem.*	What are civil rights? What is segregation? Desegregation? When did the civil rights movement take place? Who were some famous people/events during the civil rights movement?
APPLICATION *Ask questions that ensure the ability of students to apply learning to new situations.*	What is the status of this issue today? How have civil rights evolved over the years? What were people's goals who joined the civil rights movement? What challenges did those who fought for desegregation during the Civil rights movement experience? What were some of the pros and cons to the civil rights movement? What is the difference between segregation of the past and segregation of today?
CONNECTION *Ask questions that ensure the ability of students to apply learning to their lives.*	Are there any reforms that have been passed since the civil rights era that have impacted you? If so, how? Where do you see segregation the most prevalent in your life? How is segregation apparent in our school systems? Why is it important for you to know your civil rights as a U.S. citizen? What steps can you take locally and nationally to achieve social justice?
SYNTHESIS *Ask questions that encourage students to create new information from existing data.*	Why might some people refrain from taking a political stand? Why do people struggle for social justice? Given what we know about the successes and failures of the past, what do you think we need to make change happen today? Why is social injustice still an issue? How can we ensure justice for all? What challenges might you face in taking a stand against injustice?
METACOGNITION *Ask questions which prompt students to think about their own thinking process.*	What factors came into play when you were deciding which issue needed the most attention? How did you decide who your audience would be to share your solution?

Justice for All: *Facilitation Grid*

Students	Defines segregation	Explains "Separate but Equal"	Describes cause-and-effect of key events during the civil rights movement	Describes steps taken towards desegregation in the past	Explains civil rights of a citizen	Compares and contrasts segregation of the past and present	Identifies recent examples of segregation and efforts to desegregate	Analyzes the difference between equality and equity with examples

M = mastery   *P = peer tutor level*   *HW = needs homework for reinforcement*

W = working on it   *ML = needs a mini-lesson*

* The sample facilitation grid should be clearly designated as a sample and may only cover a single week

Unit Overview
What changes would you like to make in your life and/or in the lives of people in your community? Are we still a segregated nation? In this high school unit, students will conduct research on current issues regarding segregation in American schools. They will develop a call to action to address an issue and determine who has the ability/power to help them make a difference. Students will deepen their understanding of their civil rights and explore the difference between equality and equity.

Common Core State Standards Addressed
CCSS.ELA-LITERACY.RH.11-12.1 CCSS.ELA-LITERACY.RH.11-12.2 CCSS.ELA-LITERACY.RH.11-12.7 CCSS.ELA-LITERACY.W.11-12.1 CCSS.ELA-LITERACY.W.11-12.4 CCSS.ELA-LITERACY.W.11-12.8 CCSS.ELA-LITERACY.SL.11-12.1 CCSS.ELA-LITERACY.SL.11-12.4 CCSS.ELA-LITERACY.SL.11-12.6

National Standards/Content Addressed
National Social Studies Standards NSS-C.9-12.2 NSS-C.9-12.5 NSS-USH.5-12.9 NSS-USH.9-12.10

Enduring Understandings	Essential Questions
◆ The civil rights movement was a culmination of many events between government, groups, and individuals. ◆ Individual/human rights are not free, they must be fought for. ◆ Non-violent protests are necessary in effecting change. ◆ Empathy and tolerance are necessary in defending human rights. ◆ Citizens have the ability to create change. ◆ People can make their political voices and opinions heard by organizing, supporting, and reaching out to local and state organizations/agencies.	◆ What is the ongoing legacy of the civil rights movement? What lasting effects did it have on the U.S.? ◆ How does the press shape our perception of current events? ◆ How can the average citizen begin to make an impact and effect change in today's society? ◆ Why is the average person willing to risk their safety to defend something they are passionate about?

Twenty-First-Century Skills Addressed

Core Content and Interdisciplinary Themes
♦ Subject-Area Mastery
♦ Civic Literacy

Learning and Innovation
♦ Critical Thinking and Problem Solving
♦ Creativity and Innovation
♦ Communication and Collaboration

Information and Media Literacy
♦ Information Literacy
♦ Media Literacy

Life and Career
♦ Initiative and Self-Direction
♦ Social and Cross-Cultural Skills
♦ Productivity and Accountability
♦ Leadership and Responsibility

Appendix H
Rubric to Assess a Benchmark Lesson

	Novice	Apprentice	Practitioner	Expert
Topic	selects a concept (not skill) that is meaningful to the students	selects a concept (not skill) that is key to understanding the content of the unit and is meaningful to the students	selects a concept (not skill) that is key to understanding the content of the unit, is meaningful to the students, and is based upon need as determined by assessment data from the classroom and/or standardized test	all of *Practitioner* plus chooses a title that is provocative, related to the concept/topic
Opening	states the objective of the benchmark up front	explains why the content to be covered is important for the students to know	• begins with a reflective question to focus students on the need for the content • uses students' responses, a news story, a metaphor, or some other technique to build a "felt need" for the concept	all of *Practitioner* plus uses a multi-sensory approach to building the felt-need (e.g., print, sound, visuals)
Content	a significant amount of content related to the topic, covered quickly	• hones content to that which can be reasonably "digested" in ten minutes • includes at least three clear points	• narrowly-focused content that can be reasonably "digested" in ten minutes • a number of clear points made regarding the concept • connects the content to the *ALU* to build a felt need to learn related skills • logical presentation sequence that builds to content mastery	all of *Practitioner* plus includes facts, statistics, charts, graphs, video, sound, etc. to illustrate points
Delivery	includes two to three of the six criteria under *Practitioner*	includes four to five of the six criteria under *Practitioner*	• repeats key points • speaks clearly, articulates, and uses appropriate volume for the venue • uses pauses to allow the students' brains to process a point • uses appropriately sophisticated vocabulary • does not read from notes or screen, rather speaks as if knowing the content • makes eye contact with audience	all of *Practitioner* plus uses tone, speed, and volume as tools; uses appropriate metaphors, anecdotes, and/or analogies to make points
Logistics	• 10–15 minutes in length	• 10–15 minutes • all necessary visuals or materials set up in advance	• 10–15 minutes • all necessary visuals or materials set up in advance • stands or moves around the room to engage the audience and ensure visibility for all	all of *Practitioner* plus creates a physical room arrangement and ambiance to position the audience for optimal learning
Closing	summarizes key points	• summarizes key points • closes with a clear, final statement	• reiterates how the related skills will help students in solving the *ALU* problem • summarizes key points • closes with a metaphor, quote, or other technique to punctuate the content	all of *Practitioner* plus ends with a thought-provoking question to promote continued thinking about the content

Appendix I
Learning Styles and Readiness Grid

When you stand before your class to teach a skill, you can be sure that students are not in the same place cognitively nor in terms of learning styles. Consequently, instruction will only be moderately effective. Differentiated instruction involves using varied *learning activities* to meet the needs of all learners. Select a skill you might teach. Consider the student who lacks the prerequisite knowledge to learn the skill, the student who is cognitively ready to learn the skill, and the student who already knows the skill you're about to teach. Then, for each category of student, consider three possible levels of learning style. Brainstorm nine different ways a student could address the same skill, preferably independent of the teacher. You may never have nine different activities going on at the same time for a skill, but you might choose, say three. These would become choice activities on your *activity list*.

	Distal Zone A student who will be challenged to learn this skill or lacks the prerequisite skills.	Proximal Zone A student who is ready to learn this or is on grade level.	Current Knowledge A student who is ready to move beyond this or is above grade level.
Visual			
Auditory			
Tactile/ Kinesthetic			

Appendix J
The "Great Student" Rubric

	Novice	Apprentice	Practitioner	Expert *All of Practitioner plus*
Individual Responsibility	comes to class ready to learn: ● brings completed homework ● has materials and necessary tools ● with prompting, starts tasks	● starts tasks without prompting from teacher ● uses the "Help Board" rather than interrupting the teacher ● completes activities for group work	● completes all work to be handed in on time ● follows through on all group responsibilities when in need of help: ● re-reads directions ● reviews notes ● quietly asks others for help ● adds name to "Help Board" ● if unable to continue without help, moves on to something else productive	● when finished early, works to improve upon the work to be handed in or works on challenge/optional activities
Folder Organization	brings any current and prior work needed for class each day	work is organized to easily access work in progress and completed work	● stores current schedule and activity list, direction sheets, current unfinished work, and completed work for the unit in ways that allow easy access ● stores papers from previous units at home	● able to explain organization strategy and changes made over time
Focus	● with prompting from teacher or peer, starts tasks ● if off task, with prompting from teacher or peer, resumes task	● recognizes loss of focus and gets back on task without teacher or peer prompting ● when working individually, chooses a seat to minimize distractions	● stays on task throughout an activity ● switches from one activity to the next with minimal "down time" ● refrains from distracting others ● reserves off-task conversations for out-of-class time	● can explain the strategies for: ● effectively staying focused during school and homework
Participation	participates in group lessons and activities	● comes to group lessons and activities prepared ● asks and answers questions to clarify content or directions ● offers ideas	● actively listens to others and relates comments to their contributions ● uses text to back up opinions ● asks higher-order, content-related questions	● offers praise and constructive criticism to peers ● accepts and utilizes constructive criticism

This *Great Student Rubric* was inspired by Paul Tough's book *How Children Succeed.*
Tough, P. (2012). *How children succeed: Grit, curiosity, and the hidden power of character.* New York: Houghton Mifflin Harcourt.

	Novice	Apprentice	Practitioner	Expert *All of Practitioner plus*
Grit and Optimism	◆ sets individual clear goals each class ◆ identifies skills and topics that are a struggle and believes growth is possible	◆ perseveres with even difficult tasks ◆ when struggling, identifies reasons behind failure and tries new strategies	◆ consistently hands in quality work on time ◆ persists through challenges to achieve quality work ◆ analyzes failures and setbacks and develops strategy for breaking through	◆ articulates strategies to develop grit ◆ explains how optimism affects success in class
Self-Control	◆ does everything possible to get to school each day ◆ reserves off-task conversations for lunch time ◆ brings prior work necessary for class each day ◆ meets pacing guide for each class	◆ gets to work right away without reminders ◆ maintains appropriate volume in class ◆ identifies at least two strategies to stay focused in class ◆ resists distraction ◆ uses directions to increase success	◆ uses rubric to help guide learning throughout the unit ◆ accurately self-checks work in class ◆ uses directions and notes to help answer questions before asking others ◆ refrains from distracting others ◆ refrains from interrupting others when speaking	◆ explains organizational strategies and changes made over time ◆ explains the strategies used for effectively managing time in school and at home
Collaboration: Gratitude and Social Intelligence	◆ identifies a clear role during partner or small group work ◆ is polite to peers (including *please* and *thank you*) ◆ is polite to teacher (including *please* and *thank you*) ◆ keeps temper in check	◆ adapts to different social situations ◆ allows others to speak without interruption (actively listens) ◆ follows through on partner or small group responsibilities ◆ helps group meet goals ◆ works to resolve differences with others	◆ able to find solutions to conflicting opinions with others ◆ shows appreciation ◆ puts forth effort to make a difference for others in class ◆ makes suggestions to group to work more effectively	assists group members in reaching consensus and resolving conflict
Curiosity and Zest	identifies topics in class that are interesting/exciting to explore	demonstrates enthusiasm for learning and applying content	◆ asks questions to aid in learning more effectively ◆ approaches new situations with excitement and energy	makes real world connections (can be cross-subject) to content from class without prompting

Appendix K
Creating a Culture of
#STEMLATIC

INSTRUCTIONAL BALANCE:	Scientific Method ♦ Seeks to explain what exists	Engineering Design Process ♦ Seeks to design that which does not exist

	Scientist *NGSS Cross-Cutting Concepts* ♦ Patterns ♦ Cause-and-Effect ♦ Scale, Proportion, and Quantity ♦ Systems and System Models ♦ Energy and Matter: Flows, Cycles, and Conservation ♦ Structure and Function ♦ Stability and Change	Technologist ♦ Information Retrieval ♦ Communication ♦ Collaboration ♦ Simulation ♦ Modeling ♦ Design ♦ Presentation	Engineer *Design Process*  ♦ Formulate ♦ Explore ♦ Ideate ♦ Sift ♦ Simulate ♦ Advocate	Mathematician *Math Practice Standards* ♦ Make sense of problems and persevere in solving them ♦ Reason abstractly and quantitatively ♦ Construct viable arguments; critique others' reasoning ♦ Model with mathematics ♦ Use appropriate tools strategically ♦ Attend to precision ♦ Look for and make use of structure ♦ Look for and express regularity in repeated reasoning
STEM MINDSETS				

	Engagement (not compliance) ♦ Felt Need ♦ Problem-Based Learning ♦ Audience ♦ Belonging–Collaboration ♦ Executive Function (access)	Student Responsibility for Learning ♦ Self-Assessment ♦ Goal Setting ♦ Scheduling Time ♦ Resource Sign-Up ♦ Peer Experts	Academic Rigor ♦ Higher-Order Thinking ♦ Content Application ♦ Strong Rubric ♦ "Reach" Expert Column ♦ Teacher Facilitation
LATIC			

Index

expectations and 46–49; collaborative learning and 99; concepts and skills in 32–34, 70; content and 31, 39–41; curricular standards in 32–33, 39, 41; empowerment and 24; facilitation of learning and 24; felt need and 184; final product in 38–40, 54–55; global citizenship and 175; home groups in 110–111, 192; interdisciplinary 208; introduction of 111–112, 188, 191; known and unknown in 37–38; learning challenges and 140–142; problem-based tasks and 31–41, 43, 54, 104, 112, 190; problem-based task statement 32, 41–43; reflection and 111–112; related subjects in 46; scaffold for learning and 77–79, 84, 104; sociograms and 192; student engagement and 24; student responsibility for learning and 24, 31–32, 106–107; unit design in 31–41, 43
authentic tasks: context for learning in 27; problem-based learning and 35–36

Bach, Cyndie 3
bar graph *123*
benchmark lessons: concepts and 70, 80, 82–84; conducting 80–84; co-teaching classrooms 194; example of *82*; felt need and 83; inspiration and 78–80, 84, 111; learning activities and 78–82; learning map and 74–75; length of 80, 83; limited resource sign-up sheets 129–130; objectives of 81–82; opting out of 84; primacy-recency effect 80; priming plan and 191; problem-based tasks and 79–80, 84; recording 88; as required activities 117; rubric for 253–254; scaffold for learning and 84; scheduling and 114; small-group mini-lessons and 89; student response in 83; student work folders 120; triggering awareness in 79; virtual classrooms and 203; whole-class 70, 79
Bloom, Benjamin 144
Bloom's Taxonomy 145, 169
Book of Learning and Forgetting, The (Smith) 26
brainstorming: collaborative learning and 160, 181; home groups and 110; problem-based tasks 32; tools for 181
breakpoint formative assessment 150–151, *152*
Building Executive Function (Sulla) 156, 166, 204

Catcher in the Rye, A (Salinger) 106
causal maps 46
cause-and-effect relationships 61, 174
choice activities 117, 255
Choice Theory (Glasser) 107
classic learning 26
classroom design: collaborative work space in 160–161, 166; computer areas 163; desks in 160–162; discourse centers 162–163; dual-purpose furniture in 166–167; efficacy and 15; exercise for 160; flexible seating in 158–160, 167; functional 158–160; "hoteling" in 162; individual work space in 161–162; interactive whiteboards in 165; limited resource area 164–165; media-based collaboration 166; resource and folder area 163; round tables in 161; small-group mini-lesson area 164; student input in 167, 207–208; study carrels 162; teacher's desk in 167; walls in 165; whole-class 165–166
clover tables 161
Coleman, James 137–138, 183
collaborative learning: brainstorming and 160, 181; in the classroom 182; classroom design for 160–161, 166; computer technology and 95; conflicts in 182; consensus and 95; critical thinking and 182; final product in 180; higher-order, open-ended thinking and 95, 160, 180; media-based 166; problem-based tasks and 30–31, 35, 39, 180–181; problem-solving and 182; roadblocks in 181; structure of 181; team norms of engagement in 181
collaborative work space 161–162, 166
Common Core 197
compliance model of education 8, 10–11, 114–115
comprehension questions 145, 147
comprehensive formative assessments 150, 151, *152*
computer technology: classroom design for 163; classroom use of 176; collaborative learning and 95; digital generation and 14–15; global citizenship and 174; infusion of 175–176; integration of 5–6, 175; introduction of 3, 75–76; just-in-time-learning and 176; learning activities and 104; problem-based tasks and 176; skill building 86–88; virtual learning and 18

double-entry journals 118
dual-focus facilitation 194
dynamic disequilibrium 18

education: compliance model 8, 10–11; efficacy model 5, 8; purpose and 5; reality pedagogy 9; *see also* learning
educational equity: defining 200; differentiated learning activities and 200; high academic standards in 171, 200; opportunity and access for 9; problem-based learning and 200; student success and 200
efficacy model: analytic rubrics and 113; content in 8; empowerment and 9, 135; facilitation of learning and 135–136, 145, 157; goals of 21; schools and 5; student engagement and 8
Emdin, Christopher 9
empowerment: analytic rubrics and 123; efficacy and 9, 135; executive function skills and 112; peer experts and 124; student responsibility for learning and 24, 106, 122, 179
English language learners: differentiated learning activities and 202; home groups for 110; scaffolding for 202; small-group mini-lessons 202; visual cues for 202
equity-focused instruction *see* educational equity
executive function skills: analytic rubrics and 61–62; categorizing information 62; cause-and-effect relationships 61; design process and 199; empowerment and 112; facilitation grid for *156*; Great Student Rubrics 191; higher-order, open-ended thinking and 169–170; learning dashboard and 127; as life skills 156, 204; multiple points of view and 61–62; predicting outcomes 62; problem-based tasks and 205; scheduling and 122, 129; student responsibility for learning and 115, 122, 178, 205; student work folders and 120; unintended consequences 62
Expert level: extended content in 58; higher cognitive levels and 58–60; metacognitive leaps and 60; performance in 50; quantitative leaps in 58
extended content 58

facilitation grids: co-teaching classrooms 194; executive function skills 156, *156; see also* content facilitation grid
facilitation of learning: activity lists and 138; assessment and 146; content in 136–137; efficacy and 135–136, 145, 157; formative assessment and 143; help boards and 125; instructional design and 137, 139; learning activities and 68–69, 136–137; management in 136; proactive decisions and 139; process and 136, 146; sitting among students in 137, 144, 154, 183; by teachers 27, 29, 91, 122, 167; tools for 139–140, 142–143; virtual 203
facilitation questions: application questions 145, 147–148; comprehension questions 145, 147; connection questions 145, 148; content mastery and 144, 146–147; delving further with 142; design of 139–140; development of 145, 147–149; leveling up approach 144; metacognition questions 145, 148–149; synthesis questions 145, 148
facilitation roadmap: celebrating success 143; connecting with resources in 142–143; delving further in 142; direct instruction and 142, 204; encouragement and 143; example of *141*; guiding instruction with 139–143; learning challenges and 140, 142; observation and 142; suggesting steps in 142
felt need: benchmark lessons and 83; in the classroom 173–174; content mastery and 48; information retention and 26, 29; instructional design and 202, 206; learning and 23, 25–29, 31–33, 35, 37, 75, 173, 206; open-ended problems and 37; problem-based tasks and 28, 68, 169, 185; skill building and 27; teaching from 184
final product: homework and 98–99; problem-based tasks and 38–40; problem-based task statement 43
flipped classrooms 202–203
flow 70–71, *71*, 140, 142
formative assessment: breakpoint 149–151, *152*; comprehensive 149, 151, *152*; content facilitation grid and 143–144; continuous 135; daily use of 156; gathering data for 143; instructional design and 137; student-directed 149, 151, *152*; student progress

and 137, 149, 193; temperature gauge 149–150, *152*; types of *152*

formative assessment grids: content facilitation grid 152, 154–155, *155*, 156; task management grid 152–154

For White Folks Who Teach in the Hood…And the Rest of Y'All Too (Emdin) 9

Friedman, Thomas 174

furniture 166–167

Game of Classroom 190

Geurin, David 38

gifted learners: attributes of 203–204; graphic organizer for 204; higher cognitive levels 60; metacognitive leaps and 60; small-group mini-lessons and 92

Gladwell, Malcolm 19

Glasser, William 12, 107

global citizenship: in the classroom 174–175; divergent/convergent thinking for 29; efficacy and 5; learning activities and 175; preparation for 7; skill building and 174; technology and 174

global positioning systems (GPS) 134, 149

grading 64–65, 120–121, 185; *see also* assessment; self-assessment

graphic organizer: analytic rubrics and 64; assessing task statement content 39, *40*; developmental progression in 57, 63; final product in 64; gifted learners and 204; task management grid and 153, *153*

Great Student Rubrics 190–191, 193, 256–258

Heifetz, Ron 8

help boards: alternate forms of 125; classroom space for 165; digital 12, 125; peer experts and 96; physical space for 125; student responsibility for learning and 106, 124–125

high academic standards: analytic rubrics and 60, 171; in the classroom 172–173; classroom wall materials and 172; educational equity and 171, 200; student achievement and 171; word choice and 172

higher cognitive levels 58

higher-order, open-ended thinking: in the classroom 170–171; collaborative learning and 95, 160, 180; executive function skills and 169–170; felt need and 169; student engagement and 170

high social capital: academic performance and 183; benefits of 183; in the classroom 184; community relationships and 183; defining 183; student achievement and 183–184; teacher-student relationships in 183–184; *see also* social capital

holistic rubrics 49, 66

home groups: belonging and 110; brainstorming and 110; size and composition of 110; student-created 111; student responsibility for learning and 110, 124–125; table journals and 127

homework: cognitive benefits of 97; final product and 98–99; generating ideas in 98; grappling with content in 98; meaning and purpose of 97–98; peripheral content as 97; practice activities and 97; prior knowledge and 98; reinforcing content in 98; self-reporting on 146

"hoteling" 162

how-to podcasts: creation of 87; focus of 88; learning activities and 68, 86–87; learning centers and 94; skill building and 109

how-to screencasts: creation of 87; focus of 88; learning activities and 68, 86–87; skill building and 109; voice-over in 87

how-to sheets: components of 86; focus of 88; just-in-time-learning and 86; learning activities and 68, 73, 86–88, 191; learning centers and 93–94; resource area for 112, 118, 123; skill building and 101, 109; student responsibility for learning and 106, 118; visual learners and 86, 88

how-to videos: focus of 88; learning activities and 68, 86; learning centers and 94; skill building and 109

"Hydroelectric Power": activity lists *116*, 117–119; analytic rubrics and *219–220*; application of knowledge in 118; expert column 60; felt need and 28; practitioner column *57*, 59; as problem-based task 217–218

hyperlinked rubrics 207

IDE Corp. 47, 109, 210

IDE Design Process 218

inclusive classrooms 193

independent learning: computer technology and 26; how-to sheets and 86; learning centers and 93; learning map and 74

191; initial engagement and 187–189; learning activities and 191

priming plan tasks 190

problem-based learning: defining 23n1; equity-focused 200; felt need and 23, 169; real-world 197, 200

problem-based tasks: analytic rubrics and 45–46, 48–49, *49*, 54, 65, 109, 113; application of 33–34; assessment 64–65; audience and 38; authenticity and relevance in 35–36; benchmark lessons and 79–80, 84; collaboration and 30–31, 35, 39, 180–181; computer technology and 176; connected learning and 179–180; content and 39–40; executive function skills and 205; felt need and 28, 68, 185; final product in 38–40, 54; generating ideas in 98; graphic organizer for 39, *40*; individual learning and 30; introduction of 188; learning challenges and 140, 142; learning map and 100; motivation and 32, 111; open-ended 29–30, 37; optional activities and 117–118; prior knowledge and 190; real-world problems and 31, 35, 179–180; reflection and 111–112; scheduling and 121; student engagement and 135; student input in 31–32, 207–208; student responsibility for learning and 121; teacher-designed 23

problem-based task statement: designing 32, 43; example of 41–43; final product in 43; motivation and 48

problem-solving 182, 189

process-oriented mini-lessons 89

project-based learning 23n1

protocols 191

Pythagorean Theorem 26–27, 33, 55, 72, 74–75

QR codes 87

qualitative criteria 51, *53*

quality work board: classroom space for 165; forms of 126; learning map and 73; student responsibility for learning and 126–127

quantitative criteria 51, *52*

reality pedagogy 9

real-world problems: design process and 18, 199; motivation and 34; problem-based tasks and 30, 34–35, 179–180, 197,

200; sources of 34–35; STEM/STEAM education 196–197

reflection: instructional design and 111–112; scheduling and 119–120; students and 81, 111–112, 119–120, 207–208; teacher 19

reflective practitioners 19

relevance 35–36

required activities 117

resource area: analytic rubrics and 112, 123; classroom design for 163–164; digital 123–124, 163–164; how-to sheets and 112, 118, 123; physical space for 123–124; sign-up sheets 132; student responsibility for learning and 123–124

Response to Intervention (RTI) 17, 187, 192–193

roadblock management chart 181

Rose, David 201

round tables 161

rubrics: assessment and 48–49; goals of 48; holistic 49, 66; hyperlinked 207; nested 46, 61; student input in 208; as technical change 8; *see also* analytic rubrics

Rubric to Assess a Benchmark Lesson 84

Salinger, J. D. 106

scaffold for learning: activity lists and 113–114; benchmark lessons and 84; content mastery and 78; instructional path for 78, *78*, 79; interactive websites and applications 95; learning activities and 77, *77*, 78, 100; participatory structures in 99; skill building 85, 99; teacher planning and 78

scheduling: activity lists and 119–120; benchmark lessons and 114; easing students into 119; executive function skills and 122, 129; limited resource sign-up sheets and 128–129; reflection and 119; small-group mini-lessons and 114, 131; structures for 112; student responsibility for learning and 114–115, 119–122; time management and 112–114; virtual classrooms and 113; *see also* time management

schools: citizenship and 7; dominant paradigm of 7–8; emphasis in 7; social capital and 138; society and 6–7; student input in 208; teacher-student relationships in 183; *see also* education

scientific method 197

screencasts *see* how-to screencasts

self-assessment: analytic rubrics and 113, 122; learning dashboard and 177; learning styles and 177; small-group mini-lessons and 131; student responsibility for 76, 146, 207–208; teacher 210

sign-up sheets: learning centers and 94; resource area 132; small-group mini-lessons 131, *131*, 132; teacher conferences 130; *see also* limited resource sign-up sheets

six hats method 181

skill building: analytic rubrics and 99; content facilitation grid and 154–156; differentiated learning activities and 85–89; felt need and 27; how-to sheets and 101–102; individual learning and 95; interactive websites and applications 92; introduction of 85–86; learning centers and 94; learning map and 99–102; learning styles and readiness grid 101, *101*, 102, *102*; leveling up approach 71–72; scaffold for learning and 99; small-group mini-lessons and 89–92; zone of proximal development (ZPD) and 101

small-group discussions 191

small-group mini-lessons: academically-focused 89; benchmark lessons and 89; as choice activities 117; classroom design for 164; gifted learners and 92; learning activities and 68, 73, 89–92; length of 91; note-taking skills and 83; opting out of 91; peer experts and 92, 96; process-oriented 89; recording 88; scheduling and 91, 114, 131; self-assessment and 131; sign-up sheets 131, *131*, 132; size of 132; skill building and 89–92; social capital and 183; structure of 89–91; student responsibility for learning and 12, 106, 130–132; virtual classrooms and 203

small learning communities (SLC) 138

Smith, Frank 26

social capital: benefits of 183; communities and 137–138, 183; small-group mini-lessons and 183; small learning communities (SLC) and 138; teachers and 137–138, 164; *see also* high social capital

social networks 214

society 6–7

sociograms 192

solution pitch 46, 55

solution statement 46

Sousa, D. 12

special education students 18, 119

standing desks 166–167

#STEMLATIC 259

STEM/STEAM education: classroom design for 163; concepts in 196–197; creating a culture of 259; design process in 18, 40; focus on 17; instructional design and 187; learning centers for 93; materials for 195; mindsets for 196–197, 259; moral imperative of 196, *196*; problem-based tasks and 195–197; real-world problems 196–197; workforce needs 195–196

student-directed formative assessments 150, 151, *152*

student engagement: activities for 189; creating a culture of 259; efficacy and 135; empowerment and 135; first day 188–189; instructional design and 9–10; learning activities and 68–69, 76–77; learning and 37, 107; problem-solving and 189; scenarios for 10; self-assessment and 76

student responsibility for learning: activity lists and 112–113, 117–120, 206; analytic rubrics and 12, 113, 122–123, 207–208; in the classroom 179; classroom design and 208, 210; creating a culture of 259; decision-making and 178; efficacy and 179; empowerment and 106, 112, 122, 179; executive function skills and 112, 115, 122, 178, 204–205; help boards and 124–125; home groups and 110, 124–125; individual learning paths and 176–177; initial engagement and 189; instructional design and 9, 11–12; learning activities and 76–77, 206; learning dashboard and 127; lifelong learning and 178; limited resource sign-up sheets and 118, 128–129; peer expert board and 124; practice activities and 206; problem-finding by 208; quality work board and 126–127; resource area and 123–124; scheduling and 114–115, 119–122; school design and 208; self-assessment and 146, 178; skill building and 107; small-group mini-lessons and 12, 106, 130–132; structures for 109, 112–113; table journals and 127; time management and 20, 28–29; work folders 120 students: daily work scheduling 121–122; empowerment and 9; positive language for 143; reflection and 81, 111–112, 119–120, 207–208; self-assessment and 113, 122, 131, 207–208; skill building 6–7; triggering awareness in 185; voice and 208

students with disabilities 110

student work folders: analytic rubrics and 121; assessment and 120–121, 153–154; benchmark lessons and 120; classroom design for 163; content facilitation grid and 154; digital 109, 120; executive function skills and 120; organization of 120; student responsibility for 106; teacher review of 109; two-pocket 109, 120, 204–205

study carrels 162

Sulla, N. 156, 166, 204

summative assessment 149

synthesis questions 145, 148

table journals: example of *128, 129*; forms of 128; home groups and 127; student responsibility for learning and 127

Tapscott, Don 14

task management grid: example of *153*; formative assessment and 152–153; learning activities and 153; popular tasks and 153; practice activities and 153; student progress and 153–154

task-rubric partnership 48–49, *49*

task statements 112; *see also* problem-based task statement

teachers: administrative functions and 122; as bridge builders 85, 93, 108–109, 184–185, 188, 203, 206; conferences 194; direct instruction and 142; energy and 138–139; as facilitator 24, 27, 29, 68–69, 91, 122, 125, 135–140, 142–145, 156, 167, 203; as GPS 134–135, 149; journaling and 18–19, 109; LATIC rubric and 208, *209*, 211; reflection and 19; self-assessment 210; sitting among students by 137, 144, 154, 183; social capital and 137–138, 164

"Teachers, Schools, and Pop Culture": analytic rubrics 239–240; assessment and 121; facilitation grids 243; facilitation questions 242; final product in 55; learning map 73–74, *74, 100*; as problem-based task

237–238; scaffold for learning *241*; solution pitch 55; transfer task 244

teacher's desk 167

team norms of engagement 181

technical change 8

temperature gauge formative assessments 150, *152*

time management: activity lists and 113–115, 118; scheduling and 112–114; student responsibility for 20; *see also* scheduling

transfer task 65–66, 185

"Tree of Whys" 34, *34*

two-pocket folders 109, 120, 204–205

unintended consequences 62, 198

Universal Design for Learning (UDL): access for all in 201–202; final product and 38; framework for 201–202; instructional design and 17, 187, 201–202

videoconferencing 166

video gaming 71

video recording: benchmark lessons and 88; policies for 89; quality work and 126; skill building and 89; *see also* how-to videos

virtual classrooms: benchmark lessons and 203; scheduling in 113; small-group mini-lessons and 203

virtual learning 18

visual learning styles: choice activities and 255; how-to sheets and 86; skill building and 101, *101, 102, 103*; transcripts for 88

vocabulary: felt need and 26, 172; high academic standards and 172

Vygotsky, Lev 69, 71, 101

whole-class lessons: benchmark lessons 70, 79–80, 83, 109; dominant paradigm of 165; effectiveness of 76, 79; individual needs and 76; sets of materials for 93

Wiggins, W. 65

word walls 119

World is Flat, The (Friedman) 174

Wright, Frank Lloyd 201

zone of proximal development (ZPD): body of knowledge and 69–70; components of 70, *70*; differentiated learning activities and 72; differentiation grids *101, 102*; skill building and 101